D1597593

Drew Studies in Liturgy Series
General Editors: Kenneth E. Rowe and Robin A. Leaver

Moving toward Emancipatory Language

A Study of Recent Hymns

Robin Knowles Wallace

Drew University Studies in Liturgy Series, No. 8

The Scarecrow Press, Inc.
Lanham, Maryland, and London
1999

Published in the United States of America
by Scarecrow Press, Inc.
4720 Boston Way
Lanham, Maryland 20706

4 Pleydell Gardens, Folkestone
Kent CT20 2DN, England

BV
312
.W37
1999

"Borrowed Light" by Thomas H. Troeger, © 1994 Oxford University Press, Inc. Used by permission.
"Lead on, O Cloud of Presence" by Ruth Duck, © 1992, published by GIA Publications, Inc. Used by permission.
"Rhyme's Reasons" by John Hollander, © 1989, published by Yale University Press. Used by permission.
"O Holy Spirit, Root of Life" by Jean Janzen © 1991. Used by permission.
"God of the Sparrow" © 1983, Jaroslav J. Vadja. Used by permission.
"Bring Many Names" by Brian Wren, © Hope Publishing Co., Carol Stream IL 60188. All rights reserved. Used by permission.
"Of Women and of Women's Hopes We Sing" by Shirley Erena Murray, © Hope Publishing Co., Carol Stream IL 60188. All rights reserved. Used by permission.
Hildegard of Bingen's Book of Divine Words, edited by Matthew Fox, © 1987, published by Bear & Company. Used by permission.
Symphonia, trans. by Barbara Newman, © 1998. Used by permission of Cornell University Press.

British Library Cataloguing in Publication Information Available

Library of Congress Cataloging-in-Publication Data

Wallace, Robin Knowles.
      Moving toward emancipatory language : a study of recent hymns /
   Robin Knowles Wallace.
            p. cm. -- (Drew University studies in liturgy ; no. 8)
      Includes bibliographical references (p.   ) and index.
      ISBN 0-8108-3640-8 (cloth : alk. paper)
      1. Hymns, English--history and criticism. 2. Liberation theology. 3.
   Feminist theology. I. Title. II. Series: Drew studies in ligturgy ; no. 8.
   BV312.W37   1999
   264'.23'014--dc21   99-11657
                                                            CIP

∞™ The paper used in this publication meets the minimum requirements of
American National Standard for Information Sciences—Permanence of
Paper for Printed Library Materials, ANSI Z39.48–1984.
Manufactured in the United States of America.

Contents

Series Editors' Foreword

One of the fruits of the liturgical renewal movement in the late twentieth century has been the renewed attention to study of the liturgy in all of the churches. This monograph series aims to publish some of the best of this new scholarship. Fresh studies of Episcopal, Roman Catholic, and Orthodox liturgy are included, along with studies of the full range of Protestant liturgies.

Much liturgical writing to date has concentrated on liturgy as text. This series does not ignore such studies but seeks to reflect more recent thinking that understands liturgy not only against the background of theological principle, liturgical tradition and ritual text, but also in terms of liturgical practice and setting.

Clarity of focus, relative brevity, and freshness of scholarly contribution are the principal criteria for publication in the series. Newly written studies, as well as revised dissertations, form the majority of titles, but edited collections of essays and texts are included when they exhibit a unified topical focus and significantly advance scholarship in the field.

Series Editors:

Robin A. Leaver
Westminster Choir College of Rider University
and Drew University

Kenneth E. Rowe
Drew University

Foreword

Conspiracy *n.* from Latin *conspirare*, to breathe together, conspire, agree: *con-*, together, and *spirare*, to breathe.

Theory *n.* a scheme or system of ideas or statements held as an explanation or account of a group of facts or phenomena; a hypothesis that has been confirmed or established by observation or experiment and is propounded or accepted as accounting for the known facts.

Robin Knowles Wallace's *Moving toward Emancipatory Language: A Study of Six Recent Hymns* is a liturgical conspiracy theory. Using insights drawn from the fields of criticism in linguistics, rhetoric, theology, and scripture, Wallace constructs a compelling argument for the necessity of emancipatory language in congregational singing and Christian identity. Her theory of "con-spiring," singing praise of God within communities of faith and freedom, strikes a new note, yet this text draws on a classic understanding of the role of hymns in congregational life, as Carlton R. Young writes in *My Great Redeemer's Praise:*

> The church's traditional use of congregational song has been twofold: the praise of God and the teaching of doctrine, the joining of *doxa* and *logia*, praise and belief; and preaching joined with song as a means of converting the unconverted and sustaining the converted. (140)

To interpret Wallace's work as liturgical conspiracy theory locates it within the fields of liberation and feminist and ecological theologies, a claim that recognizes the controversy created by those theologies in many congregations. For Wallace, the essence of emancipatory language is found in the naming God in the same breath as the marginalized, and that naming places claims on truthfulness, unity-in-diversity, and revelation in our human language of the Holy.

It is essential to state the author's claim for liturgical reformation at the outset of this text. Robin Knowles Wallace writes with the skill and passion of an evangelist. Her theories and structures of interpretation offer a means of converting the unconverted. [See "Praxis: Seeking Communal Affirmation."] Careful reading of this work may also result in sustaining the converted, those ministers of word and music who seek to deepen congregational "conspiracies" of praise and prayer. [See "Source and Sovereign, Rock and Cloud: A Multidimensional Reading."] Wallace's strategy "for creating emancipatory language is imaginative construction, aided by anamnesis (remembering and making present again) and mysterion (God's self-revelation)" (234).

From the deceptively simple question, "What is a hymn?" to a detailed analysis of the rhetorical intentions of six leading English-language hymn writers, Robin Knowles Wallace skillfully conducts the reader through the intricate movements of her work. *Moving Toward Emancipatory Language* does not limit its range to theological speculation. Composition notes from Shirley Erena Murray, Hildegard of Bingen by Jean Janzen, Jaroslav J. Vajda, Brian Wren, Thomas H. Troeger, and Ruth Duck provide valuable insights into the imaginative constructions of the composers. Using six hymn texts: "God of the Sparrow   God of the Whale," "Source and Sovereign, Rock and Cloud," "Bring Many Names," "Lead on, O Cloud of Presence," "Of Women, and of Women's Hopes We Sing" and "O Holy Spirit, Root of Life," Wallace details a hypothesis "established by observation or experiment" through congregational interviews on the ways that "revelation begins in individual consciousness and then must be translated into communal consciousness to be come socially meaningful" (Ruether 1983, 13).

For Wallace, it is not enough to ask, "Is it singable?" or "Will they sing it?" The prophetic principle declared by the prophet Amos (5.18-24), and defined by Rosemary Radford Ruether as "the tradition by which Biblical faith constantly criticizes and renews itself and its own vision" (Ruether, 1983, 24), provides the essential question of this text: "What difference will it make if they do?" For Wallace, hymnic devices such as meter, rhyme, and metaphor are the conspiracy means of the Spirit who teaches the truthfulness, passion, and revelation of "a language that can open our hearts and lives to the One who is Holy" (244).

Heather Murray Elkins
Academic Dean
Drew Theological School

Acknowledgments

I thank the hymnwriters who so generously shared their texts and their responses to parts of this book: Jaroslav J. Vajda, Thomas H. Troeger, Brian Wren, Ruth C. Duck, Shirley Erena Murray, and Jean Janzen. Gratitude is also due to the spirit of Hildegard of Bingen who, through Jean Janzen's setting, gives wings to this text.

Special thanks to my Ph.D. dissertation committee, who made this task one not only of learning, but also filled with enjoyment and the Spirit: Ruth C. Duck, Rae Moses, K. James Stein, Michael C. Leff, and Rosemary Radford Ruether. Thanks also go to Carlton R. Young who long ago affirmed my belief that congregational song is central to worship and our faith lives.

The churches, groups, and individuals who participated in the discussions that form the basis of Part IV were gracious in their responses and permission to quote.

Finally, my gratitude to Robin A. Leaver for his appreciation of my work and Heather Murray Elkins for her creative foreword.

Abbreviations

Bible = annotations from *The New Oxford Annotated Bible*
Webster's = *Webster's Ninth New Collegiate Dictionary*

Hymnal abbreviations used are as follows:
CH = *Chalice Hymnal*, 1995
NCH = *The New Century Hymnal*, 1995
UMH = *The United Methodist Hymnal*, 1989

Except where noted, quotations from the scriptures are from the *New Revised Standard Version*, 1989. All italics within scripture quotations are my own. Occasionally I have used brackets within the biblical quotes, both to clarify pronouns [Jesus, God, etc.] and to remove excessive male pronouns used for the divine.

Introduction

This book explores a strand of English-language hymn texts intended for congregational singing that, generally speaking, have poetic qualities and are strophic, based on rhyme and meter. Methodologies from the fields of rhetoric, linguistics, theology, and hymnology have been used. The strand of hymnody discussed draws particularly on the traditions represented by Isaac Watts and Charles Wesley. Until the last twenty years, these hymns would have been found primarily in Anglo-American Protestant churches in the Anglican, Lutheran, Methodist, Reformed, and Anabaptist liturgical traditions (cf. White 1990, 43). Now they may be found across denominational lines, in many hymnals, Protestant and Roman Catholic.

The fields of rhetoric and linguistics have important implications for the study of hymn texts, as may be seen to some extent in the studies of Roberta Trooien (1990), Sandra Sizer (1978), and J. R. Watson (in Jasper and Jasper 1990). Hymn texts are a relatively untapped field for theology; the systematic work of Paul Schilling (1983) and a study by Teresa Berger (1995) suggest a fruitfulness for study. Hymns have a strong influence on the theology of the laity, in particular. Much of hymnological research has concentrated on history, but there are a few works, such as those of Austin Lovelace (1982), Gail Ramshaw (1992), and Madeleine Marshall (1995), that have considered themes in hymns and their literary aspects. There is a wealth of new hymns and hymnals being published; this book considers some of these recent texts.

Part I considers this strand of hymn texts within the context of Christian worship from the perspectives of Judeo-Christian history and theology as well as the fields of poetry, linguistics, and rhetoric. Special attention is paid to the categories of genre, linguistic register, and rhetorical decorum. Part I attempts to answer two questions: What is a hymn? and what do hymns do?

1

Part II introduces and defines the concept of emancipatory language in relation to liturgical language in general, and hymns in particular. The strands of emancipatory language developed are God's identification with the margins of society, visibility and truthfulness in language about humanity, unity-in-diversity and revelation in language about God, and the strategy of imaginative construction. This section begins with the work of Marjorie Procter-Smith and then draws on concerns of language and feminism in the fields of rhetoric, linguistics, and theology (particularly liberation, feminist, and ecological theologies).

Part III uses the methodology of multidimensional reading with six hymn texts that appear in recent mainline denominational hymnals: "God of the Sparrow God of the Whale," "Source and Sovereign, Rock and Cloud," "Bring Many Names," "Lead on, O Cloud of Presence," "Of Women, and of Women's Hopes we Sing," and "O Holy Spirit, Root of Life." These texts are explored using a methodology that combines tools from the fields of criticism in linguistics, rhetoric, theology, and scripture. Each reading includes discussion of the elements of emancipatory language present in each text.

Part IV begins by reporting reactions to the studied texts from six groups (three congregations and three ad hoc groups, totaling 113 persons) as well as individual comments from fourteen pastors and worship leaders. This provides practical information about both clergy and lay understandings of the function of hymns and their responses to these texts and their emancipatory elements. A concluding chapter assesses the texts and the praxis in light of the concept of emancipatory hymnic language.

PART I
HYMNS

Make a joyful noise to the LORD,
  all the earth.
Worship the LORD with gladness;
  come into [God's] presence with singing.   Ps. 100.1-2

Let the word of Christ dwell in you richly; teach and admonish one another in all wisdom; and with gratitude in your hearts sing psalms,
hymns, and spiritual songs to God.   Col. 3.16

The standard definition of a Christian hymn was set forth by Augustine
of Hippo (354-430) in his commentary on Psalm 148: "a song of praise
to God." The word *hymn* originally came from the Greek word *hymnos*,
meaning similarly, "song in praise of gods or heroes." Scholars have
debated the difference between psalm, hymn, and spiritual song, without determining any definitions. This chapter attempts to clarify some
of the boundaries of the strand of hymnody that is the focus of this
book in order to arrive at a working definition.

    To establish that working definition, the first chapter considers a
strand of the history of English-language hymns particularly as it draws
on early Judeo-Christian tradition and the Protestant Reformation, its
relationship with theology and worship, and its function. The second
chapter focuses on related textual analysis: poetry, genre, linguistic
register, and rhetorical decorum, concluding with a working definition
of hymn. The third chapter concludes this part of the book with a description of the state of hymnody over the last twenty years and a word
about music.

Chapter 1
What Is a Hymn?

HISTORY

The church's traditional use of congregational song has been twofold: the praise of God and the teaching of doctrine, the joining of *doxa* and *logia*, praise and belief.

Carlton R. Young, *My Great Redeemer's Praise*

Early Christianity

Christianity was not the first religion to use hymns; songs of praise to a creator or sustaining god are probably as old as the oldest religion. The Jewish tradition of psalms and music in both temple and synagogue worship not only provided models for Christian hymns but gave Christianity a readily accessible body of hymnody. There are still a number of Christian denominations for whom the Psalms (from the Hebrew Scriptures) are central to their worship and hymnody, as may be seen, for example, in the Christian Reformed *Psalter Hymnal* (1988)—which includes settings of all 150 Psalms as its opening section—and in *The Presbyterian Hymnal* (1990)—which includes 101 psalm settings as its central section.

Other "songs" in the Hebrew Scriptures provided models for early Christians—the *Song of Miriam* (Exod. 15.21), believed to be the oldest in Judaism, and the *Song of Hannah* (1 Sam. 2.1-10), that was the model for the *Magnificat* of Mary the mother of Jesus (Luke 1.47-55), to name only two. The Christian Scriptures contain "songs" that are believed to have been sung in the early church in addition to the Psalms and the Magnificat, again to name only two: the *Song of Simeon* (Luke 2.29-32), known in the liturgy as the *Nunc Dimittis*, and the Philippian hymn (Phil. 2.5-11).

5

These scriptural hymns and psalms are not the type of metrical settings we often think of today as hymns. Not only is the meter of Hebrew poetry different from English language meter, but meter takes
second place to parallelism. In English these texts have neither rhyme
nor meter as they appear in the scriptures. Yet they have other poetic
qualities of image, metaphor, and vitality, in addition to their praise of
God and God's activity in the life of believers. This unmetered quality
has begun to be an issue for hymnwriting and singing again in the
twentieth century.

The early Christian church used the Psalms and other scriptural
songs as we have discussed, and relatively early, individuals began
writing additional hymns, or songs in praise of God, to be sung in worship. Most of the hymns now in hymnals that have their source in the
first millennium were either by or attributed to famous men in the
church—popes, famous preachers, and theologians.

One of the interesting characteristics of the history of hymns is how
some hymns have come from contexts outside worship. An early story
about hymns relates the use of hymns, not in worship, but as doctrinal
weapons:

> The church was torn by doctrinal factions in the fourth and fifth centu-
> ries. Arius (c. 250-336), an influential leader at Alexandria, had led the
> battle against orthodoxy over the issue of the nature of Jesus Christ. To
> him, Jesus was a derived creature and therefore not fully divine. . . .
> Though Arius was banished by his superiors, his teachings continued to
> be spread by means of appealing hymns, often sung in nightly proces-
> sionals. With the blessing of Emperor Theodosius (378-396), Bishop
> John Chrysostom of Constantinople organized processions of orthodox
> hymn singers as a counterforce (Eskew and McElrath 1995, 85).

The follow-up to this story is that Ambrose, the fourth-century bishop
of Milan, also encouraged hymn writing, in support of Nicene Christology, and those hymns eventually moved from the streets into worship.
In the Middle Ages, sacred songs continued to be used outside of worship. Carols (such as "In dulci jubilo" known today as "Good Christian
Friends, Rejoice") and *leisen* (songs in the vernacular, used in religious
processions) were in use, and some of these eventually moved into
worship (Schalk 1981, 20-21; 1990, 288-289). A parallel may be seen
in our time with the movement of songs such as "We Shall Overcome"
from the street into hymnals (*UMH* #533 and *NCH* #570).

How often hymns were sung by congregations as the church moved
from worship in small communities in homes to elaborate cathedrals

with multiple priests and choirs is not really known. What is known is that parts of the Mass were sung and that texts and music often changed according to the liturgical season. Yet, for all intents and purposes, except for isolated pieces that have survived and been translated into verse in languages other than Latin or Greek, the strand of hymnody that is the focus of this book really starts with the Protestant Reformation.

The Protestant Reformation

With the Protestant Reformation came the idea of increased participation of lay people, or congregations. John Hus (c. 1369-1415) was one of the forerunners of the Reformation, "who advocated that scripture, its teaching, and preaching should be in the language of the people, and worship centered in the common cup and in the singing of hymns" (Young 1995a, 20). Hus's followers, the Bohemian Brethren, published "a Czech hymnal in 1501, more than two decades before the first Lutheran hymnal" (Eskew and McElrath 1995, 106).

The Protestant Reformation gained momentum in part from Luther's chorales and Calvin's metrical psalms. These songs permeated the home, schools, and churches of Germany, Switzerland, and other countries where they were used (Eskew and McElrath 1995, 292).

In Germany, Martin Luther (1483-1546) described music as both a gift of God and the handmaid of theology (Schalk 1981, 19; Leaver 1992, 127). As we have seen, hymnwriting was not entirely new in Luther's day, yet his hymns brought together the aims of the reformers and created a new thing. For his own hymns Luther drew on the scriptures and themes of the Bible and the church year. His hymns that have endured in English translations speak of unchanging truths from scripture and the Christian's experience of Jesus Christ: "A mighty fortress is our God," "Savior of the nations, come," "From heaven above to earth I come," "Christ Jesus lay in death's strong bands." Influenced by the personal fervor of Luther and others like him, by the emerging nationalism of the German language, and propelled by a return to biblical consciousness, hymns functioned as a source of transformation in Luther's reformation.

John Calvin (1509-1564), French reformer active in Strasbourg and Geneva, believed in adhering strictly to the words of scripture in hymns. The settings used by his followers simply put the thoughts and as many of the actual words of the Psalms as possible into meter and rhyme. Thus like Luther's poetic hymns, these metrical psalms were shaped so that several stanzas, indeed even several different texts, could be sung to a particular tune. The *Genevan Psalter*, 1563, used by Calvinists, was a collection of the versification of Psalms by Clément Marot and Theodore Beza, with musical contributions by Bourgeois (whose tune OLD 100TH is still used in many churches every Sunday with the "Doxology" text).

Hymns in English

Myles Coverdale (c. 1488-c. 1569) was the first to introduce the Reformation hymn, and presumably hymn singing, to England with his *Goostly Psalmes and Spirituall Songes*, around 1535 (Young 1995a, 24). This collection was primarily composed of translations of German texts. Because of the strength of Thomas Cranmer's prayer book and Cranmer's skills in writing prayers rather than hymns, hymns took longer to "catch hold" in England and in the English language. George Wither (1588-1667) published a collection in 1623, *Hymns and Songs of the Church*, that is probably the very earliest English-language hymnal (Eskew and McElrath 1995, 127).

Isaac Watts (1674-1748), called variously a Congregationalist, Nonconformist, or Dissenter, wrote some six hundred hymns (Young 1995b, 55). The Church of England at this time sang metrical psalms, and those only sparingly. Watts moved the hymn "beyond the mere words of Scripture to include original expressions of devotion and thanksgiving" (Eskew and McElrath 1995, 132). Watts also believed in "Christianizing" the psalms for Christian worship; one of the prime examples of the result of this practice is his hymn "Joy to the World," based on Psalm 98.4-9, that is now so identified with Jesus Christ that it is sung almost exclusively at Christmastime. As developed by Dr. Watts, hymns could be characterized as religious, communal, lyrical, and comparatively regular, both in meter and structure (Baker 1988, 90-91).

Charles Wesley (1707-1788) and John Wesley (1703-1791) wrote and published hymns about the Christian experience of salvation and grace, that opened up the scope of hymn writing and advanced the Methodist movement on two continents. The Wesleys brought two kinds of hymns into existence, the evangelistic hymn and the hymn of Christian experience (Gealy, Lovelace, and Young 1970, 32). In his hymns, John "conflated the Puritan love of the word with his new insight into the importance of emotional excitement as an agent of conversion," whereas the prolific Charles wrote hymns "to provide a body of Christian teaching, to provide material for public praise, and to objectify his rich personal faith" (Routley 1968, 23, 30). Carlton R. Young built his study of the Wesleys around the idea of "music of the heart," saying, "[John] Wesley intuitively and pragmatically linked feeling, musical response and doctrinal teaching" to produce music that was a "heart movement"—"a heart repentant, assured, and forgiven; a heart overflowing in joyous response; a heart of love, and a heart of perfect intention" (1995a, 191, 12). Charles wrote over 6,500 hymns (Young 1993, 854), many of that were used in the Methodist class meetings, prayer meetings, and covenant services (Beckerlegge 1983, 65). The use of these hymns by persons from a wide variety of religious, social, and economic settings reflected the revival's central theme of salvation for all in Christ (Young 1995a, 30). John published the first hymnbook on North American soil, *Collection of Psalms and Hymns* (Savannah, Georgia, but printed in Charlestown, South Carolina, 1737).[1] Young calls this "the first English hymnbook meant to be used in worship" (1993, 855), suggesting that many of the earlier publications were used primarily in private devotions rather than public worship.

In the United States

In the expanding United States of the 1700s and early 1800s, several forms of hymns emerged out of the experiences of Christians to meet the needs of the frontier and slave quarters—revival choruses, gospel hymns, and spirituals (Young 1995b, 78-100; Cone 1972). In the 1830s and 1840s polemical hymns were written to be sung in churches and in meetings against slavery and for temperance and reform (Spencer 1990, 39-41).

Drawing on these roots, the Social Gospel movement evolved in the late 1800s and early 1900s and produced several hymnals, most notably, *Hymns of the Kingdom of God* (1910), edited by Henry Sloan Coffin and Ambrose White Vernon. The Social Gospel movement believed that the church had an important role in issues of social justice in that "the essential purpose of Christianity was to transform human society into the kingdom of God by regenerating all human relations and reconstituting them in accordance with the will of God" (Rauschenbusch 1911, xiii). The use of hymns to promote social justice and the vision

---

1. *The Bay Psalm Book* was published in 1640 but may be considered a psalter rather than a hymnbook.

of the kingdom of God flowed through the temperance and abolitionist hymns to hymns of the Social Gospel movement and into the hymns and spirituals that were an important part of the civil rights marches and demonstrations of the 1950s and 1960s (Wilder 1976, 29-30, and the work of Jon Michael Spencer).

Liberation Hymnody in Latin America

Another important aspect of hymnic history is the hymnody that grew out of the liberation theology movement that began in Latin America in the Roman Catholic Church in the 1960s. This movement took seriously the incarnation of Jesus Christ, as God living and suffering in human form, and Jesus' ministry on earth to the oppressed, the hungry, the sick, and the "invisible" people of his time. Liberation theology soon became an ecumenical theology as the winds of Vatican II also affected the Protestant churches in Latin America (particularly as the Roman Catholic Church predominates much of Latin America). The music of Protestant Latin America was strongly influenced by this movement.

Prior to 1960 the Protestant Church in Latin America had drawn heavily on European and U.S. hymnody, including Bach and the Wesleys, for their church music. As Latin Americans began to claim themselves as persons of dignity and as persons in struggle, instead of persons of no worth, doomed to an oppressive existence, they wrote new songs and hymns that drew on the ideas and experiences coming out of liberation theology.[2] The catalyst for this newfound dignity and the hope for the struggle was a renewed commitment to Jesus Christ as he was understood not as sanctioning the status quo but committed to the struggle as well as the people. Drawing from the rhythms and music that had been around them for centuries, these Latin American Protestants created new sounds for their worship, bringing their whole selves to worship, and thus combining the personal, cultural, and theological elements of themselves and their churches (Sosa 1983). The work begun in Latin America in the late 1960s into the 1970s is affecting U.S. Protestants as well, as each of the major denominational hymnals published since 1989 contains several Latin American songs and hymns (see, for example, *UMH* #313, *CH* #291, 292).

---

2. These compositions included the popular masses written for the Roman Catholic Church, *Misa Popular Nicaragüense, Misa Campesina Nicaragüense,* and *Misa Popular Salvadoreña.*

THEOLOGY AND WORSHIP

The better and clearer the theology, then, the more quickly the human heart will sing unbidden.　　Paul Holmer, *The Grammar of Faith*

I argue that the continuing worship of God in the assembly is a form of theology. In fact, it is "primary theology."
　　　　　　　　　　Don E. Saliers, *Worship as Theology*

What Is Theology?

Theology literally means "words about God." Specifically it is the study of religious faith, practice, and experience, of the interaction between God and the world. Karl Barth defined theology, not as knowledge of God, but the grammar of what is known when God is appropriately acknowledged, praised, invoked, and supplicated (Saliers 1994, 72-73). Paul Holmer acknowledged Barth's emphasis on grammar by entitling his book about theology *The Grammar of Faith*. Theology, says Holmer, "is that skein of thought and language in that Christians understand themselves, the Bible, God, and their everyday world" (1978, 9). The purpose of this understanding for Holmer is "to root believers firmly in the Christian life," to enable them to become "something more worthy and justified" (Holmer 1978, 50, 28). Thus theology is a grammar for saying more clearly with one's life what the God-human relationship means.

Like any other grammar, theology is fluid and responsive to human experience, so that it might speak to contemporary experience in ways that illuminate Christian faith (McFague 1987, 32). One focus of contemporary theologies is the acknowledgment that all persons speak from particular social locations that affect both their understanding and their articulation of theology. This parallels the concern of contemporary philosopher Hans-Georg Gadamer, who speaks of the "biases of our openness to the world" (1990, 152). For Gadamer these biases are not negative but arise from the historicity of our existence and are part of the horizon that we bring to the dialogue, in this case, the dialogue of theology.

The limiting nature of acknowledging our biases moves us to another concern of theology, as we experience the limits of our language and our knowing (Saliers 1994, 68).

What Is Worship?

One of the understandings of worship derives from its linguistic background in Old English: to attribute *worth* to someone. The nature of Christian worship is that this attributing of worth moves in two directions: Human beings acknowledge the worthiness of God (as in the hymn of Rev. 4.11a, "You are worthy, our Lord and God, to receive glory and honor and power"), and human beings are esteemed worthy as beings created in the image of God (Gen. 1.26) (cf. Elkins 1994, 17-19). Or to say it another way, "Worship is always two-fold: it is the action of glorifying God and the sanctification of all that is human before God" (Saliers in Leaver and Litton 1985, 40). Comparing Holmer's description of the purpose of theology with this understanding of worship, the correlation can be drawn: While we worship God for God's sake, through worship God shapes us as persons who are worthy, and through theology we understand ourselves reflecting the image of God who is worthy.

Another word that is often used in place of or to supplement *worship* is the word *liturgy*. The original Greek translates into English as "the work of the people" and is related to action of the whole community. *Liturgy* is often the word of choice when discussing those churches that depend on set prayers and an order of worship that is fairly stable and unchanging. Because hymns particularly flourish in what are often called "nonliturgical" churches, those not dependent on a prayer book, this book more often uses the word *worship*.

Yet *liturgy* brings two important understandings that will be incorporated in this study under the word *worship*. The first is that liturgy and worship are the work of the people, not solely the task of clergy or institutional hierarchies. This is one of the basic tenets of the Protestant Reformation: All Christians participate in enabling worship to happen; it is not something done by a few persons on behalf of the congregation.[3]

The second understanding brought from the meaning of *liturgy* for this text is the sense that liturgy is something done by the congregation on behalf of the world. In worship the congregation brings the concerns of the world—illness, poverty, hatred, violence, destruction—along with the joyful evidences of healing, abundance, love, reconciliation,

---

3. A very real concern for worship today is the movement toward "entertainment" worship, when worship moves from participation to observation, becoming again the work of only an elite group of persons.

and peace, so that all may be sanctified before God. Not only are Christians made more worthy by worship, but the whole of creation is deemed worthy and made more worthy by its Creator through worship.

Worship as Primary Theology

Several contemporary theologians have suggested that worship is the primary context for discussing theology. Sallie McFague draws from the language of worship the primacy of metaphor and then builds her theology around metaphor. Don Saliers elaborates on the intersection of theology and liturgy, that is liturgical theology. Teresa Berger, a German Catholic writing about Wesleyan hymns, suggests that those hymns uniquely join doxological speech and theological reflection. All three of these approaches have implications for the study of hymn texts as theology.

Metaphorical Theology. McFague begins by stating that "The primary context, then, for any discussion of religious language is worship" (McFague 1984, 2). This text begins with material from the context of worship, hymn texts, and acknowledges that what happens in worship with hymn texts is different than what happens when one analyzes and interprets a hymn while sitting alone at a desk.

McFague focuses on language that is metaphorical, containing "the whisper, 'it is and it is not.'" Rather than limiting metaphorical theology to one metaphor, she insists "that many metaphors and models are necessary, that a piling up of images is essential, both to avoid idolatry and to attempt to express the richness and variety of the divine-human relationship" (McFague 1984, 13, 20).

In her conclusion to *Metaphorical Theology* McFague raises an important question regarding our use of theological language: "How can we . . . fall into neither idolatry nor irrelevance?" (McFague 1984, 193). Her insistence on many metaphors and images helps us to avoid the idolatry of one image or metaphor, in part by reminding us that all our language is not God but only points to God. Avoiding irrelevance seems to be important for our particular time, as some believe the idea of a universe of symbols no longer speaks to humanity, and others believe that only speaking of success or self-esteem will produce church growth. Can we find language that is relevant to our lives but also has room for God? McFague posits that metaphors and models of a personal God will be relevant, because they will relate God with us and us with God.

Liturgical Theology. For Saliers worship constitutes "primary theology." Every attempt to say what worship is or does is a kind of "secondary liturgical theology" (Saliers 1994, 16). Following that definition, hymns sung in worship are primary theology, whereas this book represents a secondary liturgical or hymnic theology.

Saliers reminds us that the language of worship depends not only on words but also on nonverbal languages (1994, 140). The music of hymn texts has that influence, as does the atmosphere of worship in which hymns are sung, whether it be rigid, proper, and self-contained, or open, relaxed, and focused on the community's praise of God.

Saliers brings another theological rationale for incorporating diversity: "All of our arts must be seen in light of the comprehensive glory of God, or congregations will be starved and become spiritually anorexic" (Saliers 1994, 45). Applied to hymn texts, this means that a wide variety of images and metaphors in hymn texts are necessary, drawing on the comprehensiveness of scripture, tradition, and human experience, as well as varieties in styles of hymn tunes. Congregations will be starved and our growth stifled if we try to limit God's glory to one image, one style of singing, or one metaphor.

Doxology and Theology. Berger's interest in hymnody stems in part from its nature as a common genre of "doxological speech" used by both liturgical and nonliturgical traditions (1995, 20). *Doxology* is ascription of glory to God, thus it is worship and primary theology, as McFague and Saliers have pointed out. *Theology* is the study about God, a secondary task (moving from the second person address of doxology to a third person description). Berger's study asks the question "Theology in Hymns?" as she discusses how doxological speech can nourish and inform theological reflection (1995, 45). Berger raises methodological questions throughout, including one particularly relevant to this text, "In what sense can one speak of a 'theology in hymns,' without missing the essential characteristics and intention of doxological-hymnic expression?" (1995, 22).

This book pursues a slightly different direction—to show how doxological speech reflects current theologies. Nevertheless Berger reminds us that the essential nature of doxological material is not changed by theological study, and theology cannot be turned into doxology (1995, 173). Thus this text is a theological reflection on doxological material, in order to illuminate it so that "the clearer the theology, the more quickly the human heart will sing unbidden" (Holmer 1978, 19).

WHAT HYMNS DO

Hymns are the primary way that the liturgical year and theological imagery are appropriated by the laity.

Gail Ramshaw, *Words that Sing*

Hymns both reflect the experience of the church and are also part of the question to try and find new ways of expressing the faith.

Fred Kaan, in Leaver and Litton, *Duty and Delight*

Express and Shape Theology

Robin Leaver, British hymnologist, now working in the United States, describes the intersection of theology and hymnody in the following way:

Music and theology are interrelated and interdependent. The Bible is concerned with practical theology, the understanding and explanation of the interaction between God and [humanity], and also with practical music, the accompaniment to that interaction. Theology prevents music from becoming an end in itself by pointing [us] to its origins—in the doxology of creation. Music prevents theology from becoming a purely intellectual matter by moving the heart . . . to consider its ultimate purpose—the doxology of the new creation (Leaver and Litton, 1985, 49).

Part of the unique nature of hymns is their accessibility to the laity of the church. One does not need to attend seminary or read theology to understand hymns, although a good hymn will reveal theological depth to those who sing it repeatedly and those who search for theological and biblical threads in it. One aim of this book is to show how contemporary theologies are being expressed in hymns and how the theology of current hymns can shape believers.

For denominations that are not centered on a prayer book, the hymnal joins the Bible as their basic book of theology and of faith. In a periodical introducing the 1990 *Presbyterian Hymnal*, Leaver described "the hymnbook as a book of practical theology," practical in the sense that it can be applied in life in the community of faith and in the world (Leaver 1990, 55-57). In part this is because hymnals include all the major theological categories of faith.

A comparison of two recent hymnals can show both the spectrum of theological categories and the particular focus of each denomination's beliefs. Both hymnals begin with the themes of the Triune God—Creator, Jesus Christ, and Holy Spirit—then *The United Methodist Hymnal* particularly focuses on John Wesley's understanding of grace working through the Holy Spirit, whereas *Chalice Hymnal* (Disciples of Christ) has a stronger emphasis on our response to God's call for justice, including the categories of "Dignity and Equality" and "Care of the Earth":

The United Methodist Hymnal	*Chalice Hymnal*
The Glory of the Triune God	God Beyond All Name and Form
Praise and Thanksgiving	Praise Be to God
God's Nature	God the Creator
Providence	Majesty and Power
Creation	Grace and Love
	Providence and Care
The Grace of Jesus Christ	God Known in Jesus Christ
In Praise of Christ	Praise to Christ
Christ's Gracious Life	Advent
Promised Coming	Birth
Birth and Baptism	Epiphany
Life and Teaching	Life and Ministry
Passion and Death	Palm Sunday
Resurrection and Exaltation	Suffering and Death
	Resurrection and Exaltation
The Power of the Holy Spirit	God Present in the Holy Spirit
In Praise of the Holy Spirit	Pentecost
Prevenient Grace	Power and Work
Invitation	Gifts of the Spirit
Repentance	God's Church
Justifying Grace	Foundation
Pardon	The Church at Worship
Assurance	Gathering
Sanctifying and Perfecting Grace	Common Prayer
Rebirth and the New Creature	The Bible
Personal Holiness	Proclamation of the Gospel
Social Holiness	Invitation to Discipleship
Prayer, Trust, Hope	Affirmation of Faith
Strength in Tribulation	Infant Dedication
The Community of Faith	Baptism
The Nature of the Church	Offering
Born of the Spirit	The Lord's Supper
United in Christ	Going Forth
Called to God's Mission	Ministry
The Book of the Church:	Mission and Witness
Holy Scripture	Christian Community

The Sacraments and
   Rites of the Church
  Baptism, Confirmation,
    Reaffirmation
  Eucharist (Holy Communion
    or the Lord's Supper)
  Marriage
  Ordination
  Funeral and Memorial Service
Particular Times of Worship
  Opening of Worship
  Closing of Worship
  Morning
  Evening
  Special Days
A New Heaven and a New Earth
Death and Eternal Life
Communion of the Saints
Return and Reign of the Lord
The Completion of Creation
  (The City of God)
Psalter
Other General Services and
  Acts of Worship

Christian Unity
Marriage and Family
Healing and Wholeness
Life of Discipleship
New Life in Christ
Love and Gratitude
Faith and Hope
Trust and Assurance
Prayer and Guidance
Stewardship and Service
Loyalty and Courage
Conflict and Perseverance
Death and Eternal Life
God's World
Justice and Righteousness
Peace on Earth
Dignity and Equality
Unity of Creation
  Care of the Earth
  Consummation
Times and Seasons
  New Year
  Thanksgiving
National Songs
Psalter
Worship Resources

Express and Shape Faith

Linda Clark, professor of Sacred Music at Boston University, has carried out an extensive survey of music in churches. In writing about the survey, Clark posits music as an outgrowth of the faith life of a congregation:

> Music expresses faith; that is, it is a vehicle through which the faith within a person and a community comes forth. . . . Music also forms faith. If the hymn or anthem is new and unfamiliar, it confronts a person and a community with a reality with that they must come to terms in order to be faithful (1994, 2).

We have seen how hymnals contain the various themes of theology. What we see in Clark's work is a reminder about primary theology—that in singing hymns, faith can be both expressed and shaped.

    Carol Doran and Thomas Troeger describe it in the following manner:

Compare the number of people in a congregation who read theology to the number who sing hymns on Sunday. Week after week the hymns of your church are giving people the basic vocabulary of their faith. Hymns shape the landscape of the heart, planting images that bring meaning and order to people's understanding of life. Hymns keep congregations in touch with the history from which they have sprung, reinforcing their identity as Christians and directing their understanding of how they are to live in the world (1990, 86).

Express and Shape Worship

I see the hymn as an honest confession of faith, as a public response to God's "mighty acts" and grace.   Jaroslav J. Vajda

The hymn should function as the best possible expression of the community's prayer for that place in the liturgy for that it is chosen.
                                                                           Thomas H. Troeger
                                         both in Westermeyer, *With Tongues of Fire*

Worship contains many elements, taking the shape of praise, thanksgiving, remembrance, lamentation, confession of sin, and interceding for the world (Saliers 1994, 172). Hymns can be used as the congregational articulation of or response to each of these elements. This can be seen by looking at the categories listed under "The Church at Worship" in *Chalice Hymnal*: Gathering, Common Prayer, The Bible, Proclamation of the Gospel (related to sermons), Invitation to Discipleship, Affirmation of Faith, Infant Dedication and/or Baptism (the sacrament of initiation), Offering, The Lord's Supper (the sacrament of nurture and remembrance), and Going Forth. Different hymns will function differently at each of these places in worship. Not only are hymns appropriate for particular parts of worship, but hymns also shape what will follow, by their tone and their prominent theme and images. For example, the familiar hymn "Amazing Grace" might be sung enthusiastically to gather a community together but could be particularly moving if sung after an earnest prayer of confession as an acceptance of forgiveness. Worship then would continue in the light of what it means to be a receiver of God's amazing grace.

Express and Shape Communal and Personal Memory

Hymns keep congregations in touch with the history from which they have sprung, reinforcing their identity as Christians.
                            Carol Doran and Thomas H. Troeger, "Choosing a Hymnal"

This points us to another important function of hymns: sustaining the memory of the Christian tradition in the community and sustaining the memory of worship and encounter with God in the individual. Christian educator Maria Harris calls this "traditioning" and names it as the sixth of her seven steps of women's spirituality:

> Communality demands that we teach our children their own participation in a People with a heritage and an abundance of riches, with roots and rootedness. . . . a learning occurs in the blood and memory of a child who sings in company with others, whether the song is a hymn before God, or "We Are the World." That singing tells her she belongs to something that has roots in the past and in the earth. It is important that Spirituality be traditioned to her as a corporate rather than individualistic Way of Life (1991, 156-157).

How we understand our connectedness must be learned in community, but it sustains us even when we are alone. This accepting of tradition is not a passive event done by rote. As Linda Clark reminds us, we pass these practices on, "refurbished and changed to include the voices of the present faithful" (1994, 79).

Music has the ability to touch something deep within us. One way this is evidenced is in elderly persons who have lost many of their communicative skills but who can still be reached through hymns they knew as younger persons.

In his work on the spectrum of Christian hymnody, Carlton R. Young explains the interaction of music and memory, theology and worship, in hymns "as an active, inclusive, positive art form used by the church to facilitate the teaching and remembering of doctrine" (1995b, 140). Hymns are vital in expressing and shaping communal and personal memories, as they give persons and congregations a form for expressing faith throughout life's journey.

CONCLUSION

Throughout the history of Christianity, hymns have played an important role in joining praise of God and the expression of faith. Hymns teach doctrine and gather congregations into one voice. Hymns express and shape theology and faith, worship and memory, in ways that give voice to Christian praise and human experience of the divine. As part of worship, hymns constitute primary theology, and thus are important for the understanding and deepening of the divine-human relationship.

Chapter 2
About Texts

... one of the central features of liturgy: the language is human, but the kinds of communication aimed at transcend ordinary human notions of how language is to be used purposefully.

Peter Mack, in Jasper and Jasper,
Language and the Worship of the Church

INTRODUCTION

This chapter considers a variety of textual perspectives related to hymn texts. First, and most obvious, is the poetic shape of the text, but there are also other poetic elements: meter, rhyme, poetic devices and metaphor. Next is presented an attempt to describe the genre of the hymn, drawing on the work of Mikhail Bakhtin, who studied the shape of discourse and its setting. Third, drawing on the field of linguistics, is a description of register, that locates specific linguistic markers to define a usage of language. Fourth is the rhetorical concept of *decorum,* that considers the intersection of function and beauty. This chapter concludes with a working definition of *hymn*.

POETRY

The ballad stanza's four short lines
 Are very often heard;
The second and the fourth lines rhyme
 But not the first and third.
*
The ballad stanza in a hymn
 Waits on the music's pleasure,

> And hymnals (hardly out of whim)
>   Call it the "common measure."[1]
> *
> (The attic heart's—theology
> Reformed—this hymnal scheme
> In Emily Dickinson's—Amherst—house
> And slanted—away—the rhyme.)
> *
> "Long measure" in the hymnody
> Means even quatrains just like this,
> Whose music sets the spirit free,
> Doctrine dissolved in choral bliss.
>   John Hollander, *Rhyme's Reason*

Meter

Much of English poetry is based on the rhythm of accented and unaccented syllables. The combination of two or three stressed or unstressed syllables is called a *foot*. Rising meter occurs when the accent falls at the end of the foot, such as *the* CHURCH or *at his* BIRTH. The most common types of rising meter are *iambic*, with two syllables per foot, and *anapestic*, with three syllables in each foot. Falling meter contains the accent on the first syllable of the foot, such as JEsus or HYMnody. The most common types of falling meter are *trochaic*, with two syllables in each foot, and *dactylic*, with three syllables per foot. Other variants are the *spondee (O GOD)*, *pyrrhic (in the)*, and *amphibrach (founDAtion)*.

A line of poetry will be considered *stressed* when the number of stressed syllables outnumber the number of unstressed syllables. Likewise, it will be considered *understressed* when the number of unstressed syllables outnumber the number of stressed syllables. In general, *stressed* lines create a sense of weight, whereas *understressed* lines give a sense of lightness.

Scansion is the process of determining the pattern of feet in a poem, and it is generally marked using / for an accented syllable and - or u for unaccented syllables.[2] Two lines could have the same number of syl-

---

1. It should be noted that the first stanza's "ballad" meter is 86.86., whereas the second adds an additional syllable on the second and fourth lines to produce a stanza of 87.87. It is the 86.86. that is known in hymnody as "common meter."

2. Scansion is not an exact science, and occasionally a poem may be scanned in two different ways, as will be seen with "God of the Sparrow" in Chapter 8.

lables and have different meters, such as these opening lines from two
Easter hymns, that each have seven syllables:

```
u   /  u  /   u  /   u        iambic
The day of res - ur - rec - tion!    (UMH #303)


/    u  /   u   /  u   /      trochaic
Come, ye faith - ful, raise the strain    (UMH #315)
```

The difference in type of foot means that a tune that works for one foot
will not work for the other foot—the accents of the tune and text will
not match. The mismatching of poetic meter and musical meter can
also occur when hymn texts are not regular in their stresses. When
reading a text aloud, the reader can make adjustments for misplaced
accents, but a tune does not allow that freedom.

As the poem at the head of this chapter suggests, the ballad meter in
poetry, with its four-line stanzas of eight, six, eight, and six syllables, is
called "common meter" (or CM) in hymnody. It may also be notated as
86.86. "Short meter" (SM) has lines of six, six, eight, and six syllables
(66.86), while "long meter" (LM) has four lines of eight syllables each
(88.88). Each of these meters can be followed by a refrain or can be
doubled (CM with refrain or CMD, SMD, LMD, etc.). Most hymnals
print the meter somewhere on the hymnal page and also index the music by its meter so that familiar tunes in the same meter can be substi-
tuted for unfamiliar tunes. *The United Methodist Hymnal*, for example,
lists over one hundred meters in its metrical index.

Related to meter is the pattern of lines in a text and their arrangement into stanzas. As can be seen from the preceding paragraphs, stanzas are often four or eight lines. They can also be six lines, or three, or
whatever other pattern the hymnwriter decides. The primary defining
characteristic of the stanza relates to the completion of thought within
each stanza and ultimately to the music involved. It is possible to sing
an eight-line stanza to a four-line tune by doubling the tune's repetitions. Likewise, some four-line stanzas are sung to tunes of five lines
by repeating the last line of the text. Various other combinations are
also possible.

Although Isaac Watts wrote around six hundred hymns, he primarily wrote in three meters. Charles Wesley used at least thirty different
metrical forms (Reynolds 1963, 55) and helped to popularize the anapestic foot. Frank Baker suggests that the anapest gave Wesley a sense
of lilt in texts to express his enthusiastic emotions (Baker 1988, 73).

Some contemporary hymnwriters, most notably Jaroslav Vajda, are using less common and even unusual meters, much like modern poetry.

It should be noted that modern hymnals in the United States use interlining of texts rather than the older practice of placing the music and text separately, as is still followed in Great Britain. *Interlining* means that the stanzas of hymn texts are placed within the lines of music, in order that the syllable or word for each note is clearly placed under that note. The result is that hymn texts lose their shape of lines and stanzas, because what one actually sees is something like:

O   for   a   thou-sand tongues to sing   my
My gra-cious Mas- ter   and   my God, as-

great Re-deem-er's praise, the glo-   ries   of my
sist   me to   pro-claim, to spread through all the

God and King, the tri- umphs of his grace!
Earth a- broad, the hon-ors   of thy name.   (*UMH* #57)

Needless to say, there have been protests (Routley 1979, vii; Young 1995b, 24), and many new hymn collections (for example, Duck 1992, Wren 1989b, and Troeger 1994a) include printings of the texts as poetry as well as interlined with music.

Rhyme in Western Hymnody

Rhyming hymnody has been the norm since the Reformation. Rhyme consists of similar vowel and consonant sounds in the final accented syllable of a poetic line, such as *bell/well* or *foundation/salvation*. Near rhyme contains either vowel or consonant similarities but not both, such as *life/Christ, live/love*.

The most common pattern in hymns is rhyming the second and fourth lines, but not the first and third, notated as ABCB. In notating any rhyme scheme, one begins with *A* and uses a new letter for each line that does not rhyme, returning to the rhyming letter when it does rhyme. Cross-rhyming is the name given to rhyming both lines two with four, and one with three, notated ABAB. Occasionally adjoining lines, called couplets, rhyme in a four-line stanza notated as AABB; this form is used less frequently because it stops the flow of the stanza midway.

midway. Other combinations of rhyme are possible, including ABBA for four-line stanzas and various combinations for six- and eight-line stanzas.

Repetition of sounds within a line or between lines of a stanza, other than rhyme, play an important part of the poetic nature of hymn texts. The repetition of vowel sounds is called *assonance*. Repetition of consonant sounds is called *consonance*. Repetition of the beginning sounds of words is called *alliteration*. Repetition of the opening word or phrase of a line is called *anaphora*. Immediate repetition of words within a line of poetry is called *epizeuxis* (Quinn 1982, 80-81). Repetition of words within a line of poetry in which the repetition contains a slight difference in meaning is called *antanaclasis*. Kenneth Burke speaks of the "musicality of verse" by analyzing the sounds within poetry and the patterns of repetition, many of which he acknowledges may be unconscious on the part of the poet (1973, 369-378). Yet it is these repetitions and their variation that give poetry and hymn texts their flow, and that incline hymn texts to be sung.

Diction

The English language is an Anglo-Saxon language, that contains a combination of Latin and Norman French words, among other influences. Mary Kinzie focused on Latin and Anglo-Saxon words to discuss diction in a poem (1994, 9-12). She described Latinate words as primarily multisyllabled and more abstract than Anglo-Saxon words, which are primarily monosyllabic and concrete. The *diction*, or vocabulary, of a poem may be either concrete (dealing with things or ideas that are touchable) or abstract (related more to feelings and lofty ideas). Parallel to the diction of the poem is the tendency to use Anglo-Saxon monosyllabism for concreteness and Latinate polysyllabism for abstractness.

Hymns are concerned with lofty ideas but tend toward concrete diction, the use of monosyllabic words, as opposed to, say, the academic field of theology, that tends toward abstract Latinate polysyllabism. The use of shorter, more concrete words in hymns has two advantages. First, the shorter words move the text along with the music; one-syllable words are more likely not to clash with the meter of the music. Second, the concreteness enables the hymn to have a richness of texture and an immediacy it might not have with longer, more abstract words.

Poetic Devices

In his book *The Anatomy of Hymnody* Austin Lovelace describes twenty-eight poetic devices used in hymn texts (1982, 94-102). These poetic devices may be called *ornamentation*, yet they are used with concern for their effectiveness in communicating. Many of them were used more frequently by hymnwriters in former times who were trained in classical rhetoric from which these devices are drawn. In addition to the devices of repetition mentioned previously, those most commonly used in hymn texts today are: address, chiasmus, enjambment, paradox, personification, sequencing, and metaphor.

Address is a common device in hymn texts, as the text directs its voice to God ("O God, our help in ages past"), to Jesus ("Jesus, we look to thee"), or humanity ("Sinners, turn, why will you die?").

Chiasmus is the crossing of lines or clauses, wherein the second mirrors the first. Lovelace uses an example of a hymn by Charles Wesley in that *joy* appears in line one, *peace* in line two. The chiasmus occurs as *peace* is repeated in line three and *joy* in line four (Lovelace 1982, 96-97). This is repetition with the order reversed.

Enjambment occurs when a thought continues past the end of the poetic line; it might also be described as *run-on*. Enjambment is relatively rare in hymnody, yet when it occurs it adds emphasis to the words involved.

Paradox, the juxtaposition of two opposites, occurs often in Christian faith, notably in the contrast that Jesus *died* in order to *live* again. Paradox is a type of *metaphor*, where two things that seem contradictory are juxtaposed in order to show a jointly acceptable truth (Wheelwright 1954, 70).

Personification occurs frequently in hymn texts, as an inanimate object or concept is given human attributes, such as these found in hymn texts: "Awake, my soul" and "My faith looks up to thee." Personification is actually a form of metaphor, as something not usually considered human is addressed as such. Thus, the *soul* and *faith*, concepts that are not touchable and more difficult to define, are related to bodily functions, waking and looking up, actions more easily understandable.

Sequencing of a text, how the thought progresses, helps the reader focus where the writer intends. Sometimes the first thought is the most important, and subsequent lines merely explain it (psychological sequencing). Sometimes the text gathers thoughts together into a climax at the final or near final line (climactic or presentational sequencing).

Sometimes the text follows a chronological order, as in telling a story (Leech and Short 1981, 236-239). Doran and Troeger point out that many hymns follow a three-step spiritual meditation popular in England in the 1600s: memory (recalling the biblical story), understanding (the contemporary meaning of the story), and will (a prayer to live God's will in accordance with the story) (1986, vi).

Metaphor[3]

What Is Metaphor? "The essence of metaphor is understanding and experiencing one kind of thing in terms of another" (Lakoff and Johnson 1980, 5). In their detailed study, *Metaphors We Live By*, linguists George Lakoff and Mark Johnson suggest that not only do metaphors express our creativity and increase our understanding, but in fact, metaphors are as vital to our functioning as one of our senses (1980, 239). Metaphors have the power to create reality, they give us a way to understand reality, and they enable us to structure our experience (Lakoff and Johnson 1980, 145-158). In looking at paradox and personification, we have already begun to see how metaphor works with religious language.

How Metaphors Work. Metaphor can be analyzed as *tenor* and *vehicle*. The *tenor* is the meaning of the metaphor. The *vehicle,* or analogy, is the medium that carries the meaning. As an example, consider the Easter carol, "Now the green blade riseth" (*UMH* #311). This text is built on the vehicle of grain sown to grow compared with Jesus Christ's death and resurrection. Put very simply the tenor of this text is that the grain, representing Jesus, was put in the earth and rose from it in glorious splendor—so we too can experience resurrection. Because the text contains many points of resemblance and continuity between grain, Jesus, and us, the metaphor has a sense of naturalness and completeness.

Philip Wheelwright suggests two "ways" of metaphor: *epiphor* and *diaphor*. Epiphor is the outreach and extension of meaning through the comparison between something relatively well-known and something less well-known, resulting in personification and anthropomorphisms (relating God to human anatomy and human qualities) among other

---

3. Some of the work in this section is quoted from this writer's M.T.S. thesis for Candler School of Theology at Emory University in 1982, "The Language of Hymnody: The Hymn Texts of Fred Kaan."

metaphors. Diaphor is the creation of new meaning by juxtaposition and synthesis, seen in paradox and irony (Wheelwright 1962, 70-91).

Metaphor may also combine epiphor and diaphor, for example in the poetic catalogue, recontextualizing, and word-plays. In a *catalogue*, a list of names, things, or impressions are put in succession and play off against each other with a cumulative deepening of meaning. *Recontextualizing* uses traditional words or ideas in new or different contexts to reveal new understandings. *Word-plays* are not frequent in hymns, but they do occur; one familiar example is *Sun/Son*, in speaking of Jesus Christ.

Monroe Beardsley gives two principles for metaphors. First, the "principle of congruence" requires the assembly of possible connotations of the words, guided by the logical and physical possibilities. Second, the "principle of plentitude" calls for the attribution of all connotations that can be found to fit, so that the metaphor means all that it can mean (Beardsley 1958, 114-147). Following these principles results in a richness of explication—a wealth of possible insight into the metaphor—that is followed in this text in the section on multidimensional readings of hymn texts.

Metaphor and Religious Language. Metaphors are critical for the creative expression of poetry and in the field of religion when words are needed to understand something that and Someone who are beyond our comprehension. So we speak of what is unknown in terms of what is known, using metaphor. It is through metaphor that we can talk about the *face* of God or how God *touches* the earth, through metaphor that we call God *Savior, Friend, Rock of Ages, Source of Life*.

As discussed in Chapter 1, Sallie McFague based her theology on the nature of metaphor, and its whisper, "it is and *it is not*" (1984, 13). Gail Ramshaw calls this the "yes-no-yes" of liturgical language, where the first step is the acknowledgment of the possibility of liturgical language, the sacredness of words. The second step realizes that words fall far short of conveying what we mean about God; the Holy One cannot be contained within words. Yet, because we have only words, and because the Judeo-Christian tradition places great importance on both God's word/Word and on the words of our religious heritage, we are left speaking what we know is not complete (Ramshaw 1986, 23-24).

Christian hymns draw their metaphors from a variety of sources: scriptures, tradition, and experience. Part of the task of hymnwriters is to seek continually for fresh metaphors in order that the Word of God may be heard anew by those both inside and outside the church. Those who interpret hymn texts point to the sources of metaphor and their reverberation throughout a text.

GENRE

. . . they [former hymnwriters] are part of the cloud of witnesses that is influencing me and giving me courage to try writing a genuinely contemporary form of hymnody.
> Thomas Troeger, "Personal, Cultural, and Theological Influences on the Language of Hymns and Worship"

Perhaps one difference between a hymn text and any other religious poem is that the communities of faith who might sing the text are present in the writer's imagination, even in the room apart where writing takes place. Writing hymns is not simply an individual process; it is grounded in communities of faith.
> Ruth Duck, *Dancing in the Universe*

Mikhail Bakhtin says that each sphere in that language is used develops its own relatively stable types of utterances, that we may call speech genres (1986, 60). Christian hymns are developed within the tradition of Christian worship, drawing on scripture and the teachings of Jesus Christ as well as on the long history of faith and the contemporary realities of the hymnwriter.

Christian worship has produced several genres, or stable types of utterances: preaching, hymns, and prayers, to name the three most easily defined. Some comparisons of these utterances may help define the genre of hymn more clearly.

Hymns and Preaching

The similarities between hymns and preaching begin with their basis in scripture, and thus their use of biblical language, including images and metaphors. Both center on God or the Persons of the Trinity (Creator God, Jesus Christ, and Holy Spirit). Both are used in the context of worship, although hymns can show up in public life (schools, novels, soccer games) as do sermons (for example, those by Dr. Martin Luther King Jr.). Both draw people together—hymns by the common nature of singing, sermons by the common nature of all listening to the same thing.

There are differences as well. The most obvious is that hymns are accompanied by music and the aim is for all persons to sing. In preaching generally only one person speaks and everyone else is sup-

posed to listen. One variation of this character of preaching is the response tradition, particularly in African-American churches, with
"Amen!" and other responses arising from the congregation (Crawford
1995, 13ff.). Hymns are short, lasting generally from one and a half
minutes to maybe five minutes, while preaching may last anywhere
from twelve to forty-five minutes (longer in some traditions and at
some times in history). The primary purposes of sermons are to proclaim God's message, to teach the listeners the meaning of that message for their lives, and to convince them to apply the message in their
lives. Although hymns may do all three of those things, the original
purpose of hymns was praise of God. While the shape of a sermon can
be poetic, it is most often written in prose, in sentences and paragraphs,
while the hymn appears in lines and stanzas. In summary, while hymns
and sermons draw their inspiration from the same source, they manifest
two distinct genres within the field of liturgical language.

Hymns and Prayers

Prayers are less "listener-directed" than preaching, for their aim is not
to convict but to be in dialogue with God. Within the context of Christian worship, prayer takes three primary forms: silent prayer, pastoral
prayer and communal prayer. *Silent prayer* is between each individual
and God. A *pastoral* prayer is when the worship leader, most often the
pastor or priest, prays on behalf of the congregation, aloud, while the
congregation listens and adds their "Amen" at the end, signaling their
assent. In *communal* prayer the congregation prays a printed or memo-
rized prayer aloud together. Communal prayer is the most related to
hymns.

Hymns are like communal prayers in that both enable participation
and community-building, and also in that both are often written by an
individual and edited by committee. Hymns are often addressed to God
and often carry on a dialogue between the singer and God, much like
communal prayers. Hymns serve many of the same purposes as communal prayers: praise, thanksgiving, confession, seeking direction and
guidance. Like communal prayers, hymns are found in books, bulletins,
or occasionally memory. The duration of hymns and communal prayers
are about the same.

Unlike communal prayers, hymns are set both to music and to meter. Whereas the sentences and paragraphs of a prayer may vary widely
in length, once the hymn stanza is set, it repeats in meter and rhyme
scheme for the continuation of the hymn. In practice, hymns are often

more clear about their communal nature, in that breathing spaces are clearly marked by the music. In communal prayers if the prayer is written in paragraph style and the phrases get long, the communal rhythm may be jagged. Thus, although communal prayers and hymns share common inspiration and give the congregation a common voice, these two types of texts each exhibit specific characteristics, defining them each as a genre.

Bakhtin, Genre and Hymn

Drawing from the above discussion, Bakhtin's definitions of speech genre helps define the characteristics of *hymn* as a genre. The sphere in that the hymn is used has been defined as Christian worship flowing out of Christian tradition. Hymns and the related genres of preaching and prayer also find their way into secular culture, or perhaps more accurately, the remains of the Christianizing of culture begun by Constantine are evidenced occasionally by the appearance of these genres in the secular culture. Examples of this phenomenon are prayers given at city council meetings, preaching on street corners and television, hymns at state funerals, and the hymn, "Abide with Me," sung at soccer matches in England (Adey 1988, x).

The Boundaries of the Genre of Hymns. For Bakhtin the boundaries of each utterance are determined by a change of speaker (1986, 76-77). Hymn singing is introduced by a solo voice of a worship leader or cantor (songleader) or by the organist/pianist playing an introduction, then the congregation usually stands and begins to sing together.

Bakhtin defines other characteristics of *genre* as: the finalization of the utterance with its possibilities of response, semantic exhaustiveness of the theme (addressing the subject with some degree of completeness), the speaker's plan and typical compositional and generic forms of finalization (1986,76-77). The early church hymns most often ended with a doxological stanza, or stanza in praise of the Trinitarian God, followed by an "Amen." *Amen* came from the Hebrew tradition of the congregation adding an "Amen" as their assent to something (prayer or sacrifice) done in their name (cf. Ps. 106.48). During the flurry of translations of hymns from the Latin and Greek during the Oxford Movement, in the ages when hymns in the vernacular were still somewhat new (1833 forward), hymnal editors began the practice of concluding every hymn, no matter what its final stanza's tone, with an "Amen" (Routley 1978, 98). When hymnal editors in the second half of the twentieth century looked at the history of the "Amen" and realized that it was not necessary (because people were already assenting by their singing of the text), there was a hue and cry about "Amens" from the people in the pew (Young 1993, 581). In looking at the predominance of "Amen" as the signal of conclusion in prayers and often sermons, one gets a sense that for many persons "Amen" has come to mean "The End" and without it many hymns feel unfinished to the congregation. Some recent hymnal committees, although not writing the "Amen" at the end of each hymn, have suggested that local congregations might add it at the end of hymns where appropriate—for example, those that end with a doxological stanza, or prayer (Sanchez 1989, 35).

The other indicators for the end of a hymn are, of course, the end of the printed stanzas, upon which the people finish singing and sit down (if they have been standing). Because the community as a whole has participated in the singing of the hymn, the response is generally an internalized, "Yes, God, that is what I think" or "Help me, God, to make this true in my life" (responding to the pattern mentioned by Doran and Troeger above, 27). Perhaps the "Amen" functioned also as the people's response, their assent to the words of the hymn.

The semantic exhaustiveness of the theme of the hymn varies greatly among hymns. The hymns of Charles Wesley often ran over ten stanzas whereas many praise choruses that are sung in churches today consist of only one or two phrases repeated many times over. In any case, the hymn is planned to address a thought and address it in some manner of completeness. Typical compositional and generic forms of finalization for hymns are less clear than those for communal prayer or preaching. Hymns do still often end with a doxological stanza, or they may end with a stanza of prayer for carrying out the theme of the hymn in our everyday lives. Sometimes the text builds to a climax with a satisfying resolution for the conclusion.

Hymns as Part of the Chain of Communication. The other criterion that Bakhtin finds important for utterances is their relationship to the speaker and to the other participants in speech communication, realizing that there is a chain of speech communication in which the utterance takes place (Bakhtin 1986, 84, 94-95). Communal prayer and hymns have much in common on this point, for they are created by one person (and often edited by a committee) and yet are meant to be able to be spoken or sung by many persons who can agree with their sentiments. Hymnwriters acknowledge the presence of the faith community even as they write as well as the tradition in which they write. The quotations from Troeger and Duck at the beginning of this section confirm this. Hymns draw from the past (using scripture and tradition) and draw from the present (using reason and experience, to complete the Wesleyan quadrilateral of balancing one's spiritual life). They are in dialogue with utterances of the hymnic genre that have preceded them and are open to those that will follow.

Within worship, hymns often function as the people's response to the call of scripture, prayer, or the sermon. The call-response pattern is derived from the theological concept of God's call and our response (as seen throughout the Hebrew and Christian scriptures). As Young says, "music convenes the community, reminds it who and whose it is, prepares it for hearing, seeing, and responding to the proclaimed word and celebrated sacrament, and sends it forth for work and witness" (Young 1995a, 197). Likewise, the hymn is also responded to by the next action in worship, whether it is a prayer, scripture reading, or sermon. Hymns, like the sermon, anticipate a fulfillment in the believer's life during the week.

Related to the chain of speech communication is the tradition of editing hymn texts (England and Sparrow, 1966, 39). John Wesley was a master at editing texts, in translating them for his constituency. One of the most frequently cited examples of hymn editing is Charles Wesley's hymn now known as "Hark! the Herald Angels Sing" that originally read "Hark! How All the Welkin Rings" (Wren 1995b, 842). This editing characteristic of the hymnic genre is unheard of in the genre of classical poetry, yet plays an important part in this book as we look at certain recent hymn texts.

One large difference between hymns and communal prayers is that, except for "The Lord's Prayer" and some eucharistic prayers, many congregations have a different communal prayer each week with no continuity or repetition. (The repetition of hymns might be likened somewhat to the repetition of scripture reading, yet the nature of scripture reading in worship is very different from hymns.) Over a year of Christian worship a congregation may sing anywhere from fifty to over one hundred and fifty hymns, with some number of those repeated within the year and from year to year. A Christian who has attended worship regularly for, say thirty years, without even a great deal of concentration, would have a repertoire of several dozen hymns for which they know the tune and at least most of the first stanza. Thus, the genre of hymn includes the characteristics of revisited meaning and memory, known in the field of linguistics as *habituation*.

The Addressee of Hymns. Bakhtin suggests that each genre has its own typical conception of the addressee and this is what defines it as a genre (1986, 94-95). For preaching it is clear that the preacher addresses persons she or he wishes to guide along the Christian way, whether they be non-Christians or Christians already trying to go that way. The preacher is assumed to have a better understanding of God's way than the listener or at least has spent more time studying the questions and the scriptures. Communal prayer is addressed to God, whom it seeks to come and envelop the believers with assurance, love, forgiveness, salvation, and guidance.

Hymns are not so clear. A hymn may address variously God, the congregation, or an individual. It is one thing to consider a congregation addressing God in a hymn and another to consider a congregation addressing itself in a hymn.

When students write prayers for congregations in seminary or workshops they are often cautioned to keep their focus on God as the addressee. For when they begin addressing the congregation itself, they move from prayer (addressed to God) into preaching (addressing the congregation) (Duck 1995a, 26). Hymns seem to have this ambivalence built into their genre, the combination of prayer (addressed to God) and preaching (addressed to the congregation).

A cursory look at *The United Methodist Hymnal* for addressees finds that in hymns of "Praise and Thanksgiving," clearly God is the addressee; in hymns on God's nature one finds a mixture of God and congregation as addressee, with the emphasis on God. The section on "Providence" introduces some hymns addressed to *you* in the congregation. "In Praise of Christ" mixes hymns addressed to Jesus, with "I Love to Tell the Story" and "Come, Christians, Join to Sing" obviously addressed to the congregation. Skipping over the seasonal hymns on Jesus' life, we come to the hymns "In Praise of the Holy Spirit," in which the Spirit is most often addressed, but addressees also include the congregation: "Surely the Presence of the Lord Is in this Place" and "Of All the Spirit's Gifts to Me." Likewise the large section devoted to hymns about God's grace contains forty-eight hymns addressed to God, forty-two addressed to the congregation, and nine beginning with address to the congregation and concluding with address to God (in a stanza of prayer). If one were to suggest that only hymns addressed to God were truly members of the hymn genre, almost half of these hymns surveyed would be omitted! Therefore, one characteristic about the hymnic genre is ambivalence about the addressee, or options of addressee.

In the hymns that do not directly address God or at least one Person of the Trinity, God is nevertheless present as the hymn tells the congregation of God's mighty acts of creation and salvation for the world or for the individual. (God is then spoken of in the third person.) Occasionally there is a hymn that dares to speak in God's voice to the congregation: "Lord of the Dance" (first line: "I danced in the morning when the world was begun," *I* being Jesus) and "Here I Am, Lord" (first line: "I the Lord of sea and sky"). "Lord of the Dance" draws its popularity from its tune—SIMPLE GIFTS, the Shaker tune made popular in Aaron Copland's *Appalachian Spring*—and its publication in the 1960s as a "folk hymn." Its refrain calls us to "Dance, then wherever you may be; / I am the Lord of the dance, said he, / and I'll lead you all / . . ." Note the shifting of *he* and *I* for the Lord. The title "Here I Am, Lord," for the second hymn, comes from the first line of the refrain, where the voice changes from that of God to that of the Christian responding to God. Both of these hymns are particularly popular in mainline denominations and the second in evangelical denominations as well. Some persons have raised concerns about the potential for misuse of God's voice in hymns such as these (Ramshaw 1995b, 17). Yet others suggest that the use of the first person follows the tradition of the Hebrew prophets, raising a prophetic voice.

Distinguishing between the Genres of Poetry and of Hymns. Like much religious poetry, hymns are metrical and rhymed, and they use image, metaphor, and other poetic devices. Unlike devotional poetry, they are meant to give common voice as opposed to only individual sentiments (Duck 1995, 21-22). Unlike religious poetry, hymns are meant to be sung in common worship. This common nature and the matter of fitting a tune help define the genre and scope of hymns both in their topic and in their form. Hymns may be used as devotional poetry, read by individuals, but when that happens there are still echoes of the music and of common worship in the reading.

A slight distinction may also be made between hymnwriters and secular poets. Most often the writer of the text is known, along with any translator and composer of the music. Yet this knowledge does not have the weight that a poet's name carries with a secular poem. Few people in the congregation know (or care) about the author, what matters is that they can agree with the text and sing the tune. Most hymnwriters understand this factor and try to find out as much as possible about any congregations for whom they write (Wren 1989c). Many new one-author collections include information about the occasion the hymn was written for as well as listing the congregation that commissioned the hymn.

Comparisons of the Genres of Hymns and Folk Songs. Some scholars have compared hymns to folk songs and ballads. Like folk songs, hymns are meant to be "the music of the people," at least the people who call themselves Christian. Unlike the anonymous creators of many folk songs, the creators of most hymn texts and tunes are known. Like folk songs, occasionally different versions of hymns float around from different locales or different editors. One of the musical debates about hymns is whether the tunes ought to be accessible or should be held to a "higher" standard of music. Thomas Troeger, one of the more prolific and best contemporary hymnwriters, has seen his hymn texts limited in their use by the tunes that his first musical collaborator, Carol Doran, wrote (cf. Young 1993, 603, 707). Ms. Doran is a graduate of Eastman School of Music and writes tunes and harmonizations in the style of contemporary art songs or symphonies. Many of these tunes are challenging for an average congregation to sing and also require careful practice from the organist or pianist. Thus, even when they do appear in hymnals, they are not likely to be chosen frequently by pastors and musicians, even though the texts are rich in scripture and contemporary metaphors (see further discussion of this in Chapters 9 and 14).

Comparisons of the Genres of Hymns and Songs. In some places there is debate over whether something is a hymn or a song. The Hymn Society of the United States and Canada, an organization for hymnologists and hymnwriters, tries to bridge the gap by subtitling its quarterly journal, *The Hymn: A Journal of Congregational Song.* The delineations between song and hymn are often lines drawn in the sand, and, therefore, the current text considers any song intended for congregational singing that exhibits other characteristics of this genre to be a hymn.

Conclusion. It can be stated that the characteristics of the genre of the hymn are as follows: The sphere of hymnic language is that of Christian worship flowing out of the Christian faith tradition. The speaker is the congregation who join their voices together to sing the hymn. There is a communal sense within the genre and an emphasis on common voice rather than individual, that is, unison singing. The form of the genre is most often that of rhymed and metered poetry, set in stanzas of identical rhyme and meter. Whereas in former times an "Amen" signaled the end of the hymn, now the end is dependent more on semantic exhaustiveness and completeness of thought. The repetition of hymns within worship reinforced by the characteristic of habituation gives hymns an influence on faith that other forms of religious genre, such as preaching or most prayers do not have. The factor of the hymn tune and its influence on the popularity of the text and occasionally on its intelligibility is hard to measure. Hymns are subject to editing by hymnal committees and groups using them. The genre of hymn appears to have some ambivalence about its addressee, drawing upon the option of either God or the congregation (each other), and occasionally using both within one hymn. Similarly, the response evoked by the hymn might be internalized when the addressee is the congregation (shown forth over time in the believer's life) or a sense of assurance received by the speakers when the addressee is God. The hymn clearly functions in the chain of speech communication, as it may function itself as a response to some act of worship or prepare worshipers for the next act of worship.

REGISTER

> The most important stylistic feature in a text [that helps define a register] will be (a) that that occurs more frequently within the variety in question, and (b) that that is shared less by other varieties.
> David Crystal and Derek Davy, *Investigating English Style*

Linguistic Register

Every language has many subordinate varieties, that may be categorized according to user (*social* and *regional dialects*, that tell who we are and where we come from) or uses (*register* and *style*, that tell what we are doing) (Romaine 1994, 2, 20). The study of situational varieties of language began early in the twentieth century, but the word *register* to name them was not used until 1956 in a work on bilingualism by T. B. W. Reid (1956). Although there are slightly different definitions of *register*, this text follows the historical definition of *register* as a situation-based variety of language that shows a correlation between linguistic features and situation. A number of register studies have focused on religious language (Brook 1965, Samarin 1976, Ellis and Ure 1982, Jasper and Jasper 1990). Identifying the register of hymn texts can enrich our understanding of them.

Dell Hymes points out that register may be chosen not only to respond to a situation but also to define a situation (1974, 112). Every language contains a variety of registers, that may be differentiated from other registers in the total repertoire of the community on a continuum or *cline*. As a society changes, its register range also changes. All persons master a range of registers that reflects their language experience; this may also change over time. Register can be useful as a research tool in analyzing texts, in translation, and in language teaching. Intensive register study often includes multidimensional analysis of a large amount of text viewed in context of its social situation, expressed statistically, in terms of relative frequencies and percentages of specific items (Biber 1989, 1993; Biber & Finegan 1994). Every utterance (in speaking or writing) simultaneously exemplifies *dialect* (identifiable according to user), *register* (identifiable by communication situation), and *genre* (a message type) (Ferguson, in Biber and Finegan 1994, 25).

From his study of the rhetoric of the early Christian liturgy, George Kennedy suggests two tendencies of religious language:

> On the one hand there is a preference for natural, simple and contemporary language. . . . On the other hand, there is from the beginning some pull in an opposite direction, toward the exotic as a feature of sacral language (in Jasper and Jasper 1990, 35-36).

Another early work in the area of *register* is Martin Joos's *The Five Clocks* (1967), that delineated five styles of language. Although Joos did not specify register for his categorization, his delineation of styles has served as a systematic guide for register studies. The five types of style Joos named are *frozen, formal, consultative, casual,* and *intimate*. Consultative style is marked by the speaker supplying background information and the addressee participating continuously. Casual style is marked by ellipsis, slang, and formulas. Intimate style excludes public information, and is marked by extraction and jargon. In formal style participation drops out, the task is to inform, and form becomes the dominant character of discourse; another way of defining formal style uses the features of detachment and cohesion. This is the style most associated with Christian public worship with phrases such as "Wilt thou have this woman to be thy wedded wife?" and "Let us pray . . ." Frozen style moves beyond formal to a sense of being "set in stone," either in print or declamation. Joos claims frozen style is marked by its lack of participation and intonation; yet it offers two things: rereading and refeeling, that together can lead to wisdom (1967, 45). Hymn texts might be thought to use frozen style because they are written, but because they are often edited and appear in various versions (mentioned above in relationship to folk music and below in the multidimensional readings), their style falls between formal and frozen.

Another way to say it might be that hymns are formal in their usage and can be studied because they are frozen.

Register and Worship

David and R. C. D. Jasper's 1990 collection of essays took a linguistic approach to the study of worship. Crystal's essay in this collection looks at liturgical language from a sociolinguistic perspective. He identified liturgical English linguistic norms present a generation ago, including forms of words such as *thou, thee, brethren, spake*; words not in the everyday lexicon such as *thrice* and *behold*; the frequent use of the vocative, both with and without *O*; and distinctive idioms. He goes on to say that this register is changing so that it now resembles other formal registers of the English language, with the exception of some specific prayer forms that use archaic syntax and the vocative (Jasper and Jasper 1990, 123). Crystal's examples of religious register are primarily drawn from British liturgy, which has remained more formal than that in the United States, thus some of his examples were dying out of usage in liturgy here even before the Revised Standard translation of the Bible in 1946 and 1952. Yet he is correct in describing the change that has happened and is still happening in the register of religious language.

Crystal concludes from studying the language of the Mass that it exhibits more linguistic functions than any other domain of language (Jasper and Jasper 1990, 136). He enumerates these defining functions of a liturgical linguistic register: informational (particularly to those who are new), identifying (a strong function of liturgical language), expressive (of the depths of emotion), performative (related most directly to Roman Catholic liturgy), historical (in the sense of identifying with the historical tradition), and aesthetic (particularly when music is involved) (Jasper and Jasper 1990, 129-136).

Another distinction of the register of religious language found by Crystal is the extraordinary way that time is viewed in worship (Jasper and Jasper 1990, 137). This may be seen both in the repetition of texts from times past and also in what Saliers describes as the eschatological character of liturgy, the sense that worship, while happening right now, participates in the final glory of God (1994, 49-68).

Register and Hymns

As we move to identify a register of hymns, we need to recall these previously mentioned characteristics of religious language: the identifying function mentioned by Crystal (where language expresses the religious identity of the participants), the formal style described by Joos, and the characteristics identified by Crystal that particularly apply to hymn texts:

- special lexical words
- vocative syntactic structures both with and without *O*
- unusual word order (also related to the register of poetry)
- distinctive idioms
- expressive and aesthetic functions
- historical function as it relates to identification with the historical tradition
- distinctive timeframe

One other comment by Crystal is pertinent to our discussion of register and the specific liturgical form of hymns: "The use of unison speech is itself a highly distinctive linguistic activity. There are no other social occasions where this activity is so carefully structured, and where a written text can be followed" (Jasper and Jasper 1990, 137). Crystal did not specify hymns, but this points to important characteristics of hymnic register: a written text, the congregation participating together, with the uniqueness of singing.

In an essay on the language of hymns (in Jasper and Jasper 1990), J. R. Watson points out a number of characteristics of the register of hymns. The "hymn-ness" Watson describes relates to its register and its genre: its preference for certain rhythms and meters, the familiarity in its tune and text, the participatory factor, its expressiveness (already pointed out by Crystal), its varieties of focus (prayer, argument, ecstasy, and emotion), and its communal factor (many voices together in contrast to the single voice of the preacher or liturgist).

The only criterion of Watson that I would debate is his comment that hymns contain an absence of surprise. In one sense he is correct: Part of the "hymn-ness" of a hymn is that that identifies it as something we already know. We hear a snatch of "O God, our help in ages past" on the radio and know that it is a hymn, that it relates to Christian worship. Yet one of the things that informs this study is the element of surprise in hymns, a sense of "ah-ha!" or "O, yes: that is what I thought but I didn't know it could be brought before God in public worship!" or "I never thought of God in that way before!"

Another characteristic of the register of hymn texts is that of clear and concise words, often of one and two syllables. Longer words may occur, but part of the register of hymn texts is the use of shorter words that keep the thought moving along with the music (see above, 25).

The register of hymns includes received texts such as the Doxology ("Praise God from whom all blessings flow") and other hymns dating back to the early centuries of Christendom as well as hymns published recently in denominational hymnals. Songs and choruses that are being composed as this text is written are also part of the register of hymns, even though they may only be sung in one local church or may be spread by oral tradition. This text is limited to those congregational songs that are currently found in mainline Protestant denominational hymnals. But within the register of Christian hymnody there are many variants. These vary not only by denomination but also by worship style and belief: Differences between highly liturgical, prayer book churches and so called free churches, particularly those free not only of set prayers but also free of denominational connections. Still, there is a register of common voice that can be identified as Christian liturgical language, of that hymns are a part.

In the multidimensional readings that form the center of this text different characteristics of hymnic register will surface both in the interpretation and in the attempt to suggest the hymn's function. Either way, the linguistic characteristics of the hymn display its register and enable it to speak to and from its particular situation.

DECORUM

For Cicero, decorum was a principle that operated to civilize our lives as well as our speech. For Milton, decorum represented the "grand master peece to observe."

The locus of decorum is that moment when the discourse becomes luminous in itself through its illumination of a subject, and it is just at that moment that discourse attains its greatest practical force.

Michael Leff, "Decorum and Rhetorical Interpretation"

Rhetoric

The word *rhetoric* is used in this text in its positive connotations, rather than the negative ones engendered by its use in the media to denote empty phrases meant only for show. Here *rhetoric* is the study of how people communicate, how they persuade, how they "overcome the obstacles in a given situation with a specific audience on a given issue to achieve a particular end" (Campbell 1982, 7). "The 'bias'," says Campbell, "of a rhetorical perspective is its emphasis on and its concern with the resources available in language and in people to make ideas clear and cogent, to bring concepts to life" (1982, 3). "Bringing concepts to life" is part of the task of Christian worship, enabling persons to encounter God with faith, humility, and love. Thus, rhetoric informs the multidimensional readings that form the center of this text.

"The potential for persuasion exists in the shared symbolic and socioeconomic experience of the rhetor and audience" (Campbell 1989, 2). This relates to hymn texts, particularly in respect to a shared symbolic experience, and in part also to shared expectations of the genre and a shared register. The idea of a shared socioeconomic experience parallels the idea of social location discussed above under theology. It overlaps somewhat with register, as the rhetor negotiates in order to communicate, so that the experience may be shared.

Persuasion takes the form not only of initiating action, but also of maintaining action, such as "the Sunday sermon to the regular church goer, that urges continued support and attendance" or the repetition of hymns that encourages faith (Campbell 1982, 14). Thus, concepts of rhetoric have been used to study religion and worship, as may be seen in the studies of Kennedy linking the Bible and rhetoric (1984), those of Jasper and Jasper in liturgy and rhetoric (1990), and James Murphy's work on preaching and rhetoric (1990). Additional rhetorical elements that apply to hymn texts are discussed in the chapter on the methodology of multidimensional reading.

Decorum

Rhetoric includes the art of persuasion and the art of "social accommodation," adapting one's speech in community (Leff 1990, 108). Speaking through the *persona* of Crassus, Cicero suggests that "social accommodation" can enhance both the persuasive element and the aesthetic element: "the thing most useful is also in a way most becoming" (*De oratore* 3, 224, quoted in Leff 1990, 125).

Although the principles of how one persuades in rhetoric have varied throughout the centuries, the only invariant principle has been *decorum* (Leff 1995). Decorum is social accommodation, using language in a way that is persuasive not only in a particular situation but also in a way that is appropriate and fitting, that thus also is aesthetically pleasing.

The early Roman tradition of decorum blossomed in Cicero but was quickly limited after him. Elaine Fantham, in her essay on Cicero and decorum, discerned two threads: extrinsic accommodation (adjustment to context and circumstance) and intrinsic merit (holding to an absolute standard of aesthetic worth) (1984, 123-125).

In her study of rhetorical and historical consciousness in the Renaissance, Nancy Struever added a third thread, an emphasis on decorum or the search for the appropriate, that served as a general characteristic of fourteenth- and fifteenth-century ethics: What does the decorum of the situation demand? Struever suggests that decorum is not merely restraint but rather a way to make judicious choices given "the difficult freedom of a plenitude of meanings" (1970, 164, 179, 183). Thus she adds to decorum concerns not only for aesthetic form and appropriate function but also that of ethical choice. For Struever, rhetoric is a methodology that can hold together both long- and short-range views (bridging the uniqueness, in the case of this text, of the time dimension in worship and hymns), both principle and decorum (1970, 186).

As part of the contemporary revival of the understanding of decorum, Leff points out that decorum engages "both the immediate environment and the intrinsic appeals of language" (1990, 118). Building on Fantham's work, he suggests a progression of the strands of the multidimensional nature of decorum, moving from the extrinsic accommodation to the circumstances that frame the rhetorical act, through decorum as "the mediating link between form and content manifested within the discourse," to the intrinsic nature of "decorum as an organizing principle governing the internal form of a discourse" (Leff 1990, 118, 121).

Decorum, Worship, and Hymns

Decorum relates not only to the form and function of language in worship but also to the placement of certain texts within the flow of worship. As hymnwriter Ruth Duck says,

> Concern for worship means that the words of a hymn should be appropriate to the part of a service in that it appears. Almost any act of worship can be sung, from opening words to prayers to closing blessings. Hymns then should be placed where they belong in the order of service (1995a, 104).

For example, a hymn of confession should be placed before the words of forgiveness rather than after—one confesses in order that one might be forgiven. Words of joyful praise cannot be easily sung in the midst of lament. Even a favorite song, sung at an inappropriate time, can shake persons and leave them feeling violated (Roberts in Procter-Smith and Walton, 1993, 152).

Hymnwriters Doran and Troeger state the sense of decorum as it relates to hymns in a theological way:

> When we are making decisions about music for worship we are doing far more than choosing this or that piece. We are building (or blocking!) ways for the congregation to offer "a more profound Alleluia," a more complete and faithful expression of praise to the One who has made us and redeemed us and sustains us every moment of our lives (1992, 56).

Not only is decorum a vital principle in the order of hymns in worship, but it is particularly vital to observe when new texts are introduced to a congregation. Schmitt has these cautionary words for those using her collection of Christian feminist prayers:

> For congregations interested in using the prayers in Sunday worship, preparation is vital unless the people are already aware of the issues of female language for the Divine. To use the prayers without such preparation would be detrimental to their purpose of enabling people of the faith to open to this dimension of the Divine (1993, 38-39).

The persuasive and communicative motives of the authors of new prayers and hymns can be thwarted by worship planners who do not use decorum in choosing and long-range planning to incorporate these new elements and metaphors.

Again, Doran and Troeger put this into theological dimensions:

> The principle to remember is that people are more open to new hymns when there is a sound theological and liturgical basis for this use. Then the hymn is more than an innovation; it is a coherent part of the service that is supported by all the surrounding elements of worship. At the same time, the new hymn can provide a fresh sense of the Spirit to renew and strengthen what is traditional (1986, vii).

These quotes from hymnwriters and an author of prayers point also to decorum as an intrinsic principle: that writers for worship let the concept of decorum shape how they write. Thus, they write not only to a particular situation in a particular form, but most hymnwriters also hold themselves to an absolute standard of aesthetic worth. Recent publications of various writers' work show their willingness to be critiqued by others and show the cross-fertilization among various writers and composers to produce hymns that are not only theologically in-

sightful and appropriate for Christian worship, but also beautiful in
their own right.

Relationship to Genre and Register. Part of decorum in hymn texts is
using the proper form, its genre, and also its proper register. To include
slang, swearing, or other registers of language would be inappropriate.
Yet decorum does enable certain linguistic elements that are not generally part of the register of hymn texts to be used occasionally. Precedence for this may be found in the Psalms, where daily life with the
range of its emotions is brought to worship.

As the language of hymn texts (and worship in general) begins to
include women, for example, questions arise about the inclusion of
concepts and words such as *birthing, womb, nursing* (as in *feeding*),
nourishing, She for God.[4] Other stretching of the register of hymnic
language comes from the intersection of church and society, so that one
hymn includes the line "for freedom you march, in riots you die"
(*UMH* #257). The move toward honesty in worship language has produced lines that stretch the register in other ways, as in a hymn on marriage: "when love explodes and fills the sky," "when love is torn . . .
till lovers . . ." (*UMH* #634). Recent hymnals include even more evidence of the stretching of hymnic register and the need for decorum in
using hymns so that as Leff suggests there may be luminous moments
of illumination and discourse may attain great practical force (1990,
126).

Related to decorum is the stretching of the notion of the genre of
hymn. In the section on the history of hymns, mention was made of the
movement of some songs from the streets into worship (during the time
of the Arian controversy and again during the Reformation). This has
happened in our day as "We Shall Overcome" moved from civil rights
marches into mainline denominational hymnals. Decorum gives worship planners a principle for including this hymn and other "secular"
songs in Christian public worship. This has also happened repeatedly
with secular music moving into the church, folk tunes adapted for
hymn texts and the choral section from Beethoven's *Ninth Symphony*
given new texts for use in worship. The principle of decorum helps to

---

4. Yet, these metaphors appear in the scriptures (cf. Is. 49.14-15) and were
used frequently in mysticism; for example, see Caroline Bynum, *Jesus as
Mother: Studies in the Spirituality of the High Middle Ages.*

enable an enriching of worship as well as a guidance toward what is appropriate.

CONCLUSION: WHAT IS A HYMN AND WHAT DOES IT DO?

Hymns are metrical songs that gather up the elements of the public worship of the people of God. They are poetic, metrical, mostly rhymed, metaphorical, and written to be sung by Christians in common worship. Historically they have flourished at times of crisis and change in the church and in the world. Although the style of hymns is rather formal, the diction tends toward concrete monosyllabism. The poetic device of address, or the linguistic use of the vocative, is one of the markers of a hymn, even while it remains ambivalent, shifting between God and congregations in the light of God. As part of speaking in a common voice, the singing of hymns unites many voices together. Hymns function in a chain of communication within a worship service and also throughout history. Their repetition gives them an important part in both individual and communal Christian memory. There is a register of hymnic language that includes a special lexicon that is currently in flux. Some of that flux is presented in the next chapter.

Chapter 3
The State of Hymnody

INTRODUCTION

> So each generation of the church must try to test itself anew to see
> whether its song is true, to see whether its doxology is theology.
> Martin Franzmann, *With Tongues of Fire*

In the second half of the twentieth century the language base of the
church has shifted from the King James Version of the Bible to language of the Revised Standard Version (1946, 1952) and now the New
Revised Standard Version (1989) of the Bible. Changes were also initiated by theologians such as Bishop John Robinson (*Honest to God*
1963) who called for a shift in the language of the church so that "average persons" might understand it (Young 1995b, 71).

These changes have borne fruit in a flurry of hymnwriting and publication. As Erik Routley has said, "hymns have flourished most vigorously on the far edges of the church: at what some might call its growing points and others its vulnerable or even heretical points" (1982, 6).
The church, like society and culture, is in a great time of change, affected by science, technology, the shrinking of the global community,
economics, civil rights, and a sense of ecumenism. Whether one calls
the resulting hymns "growing points" or "heretical" will be determined
by a wide variety of factors, including social location, understanding of
hymnic (and religious) register, and the decorum observed (or not observed) in the hymn's usage. Some of these factors have already been
discussed; others form the focus of Part II of this text.

The State of Hymnwriting Today

Hymnwriting is currently enjoying a renaissance, much as it did during the Reformation and the time of dissent in the English church (Watts and the Wesleys). Hymns then and now are written by new converts, with little or no theological training, as well as by persons steeped over a lifetime in theology and scripture. Hymns from the early church up through this century have been preserved, translated, edited, and passed down, and new ones are being written as this text is being written. This explosion of hymnwriting is related to the debate in the church as it faces the problems of today's world and seeks to find God's word for this time and place. New hymnwriters continue the dialogue begun back before recorded history, seeking to find meaning in life, as persons are in dialogue with God and with each other.

Those currently writing hymns in English vary greatly in denomination and social location, but some common topics may be found among hymns published in denominational hymnals: justice, peace, the "pilgrim" nature of Christian life, science and technology, violence and promise of cities, care of the earth, Christian unity and reconciliation, the charismatic movement, worship renewal, and care for inclusive language (Westermeyer 1995, 183-184; Young 1995b, 70-75; Sydnor 1990, 58).

HYMNALS AND OTHER HYMN RESOURCES

One natural dividing line for denominational hymnals in the latter part of this century is the distinction of the *Lutheran Book of Worship* 1978 as the first major denominational hymnal using inclusive language about humanity (Sydnor 1990, 59). Since then "as many as thirty-five denominational and commercial hymnals have been produced in the United States" (Westermeyer 1995, 170). These include hymnals published by the United Methodists, Presbyterians, Christian Reformed, Baptists, Episcopalians, Mennonites and Brethren, Unitarians, Assemblies of God, Churches of Christ, Anabaptists, Evangelical Covenant, Roman Catholics, and nondenominational publishers (information from The Hymn Society Book Service, January 1998). Commentaries and other resources have been published in conjunction with many of these hymnals. Thomas Smith, former executive director of The Hymn Society of the United States and Canada, views this activity in developing hymnals as a positive sign that congregational song is alive and well (Westermeyer 1995, 170).

In the year in that this writing was begun, 1995, three new hymnals were published by religious bodies in the United States, *Chalice Hymnal* (the Disciples of Christ), *The New Century Hymnal* (the United Church of Christ), and the *Moravian Book of Worship*. Several books on hymnology were published: by Carlton R. Young (one general hymnology and one focused on Wesleyan hymnody), by Paul Westermeyer (interviews with ten contemporary hymnwriters), by Jon Michael Spencer (on liberating black hymnody), by Madeleine Marshall (including brief close readings of thirty-six texts), and the revision and expansion of a 1980 hymnology textbook by Harry Eskew and Hugh McElrath.

CROSS-CULTURAL CONCERNS

With the publication of *The United Methodist Hymnal* in 1989 and *The Presbyterian Hymnal* the following year, the church gained "two inclusive, global, and ecumenical resources" (Young 1995b, ii). *The Hymnal 1982* of the Episcopal Church had included seven "Afro-American spirituals" as a move toward cross-cultural inclusion. The United Methodists and Presbyterians not only included a more significant number of hymns from the African-American tradition (with new accompaniments to reflect African-American performance practice) but also included hymns from Native American traditions, Hispanic traditions, Asian traditions, and African traditions. This included translations of these materials into English, and, in many cases, the inclusion of the original language. *The United Methodist Hymnal*, for example, includes thirty-one sources under "Traditional hymns and melodies and prayers" in its "Index of Composers, Authors, and Sources," including Chinese, Croatian, Gaelic, Hindi, Indian, Laotian, Malawi, Punjabi, Taiwanese, Thai, and West Indian.

Hymns originally written in English that have become popular in other traditions appear in recent hymnals with different languages. Thus, "Jesus Loves Me" appears in *The United Methodist Hymnal* (#191) in English, Cherokee, German, Japanese, and Spanish whereas *The New Century Hymnal* version of "Jesus Loves Me" (#327) includes Armenian, Samoan, Lakota, Spanish, Japanese, Hawaiian, German, Hungarian, Korean, and Ghanaian. Not only are languages other than English included in recent anglophone hymnals, but they are not always relegated to following the English text—they are often the first language interlined and placed as the title.

This inclusion of other sources and languages might not seem a major change, but it can be a reminder that God does not "speak English only," a reminder that there are others besides ourselves who worship and praise God and who are loved as God's children. Young points out that these hymns also contain "implicit cries for social and economic justice" that need to be addressed by the church (Young 1995b, 142).

Singing hymns from other countries and cultures can be a growing and learning experience, and yet it needs to be done with decorum. Marshall raises a number of questions about singing hymns cross-culturally that need to be addressed (1995, 161-173), although I disagree with many of her assumptions and conclusions. Singing these hymns can be an emancipatory experience, I believe, but dealing with a variety of cultures is a complex topic, sadly too large for the scope of this book.

A WORD ABOUT MUSIC

Although this book is focused on the texts of hymns, the importance of music for carrying words and enabling them to be remembered cannot be dismissed without mention. One of the defining characteristics of the genre of Christian hymns is that they are sung.

Occasionally text and tune are so well matched that it is difficult to sing new words to the old tune; examples include "Joy to the World" and "O God, Our Help in Ages Past." A rousing tune may carry words that are weak theology, and because of the strength of the tune, the hymn will remain popular. A wonderful text may be given a weak or difficult tune and is never used because the tune is not pleasing. As Young says, although worship leaders choose hymns according to various theological, scriptural, and liturgical reasons, the response of congregations "is prompted primarily by whether the tune is familiar and singable" (1995b, 17).

A study of hymn tunes would include the study of melody, harmony, rhythm and meter, texture and form, tune sources, and the change in hymn singing and composition over time. Music is a complex topic and thus its discussion falls primarily outside the scope of this book. The chapters on multidimensional reading and on praxis are limited to comments on the effect of specific tunes on specific texts.

One of the things that has changed drastically in the last century and that seriously threatens the future of hymns in North America is the decline of singing as a social activity. "In fact, the only place in our society and culture today where ordinary folk can be found to sing regularly is the church" (Batistini 1988, 6). Batistini and Clark (1994, 78) have both commented on this decline and the subsequent need for churches to be involved in teaching and enabling singing not only for ritual-making but also for the society at large. "Our work may provide the best insurance humankind has that ordinary people of future generations will be able to experience the joy of music-making" (Batistini 1988, 6).

It is my belief that not only do churches need to be involved in teaching and enabling singing, but we also need to help persons focus on the words of the hymns they sing. Paul wrote to the church at Corinth, "I will sing praise with the spirit, but I will sing praise with the mind also" (1 Cor. 14.15b). When spirit and mind work together hymns can achieve their highest decorum and their greatest beauty. In the multidimensional readings and also in the chapters on praxis, this text comments on the effects of tune upon text and the linking of mind and spirit through the singing of hymns.

SOME WARNINGS

In addition to the warnings about the disappearance of singing as a common activity, hymnologists are concerned with cultural changes and with shifting priorities within churches. Here a United Methodist and a Lutheran raise their concerns:

> The church's psalmic and hymnic traditions spanning from King David via Ambrose of Milan to Fred Pratt Green and sung to psalm tone, plainsong, chorale, psalm tune, gospel hymn, hymn tunes of Ralph Vaughan Williams, and William Albright's clusters may not survive the impending cultural revolution unless those who treasure them preserve and nourish them (Young 1995b, 142-143).

> The question before the church as it completes this millennium is whether it has the courage and compassion to sing its song with all its challenge and comfort, or whether it will be co-opted by the world of marketing, the obscenity of targeting people, and the perversion of hymnody to these devious ends (Westermeyer 1995, 188).

Erik Routley, eminent hymnologist, concluded what was to be his final book with the declaration: "Even if our heathen children don't want [hymns], we will not hide [hymns] from them: another generation will be grateful if we don't" (1982, 107).

This book analyzes hymn texts so that we may better understand the relationship between hymns and religious meaning, meaning that produces faith. We also consider how current hymnwriters are recreating the tradition so that faith may grow in our time.

PART II
EMANCIPATORY LANGUAGE

> Emancipatory language seeks to transform language use and to challenge stereotypical gender references.
>
> Marjorie Procter-Smith, *In Her Own Rite*

Part II begins with Chapter 4 examining the concept of emancipatory language as it was introduced into liturgical studies by Marjorie Procter-Smith's book, *In Her Own Rite: Constructing Feminist Liturgical Tradition* (1990). That chapter concludes with a brief lexical study of the word *emancipatory*.

Chapter 5 suggests characteristics for the definition of *emancipatory*, combining Procter-Smith's work with language and feminism in the fields of rhetoric, linguistics, and theology. The concluding chapter of this part, Chapter 6, combines the understanding of *emancipatory* with hymns.

Chapter 4
An Introduction to the Word
Emancipatory

PROCTER-SMITH'S USE OF THE WORD
EMANCIPATORY

> The feminist critique that our traditional liturgical God-language is exclusively male charges that such language is in fact not clear because it is not truthful, and not beautiful because it is oppressive. This critique also observes that use of such limited language constricts our relationship with the God with whom we dialogue.
>
> Marjorie Procter-Smith, *In Her Own Rite*

Three Ways to Respond to Androcentric Liturgical Language

My use of the word *emancipatory* as it applies to liturgical language begins with Marjorie Procter-Smith's book, *In Her Own Rite* (1990). Procter-Smith uses the term first as one of "three possible ways to respond to the problem of androcentric liturgical language": *nonsexist* (removing all gendered terms), *inclusive* (balancing male and female terms) and *emancipatory* (transforming language by challenging stereotypical gender references, recognizing the interconnection between language and social systems) (63). The problem with androcentric language (discussed further below, Procter-Smith 1990) is that it posits the male as normative and not only suggests that women are less than male but renders women invisible.

Nonsexist language substitutes *people* or *humanity* for *men*, thereby expanding the possibilities of meaning, as not only women but children also become included. Often the introduction of nonsexist language in liturgy is relatively untraumatic (Procter-Smith 1990, 64). Its drawbacks are that persons hear words like *sovereign, judge, shepherd,* and *savior* as male-gender (Wallace 1993), and, argues Procter-Smith, when we remove human characteristics (including gender) entirely from the liturgy its language loses its imaginative richness (Procter-Smith 1990, 63). As we observed in the section on poetry and metaphor, metaphors related to the human experience are very important in religious language, so to lose them or to limit ourselves to words that still suggest mental pictures of men is to limit the imaginative character of liturgy (64).

Inclusive language is an attempt to balance the male references in language with an equal number of female references. Some richness is gained: *brothers and sisters, Abraham and Sarah, Moses and Miriam.* The problem with inclusive language, points out Procter-Smith, is that male and female terms are not always equivalent and may have very different connotations, for example, *Lord/Lady, Madam/Sir, Master/Mistress* (Procter-Smith 1990, 65). This limitation on the strategy of inclusive language is what motivated Procter-Smith to suggest a third response to the problem of androcentric language, the model of emancipatory language (65).

Emancipatory language is applied by Procter-Smith to both language for humanity (*In Her Own Rite,* chapter 3) and to language for God (*In Her Own Rite,* chapter 4). She considers verbal emancipatory language, visual emancipatory language (images of women in the media as well as in worship), and physical emancipatory language (nonverbal behavior, including eye contact, gestures, postures and movements in worship). Because this present paper is focused on hymn texts, we will focus on Procter-Smith's discussion and suggestions for verbal emancipatory language.

Emancipatory Language about Human Beings

The theological assumption underlying emancipatory language is that God is engaged in struggles for emancipation, including the emancipation of women, and identifies with all those who struggle (Procter-Smith 1990, 66). The problem with androcentric language is that it makes women invisible (61; also Wren 1989a, 241, drawing on Thistlethwaite). Therefore, one task of emancipatory language is to make women visible, by naming them (both those present in worship and those in the tradition) as individuals and as a gender. Recent hymnals have picked up this concern. *The United Methodist Hymnal,* for example, has more hymns than any of its predecessor denominational hymnals about Mary the mother of Jesus, along with at least four other hymns naming specific biblical women and praising their actions (#197-200, 215, 272; 81, 266 [stanzas 4 and 5], 274, 276).

After women have gained a presence as individuals and as a group, emancipatory language moves to "the imaginative construction of powerful and positive language about women" (Procter-Smith 1990, 70). In this step Procter-Smith acknowledges "the practice of using language to challenge and transform language itself." For example, African-Americans took the word *black,* considered a negative word by the majority culture prior to the 1960s, and transformed it into a term of pride and power (65).[1] One of the results of this transformation is a sense of group pride and solidarity, that Procter-Smith seeks for women.

This "imaginative construction" of emancipatory language also points to the visionary and prophetic nature of language. Not only is the truth told about women's lives—"embodiment, particularity, suffering and struggle, abuse and terror"—but the future promised by God "when all women [as well as men and children] will be healed, transformed, and restored to fullness" is given voice (Procter-Smith 1990, 71). This visionary and prophetic language "may need to transcend the limits of patriarchal and androcentric language"(70).

Emancipatory God-Language

The critique itself is simple: exclusive or dominantly male language about God grants authority to men in a patriarchal culture and religion. This is particularly true when titles ascribed to God duplicate those also given exclusively to men, such as father, king, or master. Such titles operate in a dual manner. That is, they suggest not only that God is like a father, or king, or master, but also that fathers, kings, and masters are somehow like God.

An important corollary to the fundamental critique of male God-language is that the absence of female titles or characteristics carries the further implication that women are somehow less like God than are men.

Marjorie Procter-Smith, *In Her Own Rite*

---

1. Mary Daly has done similar, although less publicly known work, with words describing women like *hag* and *crone.* See her *Websters' First New Intergalactic Wickedary of the English Language.*

Procter-Smith begins her discussion of God-language with the under-standing that it is symbolic and thus complex and polyvalent, and that the meaning of language is shaped by the gender identity and social location of the user (1990, 87). Particularly in worship, there is an ur-gency and primacy about the use of God language, because how we address God shapes our relationship with God (89).

One of the reasons to consider God as female, says Procter-Smith, is the acknowledgment of women's spiritual need for language that helps us identify with God, to be in dialogue with a God who fully un-derstands "our lives, our values, our struggles and aspirations" (Procter-Smith 1990, 91). Resources for alternative female models for God have been found in scripture (particularly "the recovery of Wisdom as a bib-lical model for God . . . represented as a woman"),[2] historical tradition (particularly the medieval mystics and later sectarian Christian move-ments such as the Shakers), and theological reflection (upon the use of these models within patriarchal culture and patriarchal church) (92-94). Theological reflection uncovers the complexities of constructing female images of God within the context of our patriarchal culture, such as restrictive stereotyping of images such as mother and goddess, and the use of "androcentric categories of 'masculinity' and 'femininity'" (93).

Christian language about the Trinity has been particularly resistant to change, and in several mainline denominations battle lines are cur-rently being drawn around trinitarian language in order to define ortho-doxy and heresy in the church today. Procter-Smith suggests that "the idea of the 'three-in-one' might be a very useful way of speaking of the kind of unity-in-diversity" that she recommends (Procter-Smith 1990, 107). Although not proposing a model of her own, Procter-Smith dis-cusses three previously proposed models: The early feminist "Creator, Redeemer, Sustainer," Ramshaw's "Abba, Servant, Paraclete" (1986) and McFague's "Mother, Lover, Friend" (1987). Procter-Smith points out the limitations of each: the early feminist version contains no ex-plicitly female images (therefore is nonsexist) and it is simply func-tional without including personal terms; Ramshaw's model contains a problem with the use of *Abba* and again contains no explicit female name; McFague's only explicit female name limits women's role to that of motherhood, only one part of women's experience (108-111).

---

2. See also Virginia Ramey Mollenkott's work, *The Divine Feminine*, quoted at several places in this text.

Procter-Smith then suggests seven principles for constructing emancipatory God-language. I have followed some of these principles as I construct my definition of emancipatory language in hymn texts. Others were of less value for my work, as is discussed in the following chapter.

1. Emancipatory God-language must challenge our colonized imaginations.
2. Emancipatory God-language must include explicitly female referents.
3. Emancipatory God-language must balance diversity and unity.
4. Female language for Goddess must be chosen and used with a critical eye toward its meaning and use in patriarchal religion and culture.
5. A valuable resource for enlarging our imaginations about God-language is to be found in the varied and rich traditions of Goddess-worship, as practiced in ancient times, as continuing in the present, and as reconstructed by contemporary feminists.
6. Emancipatory God-language must be firmly grounded in the lived experiences of real women, resisting romanticization and generalization.
7. Emancipatory God-language must also take into account the particularity of women's experience: the racial, ethnic, religious, and class distinctions, that divide us from one another as women, but that also make us distinctive. (Procter-Smith 1990, 112-114)

Procter-Smith concludes her chapter on emancipatory God-language with the reminder that the context for this language is "one not of critical inquiry but of faith" (Procter-Smith 1990, 114). As a result of this context of worship and of religious language, emancipatory God-language is metaphorical, containing the "yes-no-yes" character of metaphor. Finally, Procter-Smith acknowledges that the shift in emancipatory God-language, "from he to she, is going to be perceived as a seismic one. It changes everything" (115).

THE PLACE OF *EMANCIPATORY* IN THE LEXICON

Introduction

Emancipatory appears in *The New Shorter Oxford English Dictionary*, vol. 1: *emancipatory, adjective: that has the function of effect of emancipating* (1630-1669, first appearance). The *Collins COBUILD English*

Language Dictionary (a dictionary constructed not by individuals or a committee but by a wide-ranging computer study of words as they are used), 1987, does not contain *emancipatory* but defines *emancipate: To emancipate someone means to free them from social, political, or legal restrictions that are considered to be degrading or unnecessary, or from having to do degrading work; a formal word.*

In a collocation study of *emancipate* (studying how it appears in sentences and what kind of words it occurs with) I found that reflexive pronouns (she emancipated *herself*) occurred most often with *emancipate*. The location that subjects are *emancipated from* and occasionally *into* is most often not an actual place but in the "realm of ideas." The sense of movement suggested by *from* and *into* is an important factor of *emancipate*. In a comparison of three similar words—*free, liberate, emancipate*—*emancipate* stands out in three ways: It is the most formal, the least used, and it appears in the reflexive more often than the other two words (Wallace 1994).

In 1994 my collocational study for *emancipate* included over two dozen usages within a period of a few months in major newspapers in the United States. A similar search at that time for the word *emancipatory* yielded only nine occurrences over a period of eight months. These usages occurred in a variety of settings, including reviews of five books, an editorial, a letter to the editor, an article on robots, and reviews of art and theater. This suggests that *emancipatory* has been used sparingly, is not overladen with connotations, and thus is open to further defining.

In the summer of 1998, as this book is being completed, the Internet enables wider word searches and clues to the place of *emancipatory* in the lexicon. *Emancipatory* is much more widely used than in 1994, in areas of language, science, education, political science, and religion. Books have included *emancipatory* in their titles, and the word is often linked with movements in society and in thought, in phrases like *emancipatory movement*. Yet my conclusions from 1994 are not greatly changed, as emancipatory is still not a common word in the lexicon and is still being defined in various fields. The next section of this chapter considers the usage of *emancipatory* by several feminist theologians.

The Use of *Emancipatory* by Other Authors

Mary Kathleen Speegle Schmitt. Schmitt has published three liturgical cycles of Christian feminist prayers. In her first collection in 1993, she cites her understanding of Procter-Smith's delineation of three approaches to male-oriented language in liturgy. She goes on to say, "This collection of prayers attempts to be emancipatory in approach" (30).

Schmitt's prayers follow Procter-Smith's suggestions of making women visible and including a variety of images. For example, her first three prayers for the season of Easter include these names of address for God: *Earth Dancer, Mother of All, Risen One, Spirit of Joy, Sister Who Journeys with Us, Embryo, Chrysalis, Butterfly, One Divinity, Woman of Transforming Power, Creative One, Soul Sister, Alluring Wisdom, Womanchrist.* Note that each prayer contains at least four names for God, so that when *Mother* is used it is not the only name. These examples also show Schmitt's use of imagination, that she grounds with scripture references for many of the prayers, as they were written for specific lections of the church year.

Rebecca Chopp. In her book, *The Power to Speak: Feminism, Language, God* (1991), Chopp frequently uses the phrase *emancipatory transformation* (3, 7, 18, 23, 37, 71, 117, and so on). There is no citation that Chopp borrowed the word from any other understanding or source, such as Procter-Smith.

For Chopp, *emancipatory transformation* relates to the discourse that proclaims "the Word to and for the world," that is, feminist theology (Chopp 1991, 3, 7). Thus she links language and transformation with the word *emancipatory.*

Through a multiplicity of strategies, discourses of *emancipatory transformation* "allow each woman to speak her self, her desires, her time and space, her hopes, her God" (Chopp 1991, 18). These discourses are guided by "terms of specificity, difference, solidarity, embodiment, anticipation, and transformation" (23). As Chopp continues her analysis and suggestions for the intersections of feminism, language, and God, she points to the community, the church, that is "called to proclaim, to give to the world news of emancipatory transformation" (124).

Elizabeth Johnson. Johnson's *She Who Is* follows Chopp's *The Power to Speak* in its use of the phrase "discourses of emancipatory transformation" (Johnson, 1993, 5). Johnson also uses *emancipatory* with *praxis* (8) and in the phrase "Christian feminist emancipatory discourse" (15). In her first chapter, where these usages occur, she reminds us that how we speak of God "represents what [we] take to be the highest good, the profoundest truth, the most appealing beauty" (4). Like Procter-Smith, Johnson is concerned that "exclusive, literal, and patriarchal" God-language has become an idol, reducing divine mystery and " denigrating the human dignity of women" (36).

Johnson relates *emancipatory* to the understanding of God's glory and shalom: "Wherever human beings are violated, diminished, or have their life drained away, God's glory is dimmed and dishonored. Wherever human beings are quickened to fuller and richer life, God's glory is enhanced" (14). Thus emancipatory language and praxis is not simply a matter of "making women feel better" but is part of letting the glory of God show forth in each moment of history.

One of Johnson's suggestions is that we place the word *God* in a new semantic field, in order to "restore the word to a sense more in line with its Greek etymology, that, according to ancient interpreters, meant to take care of and cherish all things, burning all malice like a consuming fire" (Johnson 1993, 44, with footnote to Aquinas, following Damascene). Resources for emancipatory speech about God come from "women's interpreted experience" (especially feminist liberation theology and the experience of conversion) (62ff.), from scripture and its trajectories (specifically the understandings of God as *spirit, wisdom,* and *mother*), classical theology (drawing on the doctrine of divine incomprehensibility, the concept of analogy, and the need for many names of God) (104ff.).

Once Johnson has set her guidelines for emancipatory God-language, she uses it throughout the rest of the book: *Spirit-Sophia, Creator Spirit, "friend, sister, mother, and grandmother of the world"* (Johnson 1993, 146), *Jesus-Sophia, Sophia-God, Christ the Wisdom of God, Mother-Sophia, Holy Wisdom, Love.* Johnson draws on and critiques Aquinas's translation of HE WHO IS as the name given to Moses at the burning bush; her suggestion is that SHE WHO IS is an appropriate name for God, "necessary if speech about God is to shake off the shackles of idolatry and be a blessing for women" (243). Johnson not only discusses emancipatory language for God, she also employs it in her writing and, at least for this reader, produces an emancipatory experience.

Gloria Albrecht. A 1995 publication by Albrecht, *The Character of Our Communities: Toward an Ethic of Liberation for the Church*, also uses the term *emancipatory.* Albrecht cites Sandra Harding as her source for the word. Harding used the phrase "emancipatory knowledge-seeking" in her 1986 book, *The Science Question in Feminism.*

Her concern as she looked at the sciences and their focus on "Western, bourgeois, and masculine projects" was to discover if it was "possible to use for liberating ends [these] sciences" (Harding 1991, vii). Harding's 1991 book, *Whose Science? Whose Knowledge?* followed up on her belief that "feminisms [sic] must become capable of influencing other liberatory movements as they are simultaneously influenced by them" (ix).

Albrecht speaks of *emancipatory communities* several times, described at one point as "the freedom to encounter and be encountered by differences, and the risk of solidarity with 'others'" (Albrecht 1995, 94). Throughout the book she links *emancipatory community* to the qualities of truth and justice. She suggests that these communities will come about by conversion, not "to a new truth, but to a new way of walking." Thus she links *emancipatory* clearly as not merely a mental conversion but one that goes deep into one's bones, one's very way of being and acting.

This element of community is important to our development of the concept of emancipatory language. As we see in the following chapter, it is in community that individual revelations are tested and confirmed or denied. It is in community that hymns are sung and that emancipatory language can both challenge and express faith. As Chapter 14 on praxis affirms, it is in community that the fruits of emancipatory language grow.

CONCLUSION

We have seen in this chapter how the word *emancipatory* has surfaced in a number of feminist theological works. It is an active word, linked with language, with transformation, and with praxis.

Several common threads have begun to emerge that may be woven into a description of emancipatory language for this text: Emancipatory language begins with the understanding that God identifies with and is involved with women and others on the margins of society. There is a visionary and prophetic character in emancipatory language that points to the promises of God for all humanity, which is related to the eschatological character of worship in which Christians glimpse and feel the promised vision. Emancipatory language draws on scripture, tradition, experience, and imaginative construction of language to point to the God who is greater mystery than we can ever comprehend. Using emancipatory language challenges our imaginations and those of the patriarchal church and culture, and it transforms the way we think and act.

Chapter 5
Weaving Emancipatory Language

INTRODUCTION

> . . . the church must continue seeking the most adequate language possible, even as it admits the limits of all its attempts to do so.
>
> Ruth Duck, *Gender and the Name of God*

This discussion of emancipatory language begins with the foundational premise of God's identification with and struggle on behalf of women and others. This involves discussion of theologies of liberation, the Social Gospel, and feminism. Then this chapter discusses emancipatory language about humanity under the two broad categories of visibility and justice. Discussion about emancipatory God-language focuses on two broad categories as well, diversity and revelation. The strategy used to employ emancipatory liturgical language is that of imaginative construction. Finally, this chapter suggests what results might be expected from the use of emancipatory liturgical language.

Any study of emancipatory language needs to acknowledge the limits of linguistic transformation. For to say that there is only one way of writing, singing, or hearing emancipatory language would be a contradiction in definition. There are many ways to view emancipatory language, of which this text is one perspective. I cannot speak for persons of different cultures, gender, age, or denominational background. Yet, although our particularities may be very different, we can still communicate and learn from each other.

This book is concerned with the *possibilities* of emancipatory language—providing many images, metaphors, and styles of language in order that the comprehensive range of God's glory might be given voice. The wonder of God's glory, evidenced in the varieties of crea-tion—from tiny insects to towering mountains and ocean depths, with all the hues of humanity in between—suggests that our language for God and for the interaction between the Creator and all the creation be as varied and as beautiful.

FOUNDATION:
GOD IDENTIFIES WITH THE MARGINS

> Feminism is not somehow just about women; rather, it casts its voice from the margins over the whole of the social-symbolic order, ques-tioning its rules, terms, procedures, and practices.
> Rebecca Chopp, *The Power to Speak*

An Understanding of God and of the Power of Language

God. This text draws on an understanding of God that flows through the Scriptures—that the Holy One, understood by the Hebrew people as the Creator, walks with people throughout human history, ever being revealed to those who believe and who follow. Christians believe that in order to more closely identify with humanity, God chose to come in the form of a baby who would grow to adulthood, the one known as Jesus Christ, who experienced life while touching the lives of ordinary people. After the death and resurrection of Jesus Christ, his followers understood the continuing presence with them in the form of the Holy Spirit. In order to understand the way this ultimate Mystery works and is revealed to creation, the Christian church evolved the doctrine of the Trinity. The principle understandings of the Trinity are of the One who Creates, the One who Saves, and the One who Sustains, or in more tra-ditional terms, Father, Son Jesus Christ, and the Holy Spirit.

As revealed in Scriptures, God's nature is multifaceted—Creator, Most Powerful, Judge, Mercy-Giver, Savior, Shepherd, Ever-Present, Eternal, Rock, Eagle, Strength, Shield—the list is endless. Yet both Jewish and Christian doctrine teach that this multifaceted nature is all part of one God, one Unity, whose primary character is that of love.

Recent theological studies have attempted to deal with two particu-lar questions about the nature of God and God's interaction with God's creation: (1) *Why is there suffering?* (with the corollaries: *Why does God allow suffering?* and *Did God create suffering and evil?*) and, with our new understandings of the evolving and continuing change in the universe, (2) *Where does an everlasting God fit in the changing scheme of our world?*

Process theology, a philosophical theology based on the work of Alfred North Whitehead (1861-1947) and Charles Hartshorne (b. 1897), presents some answers to these questions that undergird my understanding of emancipatory language. First, as the death of Jesus Christ shows, God goes through suffering with us and can redeem our suffering (McDaniel 1989, 24). Second, like all actuality, God is evolving, is "in process" (Cobb and Griffin 1976, 7ff.). Therefore God is a living Being, who is ever revealed to us in new situations, while remaining the essence and ultimate Source of love, truth, and justice.

One understanding from process theology that is particularly helpful for emancipatory language is that "it is God who, by confronting the world with unrealized opportunities, opens up a space for freedom and self-creativity" (Cobb and Griffin 1976, 29). The source of freedom and the source for our own self-expression come from Godself.

Language. We have already discussed the importance of language in shaping our encounter in worship with God. It matters how we name God, both as that naming reflects (or diminishes) God's glory and as it reflects on human beings. Language also has the power to "birth new meanings, new discourses, new signifying practices" (Chopp 1991, 14). In Christianity newness is an important quality related to redemption, our deliverance from sin, suffering, and death. This is seen in the sacraments as baptism is understood as giving "new birth through water and the Spirit" (cf. John 3.5) and the traditional Communion invitation called forth all those who intended "to lead a new life" to draw near to Christ's table (*UMH*, 26).

Religious language is based on metaphor and the is/is not qualities that metaphor brings to our understanding even as it shapes us (see section on metaphor above in this text). Liturgical language that loses its metaphorical qualities can become an idol, and the scriptures are clear in their warnings against idolatry. Even emancipatory language carries the caution that it is also an is/is not, that all our language can point to God but is not God.

The Identification of God with Those on the Margins

Liberation Theology. In the first chapter, under the history of hymns, we briefly discussed the liberation theology movement that began in Latin America in the Roman Catholic Church in the 1960s. This movement took seriously Jesus' ministry on earth to those on the margins of society: the oppressed, the hungry, the sick, and the "invisible" people of his time (Maduro in Musser and Price 1992, 292; Tamez 1993, 42). Unlike those in power in his day, Jesus acted in solidarity with outcasts (for example, Luke 19.1-10), with children (Luke 18.15-17), and with women (Luke 8.1-3). Jesus Christ, says liberation theology, gives us the model for solidarity with those on the margins. This is part of God's promise told through Mary's song, the Magnificat, that the lowly would be lifted up, the hungry filled with good things, while the proud, the powerful, and the rich would be brought down from their high places (Luke 1.47-55).

For liberation theologians this identification and solidarity is closely linked to the power of God to liberate, as God freed the Israelites from slavery in Egypt and as the death of Jesus Christ freed humankind from the bonds of sin and death. Liberation is both physical and spiritual. In addition, liberation is communal, as one of the earliest works of Gustavo Gutiérrez proclaimed: "The fullness of liberation—a free gift from Christ—is communion with God and with other [people]" (1973, 36). Or as Hugo Assman said, "The essence of the biblical message appears to give priority to the relational image I/community or I/brothers and sisters as the basic ethical structure within that to reflect on revolutionary commitment" *(Pueblo oprimido, Señor de la historia,* 15, quoted in Tamez 1993, 203).

Liberation Theology in the United States. For Gutiérrez and other liberation theologians in Latin America, God identifies with the poor and oppressed peoples, those in poverty, unemployed, starving, ill, in countries struggling under debt and dictators. As theologians in the United States came into contact with liberation theology, they learned much from it to apply to their own situation. Following the example of Ernesto Cardenal's work with the people in Solentiname, theologians here began seriously to consider what understandings each person brings to theology, not only what academically trained persons have to say, but what those on the margins, with whom God identifies, have to teach us.

James Cone was one of the first to focus on the perspective of African-Americans in the United States, and God's identification with the black experience, claiming "Christian theology is language about the liberating character of God's presence in Jesus Christ as he calls his people into being for freedom in the world" (1975, 8). Thus, Cone also links the identification of God with the margins as a liberative or emancipatory experience.

Women on the Margins

In the wake of liberation and black theologians, women, who have long felt on the margins of society, politics, and all too often the church, began to claim themselves as those with whom God identifies. Rosemary Radford Ruether, one of the first to set out a systematic feminist theology, identified a central principle deriving from God's identification with women: "The critical principle of feminist theology is the promotion of the full humanity of women. Whatever denies, diminishes, or distorts the full humanity of women is, therefore, appraised as not redemptive" (1983, 19). Other feminist theologians have followed this principle in their proposals for theology (Elizabeth Johnson), worship (Marjorie Procter-Smith and Ruth Duck),and ethics (Beverly Harrison).

The importance of God's identification with women for women's lives cannot be overstated. Nelle Morton, an early feminist theologian, stated this identification in a particularly poignant passage:

> Now, call on *God the Mother* or the *Goddess*. What happens? For women she appears. She says your life is the sacred gift. Pick it up. Receive it. Create it. Be responsible for it. I ask nothing in return. It is enough that you stand on your own feet and speak your own word. . . . The response from women who have become aware is an overwhelming sense of acceptance and belonging and identity. . . . *God the Mother* requires from women no transfer from the male experience to the female experience as when evoking *God the Father*. No paternalizing. No demand for payment. Women sense a "forever dependence" asked from *God the Father*. But only independence and resourcefulness from the *Goddess* (1977 essay, published in Morton 1985, 143-144).

This vision Morton presents offers the independence and grace of full personhood to women who have long been taught that dependence was their lot in life and that they were less than full persons.

Janet Morley suggests that not only does God's identification with women enable a closeness "to the God in whose image we are made: it also prevents us from distancing ourselves—as we can do with 'male' language—from the uncomfortable, even frightening closeness of the difficult God who is not made in our image" (1992, xii). Thus, Morley reminds us that in using female imagery we recapture the metaphorical nature of God-language—the One in whose image we are made is not made in our image.

The Diversity of Women and of the Margins

Over the last decade women from differing social locations have raised their voices as those with whom God identifies: African-American women (including Katie Cannon, Kelly Brown Douglas, Delores Williams), Latin American women (Elsa Tamez), Hispanic women in the United States (Ada María Isasi-Díaz), and the differently abled (Nancy Eiesland). These women are a reminder to European-American women that there are many ways of being both marginalized and part of the power structure. One may be marginalized by gender but part of a powerful race, or powerful by education and marginalized by physical ability, marginalized by poverty but powerful by gender.

This acknowledgment of the diversity of women and the complexity of oppression and power calls for Christians to stand in solidarity and humility. Solidarity means truthfully recognizing where we stand and where others stand, and then finding the common voice wherein we can work together for change (Morley 1992, 4). Humility comes as we recognize where we stand, acknowledge our complicity in others' oppression, and ask God to convert us that we may turn from oppressing toward working for God's vision here on earth.

LANGUAGE ABOUT HUMANITY

Visibility

> [This] is not to say that as women gain positive linguistic visibility they magically gain recognition and respect. But something "magical" does happen whenever people—singly or as a class—begin to sense their potential as full integrated members of society, and it is this "magic" that using nonsexist language helps to bring about.
> Casey Miller and Kate Swift, *The Handbook of Nonsexist Writing*

Gender Bias in Language. Although *sexism* is often the term used to describe male domination in language, in my analysis I use the phrase *gender bias*, following Ruth Duck:

> The word *sex* refers to mating behavior and to the biological differences such as sexual organs, that distinguish males and females. . . . The word *gender*, on the other hand, is a cultural and psychological term identifying behaviors women and men learn, that do not depend on biological differences. The embedding of gender expectations in language through the false generic, word order, and gender marking re-

flects and reinforces the male domination of society (Duck 1991, 32-33, 37).

One of the most obvious accusations of gender bias in language is that of the use of the false generic, of *he* and *man* to represent all of humanity, half of which are *she* and *woman*. This use of generic *he* means that *male* is accepted as normative. Thus, even though *he* is supposed to include both men and women, in experiments where people were asked to illustrate texts using generic *he*, they tend to draw men (Romaine 1994, 115). This is not a recent problem, as Dennis Baron lists eighty proposals offered for a gender-neutral personal pronoun since the early eighteenth century (1986, 205-209).

When *men* and *male* are seen as normative, *women* occupy what is called "negative semantic space" (Romaine 1994, 101). Because women are absent, occupying negative space semantically, qualifiers become necessary to clarify meanings when the doctor or the president is a woman—the woman doctor, the female president; the female presence has to be specifically noted in the semantic world of men. Hymnwriter Brian Wren cites Susan Thistlethwaite's terms for this concept, *linguistic visibility/invisibility.* "She argues, I believe correctly," says Wren, "that it is a more accurate and acceptable indicator of what is at stake than the common terminology of 'inclusive' and 'exclusive' language" (1989a, 241). When only *he* and *men* are used to indicate all human beings, women become invisible.

Rosemary Radford Ruether's critical principle of feminist theology is an antidote for this invisibility: "The critical principle of feminist theology is the promotion of the full humanity of women" (1983, 19). One of the tasks to which this principle is applied in Ruether's book and which this book follows is promoting the full humanity of women by shifting women out of negative semantic space and making women visible in our liturgical language.

Feminist linguistic theory deals with many aspects of the critique of language, as gender bias is encountered in daily life as well as in the codification of such language in dictionaries and grammars. In our discussion about Procter-Smith's work, we have considered the myths of "neutral" language and of "equivalent" terms. Duck points out that word order, listing the male term first, *men and women, brothers and sisters*, plays a part in securing male domination in society. Equally destructive to women is the stereotyping carried out by gender marking: for example, *strong man/weak woman, law student male/pretty female* (Duck 1991, 37ff.). One of the tasks of emancipatory language is to break these stereotypes that have become so embedded in our language and our consciousness.

Lest these issues be considered simply semantics, feminists concerned with language use have pointed out the power issues involved. Studies have considered the insults of "street remarks," the disrespect of terms of endearment (the prevalence of *Honey* in the United States) used by men when talking to women who are strangers (such as waitpersons or salespersons), and the verbal violence that accompanies abuse (Cameron 1992, 106-110). Duck persuasively points out the connections between the idolization of male metaphors for God and the prevalence of child abuse in North America (1991, 43ff.).

Language needs to be changed to include the visibility of women not only in order to be precise (Miller and Swift 1988, 8) but also to raise consciousness and empower women (Cameron 1992, 125; also Campbell 1989a, 13) and for ethical reasons (Duck 1991, 55). And, as Cameron points out, this can be an emancipatory experience:

> It is liberating to be able to put into words experiences that had previously seemed nebulous and vague, or else shameful and unmentionable; it is empowering to find other women sharing, understanding and collectively reinterpreting such experiences (1992, 7).

Issues for the Church. James White links Ruether's critical principle of the full humanity of women with a concern for liturgical language and for justice:

> No longer do we have a choice to be concerned or not about sexist language. A fundamental issue of justice is involved, and the church cannot be silent in matters of justice without being a disobedient church. . . . We must move to language that affirms both women and men (1978, 1202, 1206).

Virginia Mollenkott explained this concern for local churches in more detail:

> It seems natural to assume that Christian people, eager to transmit the Good News that the Creator loves human beings equally and unconditionally, would be right in the vanguard of those who utilize inclusive language. Yet a visit to almost any church on Sunday morning indicates that alas, it is not happening that way. Whereas a "secular" publisher like McGraw-Hill has insisted on inclusive language for almost a decade, the language of Christian preaching, prayer, and hymnody is still laden with exclusive-sounding references to men, man, brothers, sons,

and the God of Abraham, Isaac, and Jacob. And the pronoun for that
God is "he" (1983, 2).

It is disturbing to note that fifteen years after Mollenkott's writing, the
language of Christian worship in many places remains focused on God-
he and men. Even the nationally televised 1995 Christmas Eve program
from the United Methodist Church (whose worship resources since
1989 have included suggestions for inclusive language) included a
number of "exclusive-sounding references" to humanity (twenty-two
years after McGraw-Hill's move to include women and men, girls and
boys). Surely the peace on earth promised by God as told by the angels
to the shepherds was meant for all people, not just men!

Implications for Emancipatory Language. As Procter-Smith pointed
out, when all gendered terms are removed from liturgy a basic connection with the human experience is lost, that of our creation as male and
female. Therefore, one of the characteristics of emancipatory liturgical
language is its addition of images, not just substitution (Beall 1994).
So, *Sarah* is added to *Abraham*, and not only would read *Abraham and
Sarah* but just as often *Sarah and Abraham*. Phrases in worship would
include sisters and brothers, women and men, children and elderly.
   Preciseness in liturgical language can make women more visible—
"we mourn with the Mothers of the Disappeared in Argentina" (rather
than "we mourn with those who hurt"), "we pray for the healing of
Harriet" (not just "Henry's wife"), "we thank you, God, for the holy
ones of the church—Joan of Arc, John Wycliffe, Catherine of Siena,
John Wesley" (instead of only male names), "we pray for the unemployed women and men of this city" (not assuming only men lose
jobs), "we thank you, God, for this new baby girl, Sarah Anne" (including her name), and "peace on earth, goodwill to all people everywhere" (the preciseness of not reserving God's peace for only our particular country).
   Visibility in liturgical language can also reach out to include
women, children, men, elderly, the stranger, varieties of sexual preference, varieties of physical, mental, and emotional abilities—blessing
church families as well as nuclear families, acknowledging our kinship
with the earth as part of God's creation, using simple and direct language. Part of this visibility includes the breaking of stereotypes: no
longer equating darkness and sin, and, following Jesus' example in
John 9.1-3, no longer equating physical/mental/emotional differences
with one's sin or the sin of the parents. A current example of this has

been the need for the church and society to separate AIDS from "sin" so that it may be seen as the uninvited killer that it is.

As Procter-Smith cautioned, we need to beware of simply balancing images, making idols of our "equality" in language. Instead we open the doors of language for humanity, for the diversity of our congregations and of our world, the world that God created, which we have often chosen to ignore. The opening of the doors of language will mean a consideration of God's grace and promises for the world and for God's justice and truth.

Truth and Justice: "Your Kingdom Come"

> But let justice roll down like waters,
>   and righteousness like an ever-flowing stream.   Amos 5.24

Scriptural Understandings of Truth and Justice. The Hebrew Scriptures are full of references to God's truth and justice, part of God's deep love for creation and for humanity in particular. God called the chosen people to participate in that justice, to care for widows and orphans, to feed the stranger, to care for the land as part of the Jubilee year (Lev. 25). Even when that truth and justice seemed far from the lives of God's people, when they were in exile or under foreign rule, God's promises remained as their hope (e.g., read the prophets Isaiah and Jeremiah).

Christians pray faithfully the prayer that Jesus taught as a model for all praying, "The Lord's Prayer," that includes the line "Your kingdom come." Liberation theology suggests that God identifies with those on the margins of society and promises to them the fulfillment of what Jesus called *the kingdom,* or *shalom,* that includes abundance of life here on this earth (John 10.10b). This is similar to the Social Gospel movement that grew out of the social implications of the Christian gospel, as articulated by the theologian Walter Rauschenbusch (*Christianity and the Social Crisis,* 1911), in the United States in the late 1800s and first half of the 1900s.

Historical Intersections with Concerns of Truth and Justice. The intersection of God's concerns and the problems of society can be seen in scriptures and has surfaced at various times in the history of the church. During the nineteenth century the abolition movement, against slavery, drew upon the teachings of the church for its support and sustenance. William Lloyd Garrison, abolitionist and publisher, was among those who published collections of antislavery hymns (Spencer 1990, chapter 2).

The autobiography of Frederick Douglass, slave and then abolitionist, gives several insights about emancipation that relate to emancipatory language. First, emancipation is not merely a physical removal
from an awful situation. It needs to be accompanied by a mental and
emotional emancipation, so that one is enabled, at least to some extent,
to deal with the new freedom (Douglass 1994, 36-39). Second is the
importance of truth-telling. It took courage for Douglass to name
names, to write down the dates that evil events occurred, to contradict
some of the myths by bringing light to bear on what happened (cf. 102).
Sometimes emancipation is enabled by the ability to tell the truth where
truth has been hidden.

A third insight one receives from reading Douglass is related to the
language he used to describe the turning point in his career as a slave,
when he fights Mr. Covey, the "nigger-breaker" to whom he was hired
out in 1833, and finds his spirit freed. Within one paragraph Douglass
uses the words and phrases: *rekindled, revived, recalled, inspired
again, determination, gratification, triumph, glorious resurrection,
from the tomb of slavery, to the heaven of freedom, spirit rose, cowardice departed, bold defiance took its place* (1994, 65). Two things
from these phrases stand out. First, the use of *re-* words—*rekindled,
revived, recalled, resurrection*—and the related *inspired again* suggest
that what is happening to Douglass does not come from nothing and
does not represent a ninety- or one-hundred-and-eighty degree turn.
What is happening is an embrace and reclaiming of what originally
was. Douglass's original and authentic potential has been realized and
set free to flourish. The second thing that might be noted is the *to* and
from movement—*from* the tomb of slavery/*to* the heaven of freedom—
with the related phrases *cowardice departed* and *bold defiance took its
place*. Emancipation is not just removal *from* something but a movement *toward* something.

During the time of Douglass and the abolition movement, many of
the early feminist speakers drew their authority to speak from the Protestant belief that we are all ministers, female and male, all given the
imperative to proclaim the gospel (based on Acts 2.17-18 and Gal.
3.27-28). Scripture references and the doctrine of the Holy Spirit supported the authority and moral stance of these women. Telling the truth
as they had experienced it, or as they had seen it (for example, Ange-
lina Grimké and Ida B. Wells), they encouraged other women to act
and to speak out as well (Campbell 1989b, 25-32, 385-419).

The Social Gospel movement was another occasion when the
church took seriously the concerns of God for society. After looking

carefully at the prophets of Israel, the life and teachings of Jesus, and primitive Christianity, Rauschenbusch set forth the premise that "the essential purpose of Christianity was to transform human society into the kingdom of God by regenerating all human relations and reconstituting them in accordance with the will of God" (1911, xiii). His list of the woes of "the present crisis" (1911) sound all too familiar: displacement of people from their land, inequity of wages, low morale of workers, the gap between rich and poor, crumbling of political democracy, tainting of the moral atmosphere, undermining of the family, economic fears. In proposing that the church take part in solving the social crisis Rauschenbusch was clear that this is a proper response to the call of Jesus Christ.

There is a Social Gospel strand in emancipatory feminist hymnody, as it seeks solidarity and justice for women and all people in this world. Feminist concerns for peace and justice continue the flow of the Social Gospel movement, and feminists are also helping to lead the development of ecological theology (e.g., McFague and Ruether).

Speaking Truthfully about Experience. Karlyn Kohrs Campbell points out an important element of the style of the early feminist rhetors that has implications for emancipatory language: "Audience members will be addressed as peers, with recognition of authority based on experience . . . and efforts will be made to create identification with the experiences of the audience and those described by the speaker" (1989, 13). The sense of identification between the original speaker and the hearers (or singers) is vital, and comes from treating others as equals and giving credit to experience rather than social, economic, or academic standing. Cameron names this sense of truth-telling and visibility in language as emancipatory, putting into words shared experiences so that they may be collectively reinterpreted (1992, 7).

Giving credit to experience, like Frederick Douglass's truth-telling, is an important criteria for emancipatory language. Part of experience includes the terrible things that happen to women—both the fear of rape and abuse and the actual experience of them, stories from contemporary experience that sound terrifyingly similar to biblical stories—the rape of Tamar (2 Sam. 13), the killing of Jeptha's daughter (Judg. 11), the torture of a concubine (Judg. 9). Part of experience includes the particular joys of womanhood—creativity, sensuality, friendship, embodiment, the experience of giving birth. Heather Murray Elkins reminds us that "The human body, that is, a woman's body, is understood to be *imago Dei* [in the image of God]; worship enables embodied revelation, not able-bodied domination" (1994, 124-125). Elkins reminds us that not only are women's bodies sacred but that all bodies are sacred in God's eyes. Finding ways to express these joys and sorrows within Christian public worship in a way that identifies with women in a positive way rather than shaming or degrading them is one of the challenges of emancipatory language. One of the rituals that is gaining importance where these truths of embodiment may be told is in services of healing (Ruether 1986, 149-181; Caron 1992, 92-95).

Sallie McFague broadens the concern about embodiment to include not only human bodies but the bodies of all God's creation, calling us "to think and act as if bodies matter" (1993, viii). The urgent need for ecological care and action also needs to be dealt with by the church in a just and truthful manner.

Implications for Emancipatory Language. Rita Nakashima Brock puts together the idea of liberation and embodiment when she says, "I believe a liberating faith lies on the borders of our thinking where *heart* links thinking with feeling, perception, and the body" (1988, xvi). It is the wholeness of human beings, promised in *shalom*, with which emancipatory language is concerned.

Truth also is vital for emancipation, as Jesus said, "The truth will make you free" (John 8.32). Saliers connects this with worship, where we are freed from our guilt and sin to live truthfully (1994, 150). Emancipatory language and emancipatory praxis can enable the redemption provided by Jesus Christ to enter our worship and our lives.

Ruth Duck has pointed out the importance of dealing truthfully with sin and gender, using as an example a hymn that contains the line "to give and give and give again." This is not a helpful hymn, suggests Duck, for women whose "sin" may be giving too much; these women need to hear a word of grace, rather than sanction of doormat behavior (in Procter-Smith and Walton, 1993, 61). Dealing truthfully with sin will always emphasize the grace of God, which frees.

The criteria of truth-telling and justice means that any liturgical text must be considered not only word by word but also checking for defects of "self-centered individualism, irresponsible otherworldliness, questionable atonement theories, or plain triviality" (Schilling 1983, 220). Duck said it well in a paper about feminist emancipatory hymnody:

> Emancipatory hymn texts incorporate the dimension of social justice as a central concern of faith. . . . Defining emancipatory hymn texts goes beyond language about gender to the content and central themes

of hymns. . . . Emancipatory hymns consciously affirm the search for justice and human development for all in communities in which difference is cherished and nurtured. They go beyond eliminating or balancing gender reference to supporting human liberation in its diverse forms (1993, 4-5)

As emancipatory language brings visibility to women and others on the margins of the church and society, it does so in truthful and just ways, in order to show God's love and concern for all persons.

LANGUAGE ABOUT GOD

Unity and Diversity

> . . . is the existence of so many religious types and sects and creeds regrettable? To these questions I answer "no" emphatically. . . . If an Emerson were forced to be a Wesley, or a Moody forced to be a Whitman, the total human consciousness of the divine would suffer.
> William James, *The Varieties of Religious Experience*

The Problematic Nature of God-Language. We have already discussed the necessity of recognizing that all our language for God, including the word *God* itself, is metaphoric; it only points to God, it is and it *is not* descriptive of God. Yet, as Mollenkott pointed out, the pronoun used most widely in the language of Christian worship is *he* (1983, 2, quoted above). The exclusive identification of God with male pronouns and images has resulted in

> . . . the deeply felt anguish that many religious women confront throughout their lives: believing themselves to be created in the image of God, they must nevertheless struggle with a sense of personal inferiority because the language of their faith tells them that God is male (Miller and Swift 1988, 104).

Emancipatory language is concerned with these struggles and women's work to free themselves from a sense of personal inferiority into a sense of full personhood as created by God.

The use of *Father* without corresponding use of *Mother* is a part of this problematic nature of gender bias in religious language, not only because it relates God to our understanding of human fathers, but because of the nature of language, human fathers are given God-like qualities. Because human mothers have not been accorded the same, this support of patriarchal supremacy underlies the power assumed by males in our society and its resulting physical and emotional abuse of children and women (Duck 1991, 43-55). Part of the problem with *Father* is that it has lost its metaphoric qualities, its sense of *is not*, and has become understood by many as an actual name for God (e.g., Griffiss 1990, 177).

The myth of nonsexist terms has been pointed out (see discussion at beginning of this chapter). And although society is changing, words like *judge, shepherd, savior*, and even *God*, are still heard by many persons as though they were male-gender (Wallace, 1993; see also Romaine 1994, 115). This points to the necessity of shifting the power base of language in order to move away from androcentric language.

Although many persons would find Nelle Morton's words cited earlier about the Goddess empowering, Schmitt reminds us that "to pray to the Divine in female terms is fraught with difficulty for people of the Judeo-Christian tradition, because female deity has systematically been objectified as evil" (1993, 17). The use of female terms in liturgical language requires a new semantic field (Johnson 1993, 44) or at least a shift in the register.

The prophetic principle of biblical faith, the tradition by that it "constantly criticizes and renews itself and its own vision" (Ruether 1983, 24), provides not only permission for critique of religious language, but also a model and an imperative. Emancipatory language begins with critique of language and then moves to renew language to bring it more clearly in line with God's vision.

What are the implications when *she* is introduced into the register of Christian worship, not as *evil* (like Eve who "brought sin into the world" or "pagan goddesses" reviled against in the Hebrew scriptures; e.g., Judg. 2.13, 1 Kings 11.33, and Jer. 44.15ff.) but as reflective of the Holy One, who is worshiped and adored in the Christian tradition, who is all good and all truth? One of the characteristics of emancipatory liturgical language is that we risk meeting God in new ways, in ways not expressible in our traditional register of patriarchal liturgical language, perhaps in ways we cannot now name.

Diversity of Metaphors for God. As discussed in Chapter 4, Johnson draws on classical theology, particularly Aquinas, who calls for many names for God (1993, 117ff.). *Many names* are necessary because God is essentially incomprehensible, and to avoid idolatry the metaphoric nature of God-language must constantly be brought to mind. For, as

Johnson reminds us, God is a reality that eludes all our names (1993, 118).[10]

The use of many metaphors for God draws its precedence from scriptures, as God gave Moses the untranslatable YHWH, often translated as I AM WHO I AM or THE ONE WHO CAUSES TO BE (Exod. 3.14, annotations, *Bible*). Another tradition traces the introduction of the sacred name back to Genesis 4.26, during the time of Adam's grandson Enosh when "people began to invoke the name of the LORD (YHWH)." Again there is an unpronounceable name that is represented by another name. This use of a representative name is a reminder that we cannot say the true name of God.

By the time of the Psalms, the Holy One of Israel is called by many metaphors in worship: *Shepherd, Sovereign, Shield, Judge, Rock, Deliverer, the Most High, the God of Jacob, King of Glory, Light* and *Salvation*, to list only a few. So the precedent has been set in worship in the Judeo-Christian tradition for understanding and using many ways to approach God. For Christians this variety in understanding was both expanded and concretized as Jesus Christ was accepted as God yet distinct. Likewise, the presence of the Holy Spirit, understood as its own distinctive presence of God, brought forth a diversity of metaphors.

Throughout the centuries the language of worship has been influenced by mystics, those who gained immediate knowledge of God in this life through personal religious experience (Cross and Livingstone, *s.v. mysticism*). As a result liturgical language has blossomed with many metaphors for God because the Holy Mystery was revealed to different persons in various life situations in diverse ways. Yet, many of these metaphors have not been widely used. Johnson suggests that Western religious language of recent centuries pales when one considers the varieties of names from postbiblical Jewish usage (over ninety names from the first through fourth centuries), the Islamic tradition of a litany of the ninety-nine names of Allah (the one-hundredth name, believed to be the one that expresses the true essence of Allah, is honored in silence), and the multiplicity of names and images compiled by John Mbiti from Africa (Johnson 1993, 118-120). Certainly a creative God calls forth creative naming from her people.

This creativity will include biblical metaphors, metaphors from the Judeo-Christian tradition, and new metaphors as they are revealed and

---

1. In order to keep before us the metaphoric nature of our naming for God, this text uses as its preferred term *metaphor* rather than *names*.

then tested in community. Certainly these metaphors will follow the characteristics for language about humanity: They will be truthful (as metaphors, without containing the whole truth), and they will make visible parts of God that we have not previously acknowledged. Part of this visibility will mean the inclusion of metaphors from the Judeo-Christian tradition as well as new understandings that make visible the female characteristics of God, such as the tradition of Wisdom or Sophia, the metaphors of Mother eagle, Bakerwoman, SHE WHO IS, and the pronouns *she* and *her,* to represent God.

Unity within God. We need to be clear about the diversity of names, images, and metaphors for God: They all point to the unity of One God, the Holy One proclaimed by the Hebrew people, the God of Jesus Christ, who is proclaimed by Christian faith.

Judaism distinguished itself from other religions of its time by its belief that there was only one God, in contrast to the many gods and goddesses worshiped by neighboring peoples. Jesus taught his follow-ers that he was one with God and that the Holy Spirit, the Advocate, was also of God (see especially John 14). In order to understand this oneness of Jesus Christ, God as revealed to the Hebrew people and then through Jesus Christ, and the Holy Spirit, the early Christian church spent several centuries evolving an understanding of the Trinity, the Three-in-One. Our own time has seen a revival of interest in the Trinity and attempts to understand it in this day and age.

One of the concerns raised around new images for God is that they might be understood as standing outside the traditional formulations of the Trinity. Feminist theologians who have chosen to work and worship within the Christian church (e.g., Rosemary Ruether, Marjorie Procter-Smith, Ruth Duck, Elizabeth Johnson, Gail Ramshaw) are clear in their writings that these images and metaphors belong to the God who was revealed in the Scriptures and who is continually revealed throughout history even to today. Historians and theologians have carefully traced strands of female divinity that surface throughout the history of the Judeo-Christian tradition. In searching for strands of female divinity (see especially Barbara Newman, Elizabeth Johnson, Marina Warner, Jann Aldredge-Clanton, and Miriam Therese Winter), these scholars take seriously the creation of humanity in Genesis 1.26-27 as represen-tative of the image of God, both male and female were created in the image of God; therefore both genders are subsumed in the wholeness of God.

Implications for Emancipatory God-Language. The categories of unity and diversity are interwoven in emancipatory God-language, in a balance of unity-in-diversity/diversity-in-unity. The goal is not to produce equal columns of *oneness* and *three-ness* but to point to the all-encompassing Mystery that has been revealed within the Christian tradition. The many metaphors that point to God include "explicitly female referents" (Procter-Smith 1990, 112). Many metaphors reach out to draw the diversity of humanity to the one God, creator of heaven and earth; many metaphors enable the message of God revealed in Christ to be heard by many people; many metaphors unite the people of God through the Holy Spirit.

Revelation and Emancipation

> Christ in the "small places" of our lives is the same spirit of liberation as She who holds the stars and spins the planets in her hands.
>
>   Carter Heyward, in "Jesus of Nazareth/Christ of Faith"

Revelation. Earlier this text described God as the Holy One who is "ever being revealed to those who believe and who follow." This revelation is available to ail Christians as part of the understanding of baptism (Gal. 3.27-28; also Acts 2.17-18). The understanding that God is revealed to humanity in community and to individuals is vital to Christian faith, and is a primary characteristic of liturgical language (Duck 1991, 20-24). Revelation has several facets: God's grace and our openness, that often coincide in the environment of worship.

Saliers speaks of "liturgy as revelatory art" (1994, 197-202). God's part in revelation "rests on the mystery of grace" (197), the grace that John Wesley called *prevenient*, offered as a free gift from God and entirely unmerited by human beings (Cross and Livingstone, *s.v. grace*). When all our liturgical actions are focused on God, we become open to revelation (Saliers 1994, 197).

One thing that enables liturgy to be revelatory according to Saliers is something we have already mentioned in regard to emancipatory language, the embodiment of worship: Worship "must seek the whole emotional range: from the ecstatic praise to the depths of lamentation, and the ordinary, daily struggle to be human" (Saliers 1994, 199). Except during revivals and pietism, mainline Protestant denominations, particularly congregations of European-American descent, have long focused on worship through the mind, not practicing any appeal by liturgy or God to strong emotions or physical response (unlike many of our African-American and Hispanic sisters and brothers).

One of the original characteristics of worship in the Wesleyan tradition was that of enthusiasm, and the sign for *Methodism* in American Sign Language is the word for *enthusiasm* (Riekehof 1993, 303). This text's understanding of emancipatory language combines heart and mind, soul and body, as God's creation and our gift back to God. Carlton R. Young's recent work on the Wesleys' "music of the heart" affirms that understanding as historic to United Methodism and vital for its continuing future (Young 1995a). Other recent denominational hymnals with their inclusion of African-American, Hispanic, and African "music of the heart" suggest that there is an understanding in these churches also that a wider range of emotions is vital to worship.

Duck reminds us that while scripture "plays a key role in mediating God's self-revelation," the center of Christian revelation is Jesus Christ (1991, 22, 24). The incarnation of God into humanity in the person of Jesus Christ gives Christianity its uniqueness, as the Supreme Being of the Universe revealed love and compassion through a person. The incarnation not only shows the great love of the Creator for the created, but also shows what an abundant life might be. Emancipatory language takes seriously this revelation of God in Jesus Christ through the Holy Spirit.

One of the stumbling blocks for emancipatory worship has been the prioritizing of the characteristic of Jesus' maleness by some sectors of the church. In Roman Catholicism, the maleness of Jesus and the circle of twelve disciples has been made a primary characteristic for sacramental leadership in the church. The traditions and language of Protestant churches as well have often emphasized the maleness of Jesus, to the exclusion of considering other important characteristics of Jesus for leadership and modeling of Christian behavior—poverty, attention to those on the margins of society, compassion, willingness to die, utter steadfastness of faith, lack of possessions. Understanding the role of Jesus Christ, or Christology, is vital for women as well as for men. Just as it is important for women to identify with God, it is important that they be able to identify with Christ. Early works of Christian feminism, such as those by Rachel Conrad Wahlberg (1975, 1978), focused on Jesus' relationships with the women he met, affirming that women were included and valued by Jesus then and now. Miriam Therese Winter's 1993 work *The Gospel According to Mary* builds on imagination and insight to present Jesus Christ as women might have experienced his presence when he walked the earth in flesh. Other recent works have focused on the theological understanding of Jesus Christ: Rita Nakashima Brock's *Journeys by Heart*, that suggests that the community around Jesus was vital in helping him to become the Christ; Kelly Brown Douglas's *The Black Christ*, that sees Christ inside Black women and men "as they fight for life and wholeness" (1994, 117), and Elizabeth Johnson's *She Who Is*, that describes Jesus Christ as *Jesus-Sophia*, emphasizing his identification with the Wisdom (She) tradition begun in Judaism (Johnson 1993, 150ff.; Prov. 16.22, Wisd. of Sol. 10, John 1, and 1 Cor. 1.30). These sources present a variety of understandings of the revelation of God in Jesus Christ, and many metaphors are needed for that revelation to speak in an emancipatory way to various persons at various times in their lives.

Revelation is related to stages of life and stages of faith, in that there is not for each person, only one revelation in life and thus only one understanding of God. Just as our lives change, our understanding of God changes and our need for certain characteristics of God changes. There may be times when we need to know that God is a Rock, One we can cling to for security in the midst of changing times. There may be times when we need to feel God's cradling arms, when we grieve or are ill. There may be times when the light of God's presence floods our souls with insight or joy. There may be times when we feel God challenging us or opening doors for us. All these times of revelation may give us new metaphors for describing what we understand of God, or they may give us the impulse to find new metaphors.

Ruether has discussed how revelatory experiences begin in individual consciousness, yet "become socially meaningful only when translated into communal consciousness" (1983, 13). Hymnwriters and writers of worship resources acknowledge that their revelations have been "called out and supported by community" (Morley 1992, xiii; cf. Duck 1992, preface). Communities of faith draw on the power of the Holy Spirit, as Elkins points out, "To truly worship, to esteem the triune being of God worthily is to trust the intercession of the Spirit within a community. 'For we do not know how to pray as we ought' (Rom. 8.26)" (1994, 19). The community of faith, the church, is where individual revelation is tested and affirmed if it resonates with the congregation's understanding. Ruether concludes that

> a religious tradition remains vital so long as its revelatory pattern can be reproduced generation after generation and continues to speak to individuals in the community and provide for them the redemptive meaning of individual and collective experience (1983, 15-16).

Janet Walton has some appropriate words to close this section on revelation, as the importance of God's continuing revelation relates to emancipatory language: "Let us invoke the Holy in ritual actions that are courageous and bold. Let us agree to believe people when they say a word, image, metaphor, or gesture is demeaning" (Procter-Smith and Walton, 1993, 241). The revelation of God to humanity draws out the response of "ritual actions that are courageous and bold." Emancipatory language also acknowledges an individual's revelation that something is demeaning because it contradicts their understanding of being loved by God. The purpose of liturgical language is not to fragment the community but to unite it in Christ (Ramshaw 1995a, 114).

Emancipation. Emancipation is a crucial element of worship and of liturgical language, as Christians sense their freedom from sin and guilt, freedom for abundant living through Jesus Christ in the Holy Spirit of God. Saliers has pointed out that the experience of emancipation, freedom from fear and guilt, is a crucial element in liturgical participation (1994, 150). As he speaks of liturgy as a revelatory art, Saliers (198-202) consistently uses the language of emancipation: *freedom, liberation from every captivity, empowered, liberated, liberating power.*

The parallels with the themes of Frederick Douglass's writings on emancipation are consistent, now viewed clearly in the light of God. We are freed "from every captivity," "empowered to stand before God," and liberated to be what we are, creatures, children of God's own. The movement *from* and *to* and the fulfillment of what was meant to be can all happen in Christian worship. In the space between the cross and the empty tomb, where worship stands "between the already and the not yet," around the book, the table and the font, the liberating and emancipating power of the mighty God can meet us.

My understanding of emancipatory language is that it enables this meeting, where the marvelous mystery of God is opened to us, in order that we might be who we are and might live in the world in the light of that understanding. We receive the light of God's love and grace that we may share them in the world (Matt. 5.14-16). Ruether affirms this understanding:

> The liberating encounter with God/ess is always an encounter with our authentic selves resurrected from underneath the alienated self. It is not experience against, but in and through relationships, healing our broken relations with our bodies, with other people, with nature (1983, 71).

Because emancipation and revelation comes from God, they are beyond our control (Saliers 1994, 197). The "transformative energies of God" (200) work both in ways we understand and in ways we do not understand. There will be limitations of our understanding and limitations on our perceptions of God's revelation, because we are human. Yet, the nature of religious language is not only that of layered meaning (therefore metaphoric), but it also opens "toward new insight and future experience" (242, includes reference to Ricoeur 1967).

To draw on another image of Ricoeur is to say that emancipatory God-language is like the opening of a fan, ultimately drawn from one Source, one Unity, yet ever widening in its freedom to draw upon revelation for many metaphors so that many may believe (Ricoeur 1978, 230).

Implications for Emancipatory God-Language. The revelatory and emancipatory aspects of emancipatory God-language draw on the freedom revealed by God through Jesus Christ throughout the history of the church to our own day and beyond. Revelation from the varieties of individual experience will be tested by congregations and then offered to the whole church. All revelation is received with the understanding that our knowledge now is only in part (1 Cor. 13.12), and the metaphoric nature of our language is affirmed.

Emancipatory God-language carries the need for openness to understanding the revelation of God in new ways, a willingness on our part to risk knowing and being known by God in new ways. The great risk God took in becoming incarnate has given us a model for that risking.

The power of our emancipation is stated in the baptismal questions as we vow to "renounce the spiritual forces of wickedness, reject the evil powers of this world, and repent of our sin" and "accept the freedom and power God gives us to resist evil, injustice, and oppression in whatever forms they present themselves." This freedom and power enables us to "confess Jesus Christ as our Savior, put our whole trust in his grace, and promise to serve Christ in union with the church that has been opened to people of all ages, nations, and races" (*UMH*, 34). Emancipatory language aims at this power to move us from sin and wickedness to resisting injustice and oppression so that we might work with people of all ages, nations, and races for the glory of God.

STRATEGY: IMAGINATIVE CONSTRUCTION

Make necessary adaptations and write new material in the vernacular, in order that the assembled community express not the status quo but the astounding mercy of God.

Gail Ramshaw, *God beyond Gender*

Anamnesis and Sources of Imaginative Construction

Anamnesis is the term used in liturgy to represent memory that is mental and physical, individual and collective, that brings divine activity into the present time and space (Procter-Smith 1990, 41). It appears in the narratives of Eucharist in 1 Corinthians 11.24 and Luke 22.19 as Jesus tells his followers, "Do this in remembrance of me." The nature of communion, individuals drawn together around the table of Jesus Christ in the physical act of eating, and the belief of Christians that Jesus Christ is present there, gives anamnesis its particular quality. Anamnesis is also elaborated in the liturgical year and recognized in the liturgies of the daily office (Procter-Smith 1990, 41). As Ruether pointed out (1983, 15-16) and as we have seen in the study of the nature of hymns, communal and individual memory is an important quality of religion, particularly Christian liturgy.

A variety of sources are available for *remembering* metaphors in the Christian tradition. Duck suggests four sources for retrieval: canonical scriptures, noncanonical scriptures, mystical traditions, and liturgical sources (1991, 89-93). We will also consider the apocryphal or deuterocanonical scriptures, for example, the Wisdom of Solomon.

Biblical scholars, most notably Elisabeth Schüssler Fiorenza in New Testament and Phyllis Trible in Old Testament, have worked to recover women's part in the biblical tradition. Their work has been vital enough to inspire others, so that *The Women's Bible Commentary* (Newsom and Ringe, 1992) included forty-one contributors. This work is important not only for recovering women who have been "lost" in our tradition and thereby critiquing patriarchal society and the church, but also because in recovering these stories we are given new understandings of how God works through women.

Ruether (1985), Newman, and others have worked with noncanonical scriptures. Ruether also includes work with some early Goddess materials that Procter-Smith suggests may be useful (Procter-Smith 1990, 96-102). This text includes reference to the Apocrypha, not commonly used by Protestants, and leaves open the door for future use of noncanonical references. Noncanonical and early materials may af-

firm metaphors that can be found or imagined within the Judeo-
Christian tradition. At this time, however, it appears that canonical
scriptures, tradition, and imagination can sufficiently yield the richness
that is called forth by emancipatory language.

The tradition of the church, in mystical writings, histories involving
women, and liturgical sources (including those of the Eastern and early
church), can yield a richness of metaphoric language for liturgy that is
emancipatory. Recent examples drawn from mystical writings include
the prayer by Anselm of Canterbury from the 11th century ("And you,
Jesus, good Lord, are you not also Mother?" *The United Methodist
Book of Worship* #398), the prayer of Mechtild of Magdeburg ("O
burning Mountain, O chosen Sun," *UMH* #104), and Jean Janzen's
hymns based on the writings of Hildegard, Mechtild of Magdeburg, and
Julian of Norwich (*Hymnal: A Worshipbook* #123, 45, 482). Histories
involving women have yielded names and stories to include when the
saints of the church are named. An example of this powerful naming
occurs in a liturgy of remembrance for All Saints (Hallowmas) that
recounts the holocaust of women hanged and burned, tortured and
drowned in the name of the church (Ruether 1986, 224-228). Ancient
Christian liturgies are also being mined for recent books of worship;
see for example #275, 388, 389, 391, and 500 in *The United Methodist
Book of Worship*.

As new biblical and historical studies of women in the Judeo-
Christian appear, new resources may be discovered for emancipatory
language. The criteria developed of visibility, truthfulness, diversity,
revelation and emancipation will need to be applied to these new metaphors and texts both by individuals and by communities, as resources
are adapted and developed.

Mysterion, the Mystery of God, and Imagination

In her discussion of imagination, Procter-Smith uses the term *mysterion*, the "imaginative dimension of the liturgy, often referred to as
'mystery'" (1990, 54). This is the word used in the Eastern Orthodox
Church for what the Western Church calls *the sacraments* (e.g., baptism and communion). The original Greek meaning, "keeping silence"
(*Webster's*) has been transformed in Christian usage to mean God's
self-revelation. Mysterion is what makes metaphors possible, it is what
"allows liturgy to be the work of the Spirit," and "it makes community
possible" (Procter-Smith 1990, 55).

Amos Wilder, who spoke of theology and the religious imagination as *theopoetic*, says that imagination is "a necessary component . . . of all remembering, realizing, and anticipating" (1976, 2). A theopoetic will enable us to recover a sense of the sacred and help sift through contemporary mythologies in order to find theological renewal. Wilder's work fits with the sense of embodiment and incarnation of emancipatory language as he speaks of drawing on "the good world of our five senses, our affections, our kinships and relationships, our skills and our talents" (1976, 56).

Mysterion holds together God's revelation with our embodiment and enables *creative ritualization*. This phrase was first used by Schüssler Fiorenza to describe the freedom of women to use "imaginative freedoms, popular creativity, and liturgical powers" to create religious ritual (1985, 135). Duck expands on this term in her book, *Gender and the Name of God* (1991):

> Creative ritualization is based on the claim that the Holy Spirit continues to move within the church, calling forth appropriate human witness and response in every age. . . . Language discovered through the method of creative ritualization is shaped by hope for God's new creation . . . (104-105)

The freedom and generativity of creative ritualization is recounted by Duck in her experience of "adapting hymn texts for inclusive language." She soon came up against the limitations of simply "translating" patriarchal language into inclusive language, and in attempting to adapt the hymn "Lead on, O King eternal" found that she needed to write a new text, "using the method of creative ritualization."[2] Emancipatory language happens when the limitations of merely translating texts is overcome and doors to new metaphors are opened as the "fan" of the register is expanded.

The use of imagination in emancipatory language will be fed by the sources mentioned above under *anamnesis*. Prayer and spiritual discipline also feeds the imagination and is vital to those providing worship resources for the church, and for those leading in worship (for a methodology that is based in prayer, see Duck 1995, 10-19). Extemporaneous prayers, in particular, can easily lapse into old, familiar, patriarchal language without a background of conscious attention to one's God-language. Through a disciplined prayer life, one is opened to revelation

---

2. See Chapter 11 for a multidimensional reading of this text.

and to a personal understanding of the unity-in-diversity of the Holy. Through a disciplined prayer life, one's compassion for the world can be nurtured, as persons are made visible in prayer and one learns to become more truthful before God. A disciplined prayer life, encompassing all of life, might help to open one's register for speaking with and about God (cf. Johnson 1993, 44).

Another source for mysterion that has caught the attention of some feminist and womanist theologians is contemporary literature. Procter-Smith cites several books as examples of the honoring of women's memory and imaginative work that show forth women's spirituality (1990, 45-51). As Kelly Brown Douglas draws *The Black Christ* to a close she quotes from Alice Walker's *The Color Purple*, claiming the protagonist's understanding of God for a womanist Black Christ (1994, 117; see also Procter-Smith 1990, 50, on Walker). The literature of African-American women is particularly important for womanist theologians, as may be seen in the "1996 Call for Papers" of the Womanist Approaches to Religion and Society Group of the American Academy of Religion, that listed eleven writers to be considered.

One other characteristic of emancipatory liturgical language that needs to be included in the discussion of mysterion is the characteristic of silence. Ultimately we stand in silence before the One who cannot be fully named or known, the Well of Silence. Emancipatory language acknowledges the futility and necessity of our struggles to verbalize our encounters with the divine alone and in community.

RESULTS OF EMANCIPATORY LANGUAGE

> So with the feminist reform of liturgical language: it will take a long time to learn the new song. The tasks are monumental.. . . We can concede that this will be a hundred-year project, but only if the church is zealously engaged in the endless and exacting tasks of reform today.
>
> Gail Ramshaw, *God Beyond Gender*

Ramshaw closes her 1995 book with the above challenge, which she has clearly named and explicated throughout the book. It is quite a task, one that is not only long-range but immediate. The definition of emancipatory language suggests that it moves beyond reform to new possibilities for language and for encounters of God and humanity, encompassing the changes Ramshaw names. As Ruether says, our metaphors and understanding "must be transformative, pointing us back to our authentic potential and forward to new redeemed possibilities" (1983, 69). Procter-Smith warned that the shift in transforming our language will change our world. Linguist Deborah Cameron concurs, "a great deal is at stake: our identities and our deepest beliefs about the world" (1992, 213).

How do these changes occur? To understand some of the changes we turn to the field of rhetoric, the study of effect of language. Karlyn Kohrs Campbell includes a description of the process whereby each rhetorical act is part of a process that can gradually enable change in belief over a long period of time (1982, 10-13). Likewise, hymns and liturgical language are part of an ongoing process, whereby persons gather weekly and participate in formulating belief. Emancipatory language aims to produce a "precipitating moment" or at least to enable the conditions from the human side for an "ah-ha!" experience, yet the reality is that the results are more gradual. Perhaps the changes might be explained by the metaphor of children growing—when you see them every day you rarely notice that they are getting taller or their face and body are maturing, but see them only once a year or every six months and their changes will astound you.

Conversion—*metanoia*, turning around—is an important concept in the Christian tradition and has been stressed by feminist theologians (e.g., see Ruether 1983, 183-192; Johnson 1993, 62-65). Emancipatory language is language committed to conversion, constant and ultimate change in individuals and communities, beginning now. We may not see great changes immediately but in the long view, in the view of the coming of God's vision, the changes are necessary and inevitable. They will happen: Individual understandings will be changed, more doors will be opened for others to enter and explore the Holy, churches will change, and earth will move a step closer to the fullness of life promised by God in Jesus Christ.

Chapter 6
Hymns and Emancipatory Language

INTRODUCTION

Singing the hymn "Rise up, O men of God" one Sunday, however, their secret dawned on me: They were men and so was God. Men were called on to do great things for God; girls were groomed to be ministers' wives. Boys could be God, girls could not. The images of childhood burrowed away in my heart and mind, limiting my dreams and the expression of my gifts in the world.

> Patricia Lynn Reilly, *A God Who Looks Like Me*

The power of hymnic language to define thoughts and then actions can be seen in Reilly's story. She struggled long and hard with the issues involved and published a book on women's spirituality with specific exercises to overcome the exclusion women have felt in the church.

Keith Watkins tells a similar story from a different perspective: The congregation was singing "O Zion, Haste" as it commissioned missionaries, and Watkins realized as he sang the final stanza, "Give of thy sons to bear the message glorious," that his daughter, whom he was sending, was not included in the hymn (1981, 16). This father became aware at that moment of the hurtfulness of exclusive language and went on to write a book suggesting ways to work and speak during the transitional period of learning to "transcend sexist language in worship." These two examples show the importance of hymnic language in the lives of believers, and have helped motivate my search for emancipatory language.

This chapter adds to the definition of the word *emancipatory* developed in the two previous chapters, as it may be specifically applied to hymn texts. I also define the body of hymns from which selections for the multidimensional readings in Part III of this text have been made.

GOD IDENTIFIES WITH THE MARGINS

As we consider emancipatory language in hymn texts, we will be looking for evidence of contemporary theologies of liberation, feminism, and ecological concerns. A primary concern of recent theologies has been the identification of God with those on the margins of the church and society. So in the close readings we look for phrases and thoughts that may be derived from these theologies. This is noted both by the inclusion of persons on the margins and by the exclusion of androcentric and patriarchal attitudes.

The first chapter of this text discussed how the theological understandings of the early church, Martin Luther, and Charles Wesley were taught to laity through hymn texts. Contemporary theologies will not take hold in the consciousness of the church unless they are made accessible to the people in the pews. One way to do this is through hymn texts.

LANGUAGE ABOUT HUMANITY

Since the 1978 publication of the *Lutheran Book of Worship*, denominational hymnal committees have been concerned with inclusive language for humanity (Sydnor 1990, 59). The United Methodist Subcommittee on Language of the Hymnal Revision Committee called in its recommended guidelines for "traditional" hymns (hymns written before 1962) to use "inclusive forms of address for persons in the assembly, in the community and the world." "New hymns" were to be "inclusive and universal in outlook, free from divisive elements and phrases that convey attitudes of superiority or indifference toward people outside the circle of singers" (Young 1993, 132-133).

Likewise two hymnals published in 1995 stated their intentions explicitly: "Every effort was made to ensure that all hymns spoke to and for all God's people, equally" (*New Century Hymnal*, x); "With great care and pastoral sensitivity, some hymn texts have been amended to eliminate or reduce archaic language, generic masculine references for humanity, and the negative use of metaphors about darkness or physical disabilities" (*Chalice Hymnal*, v). Notice that *Chalice Hymnal* specifically articulates that it will go beyond gender references to include racial and embodiment concerns.

We have already discussed some of the concerns about truth and justice and their relationship to the central thoughts of hymn texts. Specific studies of hymn texts that relate to these concerns appear in Elizabeth Smith's study of hymns by women writers (1993) and Helen Pearson's study of "The church's one foundation" (1983). Both articles point out the need not only for inclusive words and phrases but also for considering texts in their entirety, that they reflect, for our purposes, emancipatory theology and treatment of subjects.

LANGUAGE ABOUT GOD

Carlton R. Young calls for a restoration of the energy generated by the contrast of male metaphors and female metaphors and their combination (1995b, 134). This would support the diversity of metaphors for God called for by emancipatory language.

The problem presents itself in praxis, however. Young's examples of "exclusively employed female metaphors" include texts that are not yet in hymnals, hymnals that most often still include examples of exclusively employed male metaphors. How does the church restore the contrast and interplay of metaphors when published denominational resources remain heavily masculine? How can it restore what has not been the case? Can there be texts that combine male and female metaphors with integrity, rather than texts exclusive of one or the other?

This book has taken denominational hymnals as part of its communal test of individual revelation. What appears in denominational hymnals has been agreed upon as revelatory and truthful within that denomination, often by both a committee and by "test" congregations. As one begins the study of emancipatory hymnic language, language that is in the position to affect a large number of laity, it is therefore reasonable to begin with the corpus of denominational hymns. Future studies may do well to draw on emerging hymnody, not yet receiving denominational approval, for more explicitly emancipatory language.

New Century Hymnal hints at this limitation of denominational hymnals, not without hope: "Where language fails us, we live with confidence that the Holy Spirit intercedes for us with sighs too deep for words. Our hymns are a testimony to this ministry of the Holy Spirit" (1995, vii). The close readings and section on praxis (Parts III and IV of this text) show the Spirit at work within some of the hymns published in denominational hymnals.

STRATEGY: IMAGINATIVE CONSTRUCTION

One interesting facet of current hymn publishing is the inclusion of notes by the author in most single-author collections. Thus one can learn about the inspirations and situations that called forth specific hymns, such as in Duck's *Dancing in the Universe*, Wren's *Bring Many Names*, and Murray's *In Every Corner Sing*. Hymnwriters such as Vajda, Troeger, Wren, and Duck have also written about the process they use in writing, so that one can see their use of imagination and sources. By considering living hymnwriters for this text I also had the opportunity to be in dialogue with them about their texts in order to clarify writing process and word choices.

It should also be noted under the strategy of imaginative construction, the characteristic discussed in Chapter 2 of the practice of editing hymn texts. Brian Wren is the most obvious example of editing (see Wren 1996a), as he himself constantly rewrites his own hymns. In the close readings we see other marks of editing, even in texts written in the last ten years (similar to the editing by John Wesley of his brother Charles's texts).

RESULTS OF EMANCIPATORY LANGUAGE

Ruth Duck, who considers herself an emancipatory hymnwriter, has said, "Learning new hymns can help a congregation grow, as people discover new ways to articulate their faith. For most people, gentle and gradual learning, rather than a rush of new material, supports heartfelt participation and spiritual development" (1995a, 106). This coincides with the long-range goals of emancipatory language. There is also the immediate reaction of "ah-ha," of sensing that a hymn text has put into words what the singer has only just begun to understand.

To summarize, this text looks at recent hymns that are poetic, metrical, mostly rhymed, written to be sung by Christians in communal worship, found in denominational hymnals, that use emancipatory language (diverse images for God, inclusive of the varieties of human experience, truthful about human nature and existence, revealing God's continual presence), scripturally based, oriented toward the Social Gospel, and evidencing strands of contemporary theology (particularly liberation, feminist, ecological).

Part III
MULTIDIMENSIONAL
READINGS

The third part of this book contains the development of a methodology of multidimensional reading (based on the methodology of close reading) and the application of that methodology to six hymn texts. The purpose of the multidimensional readings is to understand these texts as fully as possible and to be accurate about their sources and the emancipatory aspects present in them.

The six texts appear in mainline Protestant denominational hymnals and were chosen for the possibilities of emancipatory language present in the text. Three are by men and three, by women. They are presented here in the order in which they were presented to the groups who served as praxis groups (whose responses are presented in Chapter 14). That order was focused by the appearance of two of the texts in *The United Methodist Hymnal*, the hymnal most familiar to me and to four of the praxis groups, and then a third hymn's consideration and eventual rejection by that hymnal committee. As those three texts were all written by men, the texts by the women followed, in chronological order.

Chapter 7 develops the methodology of multidimensional reading, drawing on the fields of rhetorical and literary criticism, on linguistics, and on biblical exegesis. The multidimensional analysis of each hymn text forms a chapter: "God of the Sparrow God of the Whale," by Jaroslav Vajda, "Source and Sovereign, Rock and Cloud," by Thomas H. Troeger, "Bring Many Names," by Brian A. Wren, "Lead on, O Cloud of Presence," by Ruth C. Duck, "Of Women, and of Women's

Hopes We Sing," by Shirley Erena Murray, and "O Holy Spirit, Root of Life," by Jean Janzen, based on the writings of Hildegard of Bingen. Each of these authors is living; they have graciously commented on early drafts of these readings and their comments have been incorporated to this final writing.

Chapter 7
Developing a Method
of Multidimensional Reading

INTRODUCTION

Close reading is a method that was first developed in the field of literary criticism for analyzing texts. This book, focused on hymn texts, weaves together methodologies from rhetorical criticism, literary criticism, feminist criticism, and biblical exegesis. Thus my reading is a multidimensional analysis. The focus of this reading is the text itself. The methodologies are interwoven so that multiplicity of meanings within the text might be uncovered. Different texts yield their treasures of meaning to different strands of criticism. Because some texts are rich in scriptural allusions, others in metaphor, others centered on an icon of meaning, different methods apply.

Because this multidimensional reading is centered in the text, we begin by reading the text carefully, to see what it has to say.[1] Then with the assistance of rhetorical, literary, feminist, biblical and theological tools we uncover various components of meaning in order to understand the text more deeply. Many of these tools have been described in Chapter 2 in relationship to hymns. This chapter explains how the various tools help both to uncover the meanings in the text and to describe it. Rereading and fresh examinations of the text after periods of rest also play a part. In the final section of the book (Chapter 14), we will ask about the implications of meaning for those who will sing the text.

---

1. Because this methodology has been specifically adapted for this text, first person pronouns are used.

THE FIRST COMPONENT: PRELIMINARY VIEW

> . . . what matters most is the scrutiny of meaning, the exact tracking of
> what's going on in the texts.
>
> Madeleine Forell Marshall, *Common Hymnsense*

We begin by looking at the background of the text and considering
what the author has said about the text, focused around the question
words:

Who is the author?

What did she or he intend to communicate through the text?

Why was it written?

Where was it first sung?

How did it change in subsequent publications?

These questions help us establish a *Sitz-im-Leben* for the text, locating
it in its original time and place, a tool drawn from the historical critical
method of biblical criticism. This also follows a strand of rhetorical
criticism, beginning to consider if the author's intention is communi-
cated to the listener (who in this case becomes the singer and thus participates as the one "giving" the message) (Wichelns 1958, 35).

Then, using a strand of literary criticism, we look at the poetic
shape of the text, its meter (what poetic foot is used) and the length of
its lines and stanzas. The patterns of meter in hymn texts have been
studied by Austin C. Lovelace, a contemporary hymnologist, who
pointed out that certain meters and poetic lines express different
meanings; for example, some lend themselves to stately treatment and
others to teaching (1982, 11-23). Here we begin to look at how form
follows or fights against the thoughts expressed.

This first component of meaning looks at and listens to consonant
and vowel sounds in the text. Where are the rhymes, and is there a pattern? Does the text depend on repetition of sound or words? Kenneth
Burke's essay, "On Musicality in Verse," suggests a multidimensional
reading of the consonants and vowels within a poem, searching for
repetitions of sounds and variations, all of that contribute to the "musicality" of verse (1973, 369-378). These factors can aid in the reception
of a text.

This component of multidimensional reading also looks at sentences and clauses, or segmentation (Leech and Short 1981, 214-219).
In hymn texts, segmentation is related to the literary characteristic of
line length and is determined by meter, the shape of the stanza, and
ultimately to the tune associated with the text.

A final strand that moves this first component of reading into the second component is the initial consideration of style. Style is important in communicating the ideas of the author to the intended receiver. Two of the four virtues of style named by classical rhetoric are considered at this point of the multidimensional reading: *correctness*, that is the grammar used, and *propriety*, using the proper level of style. Cicero and Augustine suggest that style is related to the duties of the orator to teach (using plain style), to please (using grand style), and to move (using middle style) (Kennedy 1984, 25). Linguistic and literary criticisms work with style also. Linguistics speaks of "registers" of speech; the use of technical or religious or slang words would mark different registers of speech. Literary criticism points out the use in English of shorter, more concrete words like *thought*, called Anglo-Saxon diction, and longer, more abstract words like *contemplation*, called Latinate diction (Kinzie 1994, 9-12). The style of the text is essential to its communication. Lastly, using a feminist hermeneutic, we pay close attention to the words used for humanity and for God, looking at the gender that is stated or implied.

THE SECOND COMPONENT: ANALYSIS

The step we are concerned with at the moment requires us to get our equations inductively, by tracing down the interrelationships as revealed by the objective structure of the [text] itself.

The main ideal of criticism, as I conceive it, is to use all that is there to use.

Kenneth Burke, *The Philosophy of Literary Form*

The second component of multidimensional reading moves into the way the words and thoughts of the text are organized and meaning is made. Here we consider the meanings of words, their lexical or dictionary meanings, the scriptures to that they allude, and the meaning the tradition has ascribed to them. Hymns are meant to be sung in worship, and in Protestant worship, scripture is central. Many hymns rely heavily on biblical references and resonance to form their meaning. This reliance both teaches biblical faith to the newcomer and recalls it for the long-time member. Hymns shape our faith by their reliance or non-reliance on the scriptures and on other sources of faith.

Cohesion is the binding together of the text (Leech and Short 1981, 243-244). At this level of multidimensional reading we look at the ways a particular text is unified. In addition to the poetic and rhetorical

devices of ways of repetition used in cohesion, this includes consideration of unifying theological concepts, particularly looking for strands of
liberation, feminist, and ecological theologies.

This component of multidimensional reading then moves further
into how the text works. What are the metaphors and salient points of
the text? What is the progression of thought? Is iconicity present?

Metaphor is integral to poetry and to religious language. Metaphor
happens when words and phrases are used to suggest a likeness or
analogy between two objects or ideas. Without metaphor we would
have no way to speak of God; God is unlike any other thing that we
know, so we can only describe God by beginning with ideas and things
that we do know. The focus of religious language on God requires its
dependence on metaphor. In addition, poetry depends on metaphor to
open up new meanings. The combination of poetry and religious language in hymn texts means a strong reliance on metaphor both for
talking about God and for opening us to new meanings and understandings about God and ourselves. Because of the importance of
metaphor in hymn texts, the salient points (high points or points of focus) will most often be related to either a specific metaphor or a progression of metaphors.

Classical rhetoric begins with the rhetorical parts of *invention*, "the
planning of a discourse and the arguments to be used in it," and *arrangement*, determining "the rhetorically effective composition of the
discourse and molding the elements into a unified structure" (Kennedy
1984, 13, 23). The sequence of thought in a text will generally follow
one of three principles: (1) presentational, that is concerned with how
the addressee hears the text, and is exemplified by the principle of climax, or "last is most important;" (2) chronological, that imitates the
purported sequence of events; and (3) psychological, that uses the "first
is most important" principle and then follows a stream of consciousness
(Leech and Short 1981, 236-239).

Iconicity is the imitation principle: "A code is iconic to the extent
that it imitates, in its signals or textual forms, the meanings that they
represent" (Leech and Short 1981, 233). Thus, chronological sequence,
that imitates the purported sequence of events, is called iconic. Michael
Leff has further developed the concept of iconicity, defining it as "the
interaction between discursive form and representational content" (Leff
and Sachs 1990, 257). Not all texts are iconic, but those that are incorporate within themselves an icon or imitation of what they are talking
about—"the medium is the message." Iconicity looks at the text as a

whole, incorporating both metaphor and the movement of narrative or argument.

In addition, as we re-look at the text as a whole we consider the importance of metaphors in the text, watching for dramatic alignment (that is, what is versus what), and watching for critical points within the work, as well as at beginnings and endings (Burke 1973, 58, 78). Here we consider again the activities of the critic: (1) see a thing clearly, (2) record what we have seen precisely, and (3) seek to judge the thing justly (Black 1966, 4).

THE THIRD COMPONENT: REREADING

> More is going on in language than we consciously know. . . . Becoming good at the method means asking the question "what does that . . . do?" with more and more awareness of the probable (and hidden) complexity of the answer; that is with a mind more and more sensitized to the workings of language. . . . It is self-sharpening and what it sharpens is you. In short, it does not organize materials, but transforms minds.
> Stanley E. Fish, *Self-Consuming Artifacts*

The third component is a step back from the text in order to give our multidimensional reading a fresh perspective at a later time. A period of rest is followed by recalling the principles of multidimensional reading. Obviously, we each come to the text with our own bias or horizon (Gadamer 1990, 152), but in this task of reading we are called to attempt fresh perspective, clarity, preciseness, and justice.

Because this book is concerned with language that is emancipatory, an important factor in this third component is a second look for characteristics of emancipatory language present in a text. Thus, we look for visibility of those on the margins of society, justice, and truthtelling about human experience; we look for unity-in-diversity, revelation and emancipation in language about God. What is not being said? Who is being left out? What stereotypes about God or humanity are promoted or challenged by the salient points of the text? Has our reading included the many dimensions of emancipatory language?

It is important to step back and then look again at the text and what we have said about it. Have we been as comprehensive as we can be? The nature of hymn texts is akin to that of scripture; that is, hearing or singing it again in different circumstances can reveal new meanings we had missed before. The task of multidimensional reading is to slow down the process so that as many of the meanings as possible might be discovered. But the meaning of the text will always open itself to new interpretation as it engages other receivers.

CONCLUSION

In the multidimensional readings that follow this chapter, elements from the first component of reading described above are covered in the introduction that follows the printing of the text and other relevant quotations. This always includes "Background of the text" and "The shape of the text" in addition to other relevant categories.

The second component of multidimensional reading, of considering word meanings, cohesion, metaphors, sequence, and iconicity, is uncovered stanza by stanza.

The third component of multidimensional reading, that of stepping back and rereading, has been followed by the writer and also accomplished through the input of her dissertation committee and the authors of the chosen hymn texts. Several stages of rereading and editing occurred during the writing of this text. The second look at the emancipatory elements of each text is presented as a final section of each multidimensional reading.

Chapter 8
God of the Sparrow
God of the Whale
A Multidimensional Reading

God of the sparrow
God of the whale
God of the swirling stars
    How does the creature say Awe
    How does the creature say Praise

God of the earthquake
God of the storm
God of the trumpet blast
    How does the creature cry Woe
    How does the creature cry Save

God of the rainbow
God of the cross
God of the empty grave
    How does the creature say Grace
    How does the creature say Thanks

God of the hungry
God of the sick
God of the prodigal
    How does the creature say Care
    How does the creature say Life

God of the neighbor
God of the foe
God of the pruning hook
    How does the creature say Love
    How does the creature say Peace

God of the ages
God near at hand
God of the loving heart
    How do your Children say Joy
    How do your Children say Home

Jaroslav J. Vajda, 1983
Vajda, *Now the Joyful Celebration* 1987, #15
The United Methodist Hymnal 1989, #122
The Presbyterian Hymnal 1990, #272
Chalice Hymnal 1995, #70
New Century Hymnal 1995, #32
Voices United 1997, #229

Having been fascinated for more than forty years in the ministry by the proper and effective motivation for Christian service, a request from Concordia Lutheran Church of Kirkwood, Missouri, provided an opportunity to compose a hymn text that would provoke answers from the users of the hymn as to why and how God's creatures (and children) are to serve him.

Jaroslav Vajda, *Now the Joyful Celebration*

INTRODUCTION

This hymn was chosen for several reasons. First, its lack of rhyme and its irregular meter immediately emancipate it from the tradition of regular metered and rhymed hymn texts. Second, it contains some theological thoughts important to ecological theology. Third, it moves beyond gendered language for both humanity and God, giving a marvelous diversity-in-unity of metaphors for the divine.

Background

Jaroslav Vajda, a Lutheran-Missouri Synod pastor and editor born in Ohio in 1919, "has authored more than 190 hymn texts and translations that now appear in thirty-six hymnals and collections in the United

States, Canada, England, Germany and recently independent Slovakia" (Vajda 1994). Three collections of his texts have been published, in addition to the inclusion of his hymns in every major denominational hymnal, since he began writing English text hymns in 1968.[1] He writes that "The task of the church, and of hymnody, is to give voice both to the cries [of the world of our day] and to the Gospel" (Vajda 1987, 9).

On October 27, 1983, Vajda completed a commission from Concordia Lutheran Church in Kirkwood, Missouri, to write a hymn to celebrate their 110th anniversary (Vajda 1987, 152). His text, "God of the Sparrow," unrhymed but metered poetry framed in six stanzas of five lines each, was sung at the celebration to a tune composed by the church organist and choir director. Before 1983 was over, another Missouri Synod Lutheran, professor of church music, Carl Schalk, had composed the tune, ROEDER, with which it would be published.[2] A survey of 125 churches conducted by Don Saliers, United Methodist professor of theology and liturgics, named this hymn as one of six new hymns from the 1989 *United Methodist Hymnal* that "have really established themselves in the congregation's repertoire" (Saliers 1993, 8). The reasons for its frequent usage include its attempt "to express the essence of worship for the contemporary Church" (Vajda 1995), thus lending itself to usage on many "ordinary" Sundays, and, this text would argue, because its use of emancipatory language gives room for many different persons to claim the text for themselves.[3]

The Shape of the Text

As one begins the multidimensional reading of this text, the lack of rhyme is immediately obvious. One of Vajda's earliest popular hymn texts, "Now the Silence," written in 1968 (*UMH* #619), also without

---

1. Vajda's earliest hymn texts were translations of Slovak and Czech hymns, on which he is a renowned authority.

2. Rev. Vajda has been very helpful in clearing up the confusion around these two versions and their respective tunes (Vajda 1996). The tune used at the premier, by the musician at Concordia Lutheran, "sang" better with "wayward child" and "olive branch." Vajda's preferred text and tune are the original words with Schalk's tune (the version used in this book). A third confusion appeared in some editions of *The Presbyterian Hymnal* (and Peter Bower's related article) where a typographical error changed 6:2 to *God of the hand*. The versions show how hymn texts may come from an individual author, but, within less than ten years in this case, alternate versions are made both intentionally and inadvertently.

3. This text has also been set as an anthem by Marty Haugen.

rhyme, established him as a writer of poetic language in meter and metaphor. The meter of 5.4.6.7.7 in "God of the Sparrow" is based on the dactylic foot, (/ u u), with variations including trochee (/ u), a cretic foot (/ u /), and several incidences of a single stressed syllable. Vajda suggests that an amphibrachic foot appears in the middle foot of the last two lines of each stanza, although I scan it as a dactylic foot. Either way, the result of this metrical scheme is a balance of stressed and un-stressed syllables, to that Schalk's tune gives an endless flow, until it comes to rest on the final word, *home.*

A second notable feature of the text is that it contains no punctua-tion. There are no commas at the end of each phrase, no periods at the end of stanzas, no question marks following the phrases *How does.* Thomas Troeger, another hymnwriter,[4] suggests that the absence of punctuation "is significant because it suggests how the questions of faith extrude beyond the limits of language" (Troeger 1992, 9). This lack of punctuation also contributes to its tensive, poetic nature.

Although there is no direct rhyme scheme, the repetition of the phrases *God of the* and *How does the creature* provides some of the predictability and familiarity that rhyme typically does for poetry. This repetition of words at the start of successive lines is called anaphora, and it is a striking poetic device as the repetition hammers home its idea, in this case *God of* and *How does.* Two rhyming words in the text, *Save* (2:5) and *grave* (3:3), contain a strong theological connection. Two word pairs that although separated by stanzas contain echoes of rhyme are *sparrow* (1:1)/*rainbow* (3:1) and the weighty words *woe* (2:4)/*foe* (5:2). Stanza three contains a "front rhyme" *grave* (3:3)/*Grace* (3:4). Kenneth Burke's essay, "On the Musicality of Verse," suggests a closer look at the various sounds in poetry (1973, 369-378). This par-ticular text lends itself to that kind of analysis, with the constant repeti-tion of the open sounds *God of the* and *does the,* and scarcity of *i* sounds. When they do occur, the *i* sounds are in positions of import: (1) the repetition of *cry* (2:4, 5) as opposed to *say* in the other repetitions in fourth and fifth lines of each stanza, and (2) *children,* that replaces *creature* in the final stanza (6:4,5). The word *cry* helps to give weight to *Woe* and *Save* in its stanza (2), and the change from the *creature* (1-5) to *your children* (6) is a turning point of the text, which is discussed below. Use of this type of analysis uncovers the echoes of rhyme in *sparrow/rainbow* and *woe/foe,* and the most important word, *home,* as the only long *o* sounds in the text.

---

4. See discussion of Troeger and one of his hymn texts in Chapter 9.

A major defining characteristic of poetry, in addition to rhyme and meter, is its use of metaphor. In this text metaphor comes both through the use of the preposition *of* and through the use of anaphora to layer images. *Of* has several properties, two of that seem relevant to this text: "used as a function word to indicate a point of reckoning <north ~ the lake>; used as a function word to indicate the component materials, parts of elements of the contents <throne ~ gold> <cup ~ water>" (*Webster's*). The lexical semantic properties of the phrase *God of the* _____, suggest first, that God is their point of reckoning; God locates *the sparrow, the whale, the hungry, the neighbor*. All the creatures, events and symbols named in the text are in relationship to God. Second, God contains *the stars, the storm, the cross, the foe*, within God-self. These claims by the words in the opening phrase of each line are "namings" of God, understood by people of the Book, in the light of the burning bush, as God spoke to Moses: "I am the *God of* your father, the *God of* Abraham, the *God of* Isaac, and the *God of* Jacob" (Exod. 3.6). What Vajda has done is to expand on these names for God, moving from a biblical litany of persons in the heritage of faith to a litany of all of God's creation.

The metaphor of the text occurs not only by the location of each named within God but by their combination and their juxtaposition. Each stanza locates God with three items of two, one, and three syllables each. The items vary from creatures and events in the natural world, to symbols of covenant, human beings, time, and space. The relationship of the three items in each stanza begins to build up the metaphor of the stanza. Then the fourth and fifth lines of each stanza raise the question of response, suggesting responses of action verbs (*praise, save, say thanks, care, love*) and nouns (*awe, woe, grace, life, peace, joy, home*). The ambivalence of using the "question words" *How does* without a question mark points perhaps to an answer within the question. These responses grow out of the namings and expand on them. As the text continues it moves the reader/singer through consideration of the varieties of God's creation and action and the creature's (including our own) response.

STANZAS

Stanza One

The text opens with the image of the *sparrow*, a small bird of the air, that because it is cared for by God, reminds us all the more that God cares for us (Luke 12.6-7). The song popular particularly in African-American congregations, "His eye is on the sparrow" (*Songs of Zion* #33) gives flight to this image of the God of the sparrow. Reference in Psalm 84:3 to *sparrow* helps to gather up all of this text from this opening line, *God of the sparrow,* to its final word, *home*:

> Even the sparrow finds a home,
>   and the swallow a nest for herself,
>   where she may lay her young,
>   at your altars, O LORD of hosts,
>   my King and my God.

Immediately follows the *whale*, a large animal of the sea, popularly associated with the story of Jonah in the Hebrew Scriptures. This popular connection, although the scripture actually says that a *large fish* swallowed Jonah, carries images ranging all the way from the children's story of Pinocchio who is swallowed by a whale to the analogy of the burial of Jesus Christ who, like Jonah coming forth from the whale alive, is resurrected and alive.

There is no direct scriptural reference to stars *swirling*, yet it contains the images from the creation of the stars in Genesis and God's promise to Abraham and Sarah that their "offspring would be as numerous as the *stars* of heaven" (Gen. 22.17), from God asking Job, "who laid [the earth's] cornerstone when the morning *stars* sang together and all the heavenly beings shouted for joy?" (Job 38.6b-7), and from the importance of the star in Christmas and Epiphany celebrations, seen by the Magi and leading them to the infant Jesus. The *swirling* of the stars might remind readers/singers of Brian Swimme and Thomas Berry's *The Universe Story* or other works on cosmogenesis, with their fluid and moving sense of creation's development.

Awe and *Praise* are called forth as the response of the creatures, familiar concepts for worship: "stand in *awe* of [God]" (Ps. 22.23, 33.8) and the appearance of *praise* 297 times in the Scriptures, in the imperative thirteen times in Psalm 150 alone (Metzger 1991). There is correlation of singing with *praise* as well, as 1 Corinthians 14.15 exhorts us to "sing *praise* with the spirit . . . [and] sing *praise* with the mind also." One additional thing to be pointed out before leaving this first stanza is that Vajda begins with creation, not with humanity. This is similar to the creation story in Genesis and has the same effect of placing us within God's creation. The reiteration of *creature* also lessens the centrality of humanity, an important point for the text and its ecological impact.

Stanza Two

Stanza two continues the emphasis on creation, with the events of *earthquake* and *storm*. This has been called a stanza on judgment, shattering "any romantic recollections of God as Creator in stanza one . . . by this rupturing burst of reality regarding the differentiation between the Creator and the creature" (Bower 1994, 148). I do not read in this stanza grave judgment, although I believe it is a strong reminder of God's power in creation and in all ultimate things. The violence and decay that are a part of creation, as described in this stanza, serve as a reminder not to romanticize either God or creation (cf. Dillard 1974). Hymnologist Paul Schilling suggests that this stanza poses a response to a troublesome question in our time: "What of the events that are neither fair nor lovely?" For Schilling this stanza openly voices "the doubts and perplexities aroused by the violence of nature, yet express truth that divine purpose will ultimately triumph, and that in the meantime God will give us strength to endure" (1991, 26-27).

The earthquake is a sign of judgment and the end of the age (Mark 13.8 and Revelation), but it also occurs at key points in the salvation events of crucifixion and resurrection, in our salvation: when Jesus dies, and when Mary Magdalene and the other Mary go to the tomb on the first day of the week (Matt. 27.51, 28.1-2). It is an earthquake that sets Paul and Silas free from their chains as they pray and sing hymns in the jail at Philippi (Acts 16.25-26). Storms play a part in Jonah's trial and Paul's travels, yet Jesus stills a storm (Mark 4.37-41), and Isaiah calls Zion a shelter from the storm (Isa. 4.6). All these are evidences of God's power in the earthquake and the storm, yet they are not desolate images. We are often unclear about what events such as storms and floods mean. Someone who has recently survived a stormy flood or an earthquake might have a different perspective on them than the scientific explanation about tectonic plates and storm, wind, and flood patterns. What Vajda suggests in this text is that God is with us in the midst of all these events.

Along comes the *trumpet blast* sounding the day of the LORD (Zeph. 1.16), the coming of the Son of Man (Matt. 24.31), the fall of Jericho (Josh. 6.5), the giving of the Ten Commandments (Exod. 20.18), and God meeting with the Israelites in the wilderness (Exod. 19.13-19), times that contain fear and awe, along with a note of grace. In churches today we have trumpet music most often at Easter and for weddings, times of joy, wherein we often forget the fear and awe that accompany resurrection and that fits the awesomeness of making covenant in marriage. Vajda has focused this stanza for us in the *cry*ing responses of

Woe and *Save*. *Woe* we hear from the prophets Isaiah, Jeremiah, and Ezekiel, *Woe* we hear from Jesus to the unrepentant cities (Matt. 11.20-22), *Woe* to you scribes and Pharisees (Matt. 23.13ff.), and *Woe* to you in the Sermon on the Plain (Luke 6.24-26). *Save* me, *Save* us, appears in those Hebrew prophets along with numerous references in the Psalms. Luke and the First Letter to Timothy promise that Jesus came to save the lost. As in the earthquake, storm and trumpet blast revelation mixes with judgment, so *cry*ing *Woe* is mixed with the knowledge that our *Save* is heard.[5]

Stanza Three

Given the cries of *Woe* and *Save*, God comes with a *rainbow, cross,* and *empty grave*. The *rainbow* is a sign of the covenant with Noah after the flood (Gen. 9.12-16) and is a colorful element in this stanza. The signs of the covenant with Christians are not named as bread and wine but are those hinted at by *earthquake* in the preceding stanza: the *cross* and *empty grave* of Jesus Christ. These are the signs of divine initiative, what we call *Grace*, calling forth our response of *Thanks* (cf. Bower 1994, 148-149).

Grace and *Thanks* each appear over one hundred times in the scriptures (Metzger 1991). John's gospel opens with the *grace* and truth revealed in Jesus Christ (1.14-16), and Paul speaks of the abundance of God's *grace* (Rom. 5.17). The epistles to the early churches constantly begin by *thank*ing God for the faith alive in the churches, and they end calling on the *grace* of our Lord Jesus to be present. The vast distance between that of creation praised in the first stanza and God lamented in the second stanza is spanned by the *rainbow, cross,* and *empty grave* in the third stanza, as creation names the *Grace* and gives *Thanks*. As the text reaches its central point, those things central to Christian faith are included, particularly *the cross, the empty grave,* and *Grace*.

Stanza Four

Stanza four contains the first actual references to humanity: *the hungry, the sick,* and *the prodigal,* (although ecology-minded persons would

---

5. To refer again to Dillard, "I often think of the set pieces of liturgy as certain words that people have successfully addressed to God without their getting killed" (1977, 59).

remind us that destroying the habitats of many species of animals leaves animals hungry and sick as well). Psalm 107.9 foreshadows the Magnificat promise that God will fill the *hungry* with good things. The gospel writers reiterate that promise in the blessings from Jesus' sermons, Luke's gospel blessing those with physical hunger (6.21) and Matthew's gospel those who hunger and thirst for righteousness (5.6). The *prodigal* is another example of those for whom God cares, familiar to Christians from the story of the Prodigal Son (although the word *prodigal* is not actually used in the words of scripture) (Luke 10.29-37).

The response of creatures in this stanza is *Care* and *Life*. Vajda says that this text grew out of his fascination for more than forty years in the ministry by the proper and effective motivation for Christian service. Although this fascination is more implicit in this text than explicit, it appears in this stanza as part of the Lutheran and Reformation concern over our motivation for good works. Here is where the layering of images is important. For if we only took the twenty-fifth chapter of Matthew telling Christians of their duty to *care* for both the hungry and the sick, as we will be accountable at the time of judgment, we would have missed our deeper motivations of *awe, praise, woe, save, grace,* and *thanks. Grace* has preceded works, and *Care* is coupled with *Life.* "I came that they may have *life,* and have it abundantly." Abundant *Life* comes out of the Hebrew tradition of *Shalom*, more than peace, shelter and enough to eat, and Jesus Christ expands our understanding of *Shalom* into a life overflowing with abundant grace and love.

Stanza Five

The fifth stanza moves our *Care* and *Life* into community, specifically to the *neighbor* and the *foe*. Jesus answered the question "Who is my neighbor?" with the tale of the Good Samaritan, expanding our understanding of loving our neighbor. In the Gospel of Matthew fourteen chapters earlier than the discussion about loving one's neighbor as oneself, Jesus says, "But I say to you, love your enemies and pray for those who persecute you" (Matt. 5.44). Thousands of Christians have suffered persecutions and been witnesses to that ministry of love and prayer. Yet for many of us, acknowledging that God is also the *God of the foe* would require more faith than we presently have. (Witness the constant killing, prejudice, racism, nationalism, and religious strife.) This hymn calls us to inclusion of both *foe* and *neighbor*, to enlarge our circle of love, grace, and forgiveness.

The biblical reference for *pruning hook* is to turning one's spear into a *pruning hook* (Isa. 2.4; Mic. 4.3), a reference to peace among peoples, but many city dwellers today lack a practical point of reference for it. Perhaps use of this metaphor can include "a teachable moment" of connecting this image with scripture and giving persons a visual image as well.

Our response to these namings of God is *Love* and *Peace*, *Love* for *neighbor* and *foe*, *Peace* with *foe* and *pruning hook*. *Love* is a central theme of scriptures, beginning with the *Shema*, central to Judaism, to "*Love* [God] with all your heart, and with all your soul, and with all your might" (Deut. 6.5). For the Christian this *Love* is extended to love of neighbor, the new commandment Jesus gave in John, "to love one another as I have loved you" (13.34). Even the *foe* is our *neighbor*, so *Love* extends to the *foe* as well. "Go in *Peace*" appears in Exodus, Judges, and 1 Samuel; "*Peace* be with you" in Luke, John, and the Epistles.

Stanza Six

God of the ages begins the sixth and final stanza. For some this will echo the Isaac Watts hymn, "O God, Our Help in Ages Past;" it also resonates with the ascription in First Timothy "to the King of the ages" (1.17). "O Lord, throughout all ages"—the psalmist claims God's presence (Ps. 135.13).

The timelessness of God's presence is immense and vast, contrasted with the next line, *God near at hand*. *God near at hand* describes personal and relational aspects of God and creation. The *God of the ages*, vast, immense and awesome, is also the God who is *near* as the psalmist claims (Pss. 34.18, 73.28, 119.151). *God near at hand* gives credence for the claim of Jesus as one's personal Lord and Savior.

God of the loving heart has no scriptural referent, but suggests both God's nature, because "God is love" (1 John 4.8), and the nature we are to have as our response to God. As the last "name" for God, it stands as the culmination of the naming in this text and changes the response of *the creature* into the response of *your children*. For in Jesus Christ, who showed us *God of the loving heart*, we were given power to become *children* of God (John 1.12). This change to *children* does not eliminate our creatureliness, but it affirms all of the images of the text in this new relationship.

It is this relationship of being God's *children* that enables the response of *Joy*. *Joy* appears over two hundred times in scripture (Metzger 1991), is one of the fruits of the spirit and is also called forth in the Psalms not from only humans but from the trees of the forest, the heavens, and all the earth. When the *children* of God say *Joy*, they also say *Home*. *Home* brings us back to the opening image of the sparrow finding her home; having experienced the text and its journey all the images are gathered up into one—*home*. *Home* is an important image for all of scripture, as the Israelites longed for *home* from exile, as Jesus gave promises of *home* in the fourteenth chapter of John and Revelation proclaims in the final vision of the new Jerusalem, "See, the *home* of God is among mortals" (21.2).

THE TEXT AS A WHOLE

What does it mean that the text builds up meaning through *sparrow, whale, stars, earthquake, storm, trumpet blast, rainbow, cross, grave, hungry, sick, prodigal, neighbor, foe, pruning hook, ages, at hand*, to *loving heart, joy,* and *home*? The turn from being mere *creatures* to becoming God's *children* is the crux of the text, the one it has been building toward since the beginning. In claiming our belonging in relationship with God as *children* we respond *Home*. *Home* works in two directions: God is at *Home* in us, and we are at *Home* in God. Yet more than just in us personally, God is at Home in all of the text—in *sparrow, whale, neighbor*, and *foe*—and they all find their *Home* in God. This enlarging of *Home* calls for a response in two directions as well: a response by our attitude acknowledging that all creation exists as God's *Home* and a response to honor the *Home* of all creatures, God's children. "How are we to serve God?" asks Vajda, and the answer comes with *Joy*, providing *Home* for God's creatures. As ones who claim to be God's *children*, we respond with *Joy*, not out of duty or for merit. The text suggests that we help to provide *Home* for God's creatures: not just those far away in (future) *ages* but also for those *near at hand*, for *neighbor* and for *foe*, for *hungry* and *sick*, for the *prodigal*, in the aftermath of *earthquake* and *storm*, for *sparrow* and *whale*, in the light of *the rainbow, cross,* and *empty grave*. *Home* provides the resting place and also the base for operations, for going out into the world, as God gives us solace and sends us out. The use of *Home* as the final resting place of the text, strengthens its iconic function. The tensions of adoration and Social Gospel are balanced in the text as we ponder, then move to respond.

The text thus moves forward from beginning to end, in a psychological progression that is equally the progression of salvation history, gathering up names for God and suggesting creaturely responses, each stanza opening a new door while encompassing what has gone before and reinterpreting it, until the final point of understanding is reached, *Home*. Troeger suggests that the lack of punctuation after *Home* reminds us "that our ultimate dwelling place is not our language about God but in the very being of God, who is beyond the control of our grammar and definition" (1992, 9).

Home is in a sense the Alpha and Omega, the beginning and the end, for it is the first thing we know and the last for that we long. Vajda's text has posed the questions not only for individual Christians but for all of God's creation, animate and inanimate, *Praise* and *Woe*, *Save* and *Care*, *Love* and *Peace*, ending with *Joy* and *Home*. *Home* stands as the climax of the text, but one that reinterprets the text as well.

ASPECTS OF EMANCIPATORY LANGUAGE

This multidimensional reading has already pointed out evidence of emancipatory language present in this text, particularly in the multiplicity of metaphors used in regard to the Holy One.

Procter-Smith suggests that emancipatory language has an emphasis on diversity while balancing unity and diversity (1990, 113). This text maintains its unity through the repeated phrases that proclaim God and suggest the creatures' response. Yet the emphasis is on the diverse images of God, images that avoid the traditional King-God-Almighty-Father-Protector images (Wren 1989a, 124) while in their multiplicity strongly reflecting the biblical tradition. Ricoeur speaks of one of our tasks as that of maintaining "as completely open as possible the fan of our language" (Ricoeur 1978, 230). The interplay of Word and Spirit in Christianity enables this opening of the fan of language, that is present in Vajda's text.

The "truth-telling" of *Woe, Save, hungry,* and *sick* are another emancipatory facet of the text, not avoiding the less pleasant aspects of our existence. There is a sense of embodiment present in the words *hungry* and *sick*; and the depth of emotion suggested by *Woe* and *Save* helps to deepen other words such as *Love* and *Joy*. Part of the truthfulness of the text is its inclusion of those on the margins of society—*the hungry, the sick, the prodigal, the foe*—who are all related to God.

The very fact of the text's shape, although not as direct as it would be if printed as poetry and not interlined within the music, is one characteristic of emancipatory language. This is a text of unusual rhythm, no rhyme, no punctuation, more like modern poetry than what we have known as hymn texts. Yet the images and their sense of truth for us, carried by a very singable melody, have enabled this hymn to find its place in the repertoire of many congregations.

Another reason for its popularity may be the basic simplicity of its register. The constant reiteration of *God* places the "everyday" words within a religious framework. With the exception of *prodigal* and *pruning hook*, the concepts are all easily understood. Children especially can sing it, draw pictures of it, and begin to identify with the images of God and their own responses. The multiplicity of images, the marking of God's presence in the varieties of God's creation, and the call for our response can all be a part of the spiritual formation of both children and adults.

Although the biblical background of the images carry this hymn in the flow of salvation history, there are also strands important to ecological theology present. Human beings are not the focus of the text—God comes first (60% of the lines) and the creatures respond (40% of the lines, but only in reaction/response to God). The use of *creature* and the naming of *sparrow, whale,* and *stars* in the opening stanza place human beings into the flow of creation, as part of it, and equal to God's other creations. Creation is honored, with our responses of *Awe* and *Praise* to God, and yet it is not adored in itself, for not only is God the focus but the difficulties of creation in *earthquake* and *storm* are not glossed over. The text lends itself to further explication in worship, which could include focus on:

- the theme of the *sparrow* finding a *home*
- the relationship of creation and God marked by *rainbow, cross,* and *empty grave*
- God of the ages, as a reminder that we human beings are not the beginning and end of creation but a part of its growth and continuance
- pondering how God calls us to say *Home* for all of God's creatures.

Chapter 9
Source and Sovereign,
Rock and Cloud
A Multidimensional Reading

Source and Sovereign, Rock and Cloud,
Fortress, Fountain, Shelter, Light,
Judge, Defender, Mercy, Might,
Life whose life all life endowed:
> May the church at prayer recall
> that no single holy name
>> but the truth behind them all
>> *but the truth that feeds them all*
> is the God whom we proclaim.

Word and Wisdom, Root and Vine,
Shepherd, Savior, Servant, Lamb,
Well and Water, Bread and Wine,
Way who leads us to I AM:
> May the church at prayer recall
> that no single holy name
>> but the truth behind them all
>> *but the truth that feeds them all*
> is the God whom we proclaim.

Storm and Stillness, Breath and Dove,
Thunder, Tempest, Whirlwind, Fire,
Comfort, Counselor, Presence, Love,
Energies that never tire:

> May the church at prayer recall
> that no single holy name
> but the truth behind them all
> *but the truth that feeds them all*
> is the God whom we proclaim.

Thomas H. Troeger, 1987
The United Methodist Hymnal 1989, #113
Troeger, *Borrowed Light* 1994a, #18
Chalice Hymnal 1995, #12

INTRODUCTION

There is a growing consciousness of how all speech and writing, including poetry, is an extension of the web of language, value and meaning that interconnects us. This awareness includes a heightened theological sensitivity to the tyrannies of language, the hierarchies of power that are reflected and reinforced by the way we talk about reality.

In content and style these hymns represent my small contribution to the great liberating movement of a more inclusive religious idiom that is being carried on by pastors, theologians, poets, liturgists, biblical interpreters, and thoughtful Christians around the world.

Thomas Troeger, *Borrowed Light*

Background

In 1987, Thomas H. Troeger wrote "Source and Sovereign, Rock and Cloud" in response to a commission by the Hymnal Revision Committee of The United Methodist Church for "a hymn on the wide ranging imagery for God that is found in the Bible" (Troeger 1994a, 196). The hymn was first sung during a chapel service at Colgate Rochester Divinity School, where Troeger taught at that time along with Carol Doran, composer of the original tune for this text (Troeger 1996).[1] Included in the text are forty names for God, thirteen each in the first and third stanzas and through a name-within-a-name, fourteen in the second stanza. Troeger says of the text, "I wanted the hymn to suggest how the scriptures themselves give witness to a dynamic and pluralistic tradition

---

1. This text has also been set for choir and congregation by Austin C. Lovelace.

of naming God. But then in the refrain I tried to establish a prophetic principle, as in Rosemary Ruether's work, that is greater than the literalism of the biblical text" (Troeger 1995).

Rosemary Ruether describes the prophetic principle in her groundbreaking work in feminist theology, *Sexism and God-Talk*, as "the tradition by that Biblical faith constantly criticizes and renews itself and its own vision" (1983, 24). For Ruether the prophetic principle enables persons to critique the Bible and tradition because that is what the biblical faith itself does. For Troeger it means that although many wonderful names for God appear in the stanzas of this text, the refrain reminds us that these names are not God—God is the truth that feeds them.

Elizabeth Johnson establishes this truth beautifully in *She Who Is*: God is mystery beyond our naming. "In sum, the classical themes of the incomprehensibility of God, the analogical nature of religious language, and the necessity of many names for God are a heritage most useful to women's desire to emancipate speech about God" (1993, 120). Troeger's text has used more names than any other hymn text known to me and he has relied on the metaphorical nature of religious language to suggest the incomprehensibility of God, without losing the understanding that God is in relationship to us. In so doing, Troeger has created a text that has great possibilities for emancipating our speech about God.

Troeger is Ralph E. and Norma E. Peck Professor of Preaching and Communications at Iliff School of Theology in Denver, Colorado. He has written three collections of hymn texts (two with music by Carol Doran, a former colleague at Colgate Rochester Divinity School) and numerous books and articles on preaching and worship. Ordained in the Presbyterian Church, he is also an accomplished flautist. His hymns have appeared in all major denominational hymnals in the United States since 1987—Christian Reformed, United Methodist, Presbyterian, Baptist, Mennonite and Brethren, Disciples of Christ, United Church of Christ—as well as in nondenominational collections.

The Shape of the Text

"Source and Sovereign" consists of three stanzas of eight lines each, set in trochaic 77.77.D meter. Because of the odd number of feet in each line, the trochaic feet produce a stressed line (as opposed to understressed); each line contains four stressed syllables and three unstressed syllables. Thus, Troeger avoids what Lovelace names as a problem of trochaic hymns, that they "give impact immediately, then fade away," and the text gains the advantage of the trochaic foot, that "it commands attention and is decisive" (Lovelace 1982, 63).

This meter of 77.77 contains "working room to express ideas adequately while retaining the terseness of short lines and strong downbeats" (Lovelace 1982, 66). Troeger has avoided the monotony in rhythm and melody Lovelace cites as a possible downfall of doubling the 77.77 (67) by use of a refrain and by contrasting the flow of the two sets of four lines. If one were simply to read the text, it might sound like:

> Source and Sovereign,
>   Rock and Cloud,
> Fortress,
>   Fountain,
>   Shelter,
>   Light,
> Judge,
>   Defender,
>   Mercy,
>   Might,
> Life whose life all life endowed:
>
>> May the church at prayer recall that no single holy name
>> but the truth behind them all is the God whom we proclaim.

Even though the tunes associated with the text (GOD'S NAMES by Carol Doran [1987][19] and ABERYSTWYTH by Joseph Parry [1879]) are

---

2. Near the beginning of his hymnwriting career, Troeger began working in tandem with a colleague at Colgate Rochester, Carol Doran, a musician. Together they produced two collections of hymns, using Troeger's texts and Doran's tunes, and another book on worship. In a telephone interview with this writer, Troeger said, "Carol Doran writes great tunes, ones people will sing five hundred years from now" (Troeger 1994b).

When The United Methodist Hymnal Revision Committee, that liked Troeger's texts but considered many of Doran's tunes unsingable (Young 1993, 603), asked to substitute another tune for one by Doran, Troeger refused (Young 1993, 707). So only three Troeger texts appear in *The United Methodist Hymnal,* all with Doran's tunes. Apparently, however, Troeger did take the question seriously, so that when *The Presbyterian Hymnal* appeared one year later, it contained eight of Troeger's texts, only four of that were paired with Doran tunes. Subsequent hymnals have included Troeger's texts both with tunes by Doran and by others.

For purposes of this text the writer followed Troeger's suggestion in regard to "Source and Sovereign": "Although most of Carol Doran's settings are eas-

77.77D in their phrasing, nevertheless even singing it, one sees the punctuation and capitalization of each new title and therefore senses the difference in flow between the opening four lines full of commas and capitalizations and the refrain that comprises a whole sentence with no commas or punctuation except for the period at the end. Notice that Troeger has prepared us for the switch in flow by moving from four names in each of the opening three lines of each stanza, to the fourth line, that contains only one name, a phrase made up of seven syllables.

Troeger has been an advocate for maintaining "traditional poetic expression" in hymnody (Troeger 1992, 8), and his own hymns are models rich in rhyme and meter, with many using traditional hymn meters. Yet as the outline of the first stanza immediately above shows, Troeger has devised an intricate pattern within the traditional 77.77D to say something new. The first four lines of each stanza begin:

one-syllable name and two-syllable name, one-syllable name and one-syllable name, two-syllable name, two-syllable name, two-syllable name, one-syllable name

The patterns varies in the third line, with stanza one:

one-syllable name, three-syllable name, two-syllable name, one-syllable name,

whereas the second stanza has the pattern of the first line repeated:

one-syllable name and two-syllable name, one-syllable name and one-syllable name,

and stanza three repeats the pattern of the second line:

two-syllable name, two-syllable name, two-syllable name, one-syllable name

The fourth line of each stanza contains seven syllables that make up one "naming" phrase. In the first stanza, five one-syllable words are followed by a two-syllable word, *endowed*. The second stanza has a similar pattern if one considers the final two syllables *I AM* as one unit, the name God told Moses at the burning bush (Exod. 3.14). The third stanza's fourth line begins with one of the three three-syllable words in the text, *energies*, and completes the line with one-syllable, two-syllable, and one-syllable words. In comparing the grouping of sylla-

---

ily singable and very beautiful, the vocal line in this one is more difficult, and if you want to focus on the words, [you] may need to consider an alternative setting, for example Aberystwyth or St. George's Windsor [sic]" (Troeger 1995).

Thus ABERYSTWYTH was used in the praxis section of this research, as it was also the choice of *Chalice Hymnal*.

bles in each line, we can see how creative Troeger has been within the
limitation of seven-syllable lines:

Stanza 1	Stanza 2	Stanza 3	+ = the word *and*
1 + 2, 1 + 1	1 + 2, 1 + 1	1 + 2, 1 + 1	
2, 2, 2, 1	2, 2, 2, 1	2, 2, 2, 1	
1, 3, 2, 1	1 + 2, 1 + 1	2, 2, 2, 1	
1 1 1 1 1 2	1 1 1 1 1 2	3 1 2 1	

Another organizing principle of this text is the use of the trinitarian
pattern. The first stanza primarily describes the First Person of the
Trinity, the Creator. Stanza two primarily names the Second Person,
Jesus Christ, God Incarnate. The third stanza primarily contains associations with the Third Person, the Holy Spirit. *Primarily* is an important qualifier. As we shall see, especially in the studying the biblical
background of the metaphors, many of them are associated with more
than one person of the Trinity. This is particularly true in the third
stanza, for the Holy Spirit has not been as fully developed in scripture
and theology as the other two Persons of the Trinity, and the metaphors
for this Third Person draw heavily on words associated with the First
Person. Nevertheless, pointing out the trinitarian nature of the text will
enable singers/readers to find some familiarity and organizing pattern
in the catalogue of names. Still, as the refrain reminds us, we must
avoid boxing in God, in this case, into three totally separate identities.
So a study of the text should include the recognition that the three Persons of the Trinity are not merely points on a triangle. Rather they are
the movement and flow within that space that is greater than anyone
can imagine.

Poetic Devices

Troeger has also drawn on traditional poetic devices throughout the text
in addition to the use of metaphor in naming God. The listing of names
is a poetic device called a *catalogue*. Yet this is not a random listing;
Troeger has relied on the poetic devices of alliteration (beginning
words with the same sounds, such as *Source* and *Sovereign*), juxtaposition (for example the density and hardness of *Rock* contrasted with the
ethereal and fragile *Cloud*), and rhyme (*Light-Might*).

Repetitions of Sounds. Alliteration and other repetitions of sounds have
an important role in this text and are found in each stanza, beginning
with the opening phrase of each stanza: *Source and Sovereign* (1:1),

Word and Wisdom (2:1), and *Storm and Stillness* (3:1). Stanza one contains alliteration in every line: *Source and Sovereign* (1:1), *Fortress, Fountain* (1:2), *Mercy, Might* (1:3), culminating in epizeuxis (repetition of a word in the same line; also creates strong sense of alliteration): *Life whose life all life endowed*. Stanza two also contains alliteration: *Word and Wisdom* (2:1), *Shepherd* (weak alliteration but strengthened by both words that follow), *Savior, Servant* (2:2), *Well and Water*. There is also a sense of repetition in the fourth line with beginning *ws* in *Way who* as well as the ending *s* on *leads us*. Stanza three is equally full of alliteration: *Storm and Stillness* (3:1), *Thunder, Tempest* (less strong but reinforced by the repetition of the *w*-sounds in *Whirlwind* [3:2]), *Comfort, Counselor* (3:3), the middle *s*-sounds of *Counselor, Presence* (3:3), and the repetition of *e*-sounds in *Energies* (3:4).

Juxtaposition. By juxtaposing certain terms, language layers meaning onto each of the terms or strengthens certain meanings of each term.[3] Each stanza of this text contains juxtapositions that are important for giving a sense of the diversity of God's names and equally for reminding us that because both names are "true" they are both therefore "not true;" God remains beyond our naming. Although the word *Sovereign* attempts to get beyond the maleness of *King*, the picture it still raises in many minds is that of a king on a throne. Yet by placing *Sovereign* after *Source* (1:1), a name for God that can be heard as female (Wallace 1993), the neutrality of *Sovereign*, its ability to represent either male or female, is enhanced. The juxtaposition of *Rock* and *Cloud* (1:2) was mentioned above. The first stanza of this text also includes the juxtaposition of two courtroom metaphors: God as *Judge* and God as *Defender* (1:3). Both of these metaphors come from scriptures as we shall see below, and each shades the other, the God who judges is tempered by the God who defends us, while the God who defends is not without strength and discernment to judge us.

The second stanza contains three equally interesting juxtapositions. As we will consider below in looking at the biblical bases for these names for God, both *Word* and *Wisdom* (2:1) are related to the understanding of Jesus Christ as the *logos*, the *word* or *wisdom* of God. Theology of the *logos* was known in both pagan and Jewish antiquity and was adopted by the Johannine writings in the New Testament (Cross

---

3. Additional richness in this text might be gleaned from lexical analysis of the unmatched pairs of words: *Source/Sovereign, Rock/Cloud, Fortress/Fountain,* and so on. However, due to the limitations of this text, the analysis focuses on the context of the text within Christian worship.

and Livingstone, *s.v. Logos*). The juxtaposition of *Shepherd* and *Lamb* (opening and closing 2:2), both important biblical names for Jesus Christ, is akin to the juxtaposition of *Judge* and *Defender* above: Jesus is the one who cares for us lambs; Jesus is like us, but as the *Lamb* is sacrificed for us. *Well and Water*, in juxtaposition in the third line, point back to the word *Source* (1:1), for the *Well* is the *Source* for *Water*, and *Water* is contained by the *Well*. In addition to the importance of juxtaposition for pointing out the *is/is not* of opposites as characteristics of the divine, the central tenets of Christianity are built around the juxtaposition of opposites: Jesus Christ is fully *human* yet fully *divine* and Jesus Christ *died* to bring *life*.

The third stanza draws even more on juxtaposition than the two previous stanzas, as it includes entire lines in its groupings. *Storm and Stillness* (3:1) repeats the pattern of the text as each stanza opens with alliteration and juxtaposition. *Storm* denotes rain, snow, or hail, winds, thunder and lighting, and noise. *Stillness* denotes quiet and minimal, gentle movement. Yet God is in each. The second line of this third stanza contains four words, each suggesting a kind of energetic movement: *Thunder, Tempest, Whirlwind, Fire*. Following the words *Stillness, Breath and Dove*, all connoting quiet and gentleness, these energetic words relate to the opening word of the stanza, *Storm*. A sense of calmness returns again in the juxtaposition of words in the third line: *Comfort, Counselor, Presence, Love*, all words that can be associated with a *counselor*: one who gives *comfort*, in whose *presence* we feel safe, and one who helps us *love* ourselves and others better.

Rhyme. The rhyme scheme of the first stanza is ABBA CDCD (*Cloud/ endowed, Light/Might, recall/all, name/proclaim*), whereas the rhyme scheme of stanzas two and three is ABAB (*Vine/Wine, Lamb/Am*, and *Dove/Love, Fire/tire*) CDCD.[21] Although the first stanza sets up the expectation of the rhyme ABBA, the text is so interwoven with poetic devices that when the more familiar cross-rhyme ABAB appears in stanzas two and three, it feels natural. It is also important with the use of catalogue that the rhymes are all full rhymes, not near rhymes, or they would be lost. This also resonates with Troeger's own fondness for rhyme "because it builds into language a sonic reminder that there is more to reality than the meaning of words" (Troeger 1996).

---

4. Troeger does not remember why he changed the rhyme scheme, suggesting it was "probably to build momentum while keeping strong end rhymes" (Troeger 1996).

Refrain. Through repetition refrains of hymn texts take on special importance. First, they become a familiar place for singers by their repetition. Second, in well-written texts, the refrain will also be affected by the stanzas so that each time we sing it we either hear something new in it or we understand its truth more deeply. In a text such as "Source and Sovereign," the refrain is vital for several reasons. First, the familiarity and the long phrases are important relief after the constant catalogue of the stanzas. With thirteen names for God passing through our eyes, minds, and mouths so quickly we need a place to rest and "shift gears." Second, as the images pile up, the truth of the refrain becomes clearer: there is no one all-sufficient name for God; as the gathered body of Christ, we remember that our understanding of God is fed by the truth within all these names; yet even while God is within these names, God is still greater than the largest collection of names we can ever make. God is greater than thirteen names, than twenty-seven names, than forty names, but there is truth feeding all of these names. The truth found by mystics and voiced by Gregory of Nyssa becomes clear: The more we grow toward God, then the more we yearn for God, as we find there is no limit to God's good (Gregory of Nyssa 1961, 149). Yet still we proclaim God, and all the more, because we begin to grasp a sense of the wonderful immensity of the Truth that feeds our understandings.

The original penultimate line of this hymn text read *but the truth behind them all.* Brian Wren, a friend and colleague of Troeger, pointed out that this version suggested "a certain neo-Platonism, that God is 'behind' reality but not intimately connected" (Troeger 1995). Troeger worked with the text and decided *but the truth that feeds them* all would "affirm God's continuing nurturance of our metaphors and symbols, just as God continues to sustain creation.[5] This also fits the theology that had profoundly influenced my writing of the hymn, especially Sallie McFague's work" (Troeger 1995).

The theological points where Troeger and McFague are in agreement are several. In *Metaphorical Theology*, McFague reminds us that scripture and tradition describe God with:

---

5. Troeger's preference for the revision did not appear, as might have been expected, in the most recent publication of this text, in *Chalice Hymnal*, probably because the committee saw the earlier version of the text. Yet the revision does appear in Lovelace's anthem setting.

naturalistic, impersonal images balancing the relational, personal ones: God as rock, fortress, running stream, power, sun, thunder, First Cause, and so on. . . . In any case, a metaphorical theology will insist that many metaphors and models are necessary, that a piling up of images is essential, both to avoid idolatry and to attempt to express the richness and variety of the divine-human relationship (1984, 20).

Troeger employs a variety of "naturalistic, impersonal images" (e.g., *Source, Rock, Cloud*) in this text alongside "the relational, personal ones" (e.g., *Sovereign, Shepherd, Counselor*). The richness and "variety of the divine-human relationship" may be seen in this text of many names, and yet the refrain points to our inability to "capture" God in any metaphor or model (McFague, 1984, 128), as McFague continues,

The balancing act involved in proper theological reflection is a difficult one. The theologian must take his or her models with utmost seriousness, exploiting them for all their interpretive potential and yet, at the same time, realize that they are little more than the babble of infants (1984, 131).

Troeger's text also demonstrates McFague's basic understanding of God as discussed in her later work, *The Body of God*. After describing the traditional "major models of God and the world," McFague proposes that we understand God as a combination of the agential and organic models, as panentheistic, everything is in God. (This would be contradicted by Troeger's earlier refrain where God stands *behind* things.) McFague goes on to explain that this model "radicalizes both divine immanence (God is the breath of each and every creature) and divine transcendence (God is the energy empowering the entire universe)" (1993, 150). In Troeger's rewrite of the refrain, McFague's understanding of God may be seen as the breath and energy of God *feeding* holy names with truth.

Patterns of Images. An interesting aspect of this text by Troeger are the images it includes that remind the long-time church member of other well-known hymns:[6]

---

6. Of this listing, Troeger says, "Although I did not have these consciously in mind while writing the hymn, I am familiar with all of these hymns. They would be a part of my soul's repertoire from years of worshipping in many traditions" (Troeger 1996).

Rock	My God is a *Rock* in a weary land	African-American spiritual
Fortress	A mighty *fortress* is our God	Martin Luther, ca. 1529
Fountain	There is a *fountain* filled with blood	William Cowper, ca. 1771
Light	Walk in the *light*	Bernard Barton, ca. 1810
Defender	O worship the King	Robert Grant, 1833
	(our Maker, *Defender*)	
Shepherd	Savior, like a *shepherd* lead us	attrib.Dorothy Thrupp,1836
Way	Come, my *Way*, my Truth, my Light	George Herbert, 1633
Breath	Breathe on me, *Breath* of God	Edwin Hatch, 1878
Thunder	Steal away	African-American spiritual
	(My Lord calls me by the *thunder*)	

Another aspect of the text, one directly related to emancipatory language, that might be considered before looking at the biblical references, is suggested by Dorothee Solle: "Fountainhead, source, spring of all goodness, living wind: That is also language for God, in that human beings have expressed their relationship to God without resorting to sexist or familial language" (Warner and Beilenson 1987, 51).[7] In this text, Troeger has not only avoided specifically gendered terms, but he has also avoided familial terms such as *father, mother, brother, son,* all used in Christian tradition in describing God. In this text, Troeger suggests a wider variety of relationships than just parental. This strengthens the possibilities of the text reaching persons who have difficult or abusive relationships with these significant persons, *father, mother, brother, son,* as it avoids conferring "God-likeness" on these relationships.

STANZAS

"Source and Sovereign, Rock and Cloud" lends itself to meditation and prayer, and to the study of the images of God found in the Bible. One could write an entire study on the biblical references and the implications of God's nature solely using this hymn text. For our purposes, however, the best known references will be used for each name, recognizing that, although this book is limited, the contexts of various scripture verses each has something to add to the understanding of the truth that feeds that name.

---

7. It might be noted that *fountain, source,* and *wind* (in whirl*wind*), all mentioned by Solle, find their way into Troeger's text (1:2, 1:1, and 3:2).

Stanza One

"God is the *source* of your life in Christ Jesus," says the writer of the first epistle to the Corinthians (1.30), whereas the writer of Hebrews says, "having been made perfect, [Jesus] became the *source* of eternal salvation for all who obey him" (5.9). Both God and Jesus Christ are named as *Source*, one of our life in Christ, the other of eternal salvation. Both God and Christ are also called *Sovereign* in scripture: "O Lord, our *Sovereign*, how majestic is your name in all the earth!" proclaims the psalmist (8.9). Writing to Timothy, Paul speaks of "our Lord Jesus Christ—he is who is the blessed and only *Sovereign*, the King of kings and Lord of lords" (1 Tim. 6.14-15).

Before he dies, Jacob blesses his son Joseph "by the name of the Shepherd, the *Rock* of Israel" (Gen. 49.24c). The prophet Isaiah calls "Look to the *rock* from which you were hewn" (51.1). Paul telling the story of Moses and the children of Israel in the wilderness says, "For they drank from the spiritual *rock* that followed them, and the *rock* was Christ" (1 Cor. 10.4b). Again, we see a name applied to both the First and Second Persons of the Trinity. *Rock* relates to *Cloud*, as both are part of the story of Moses and the children of Israel in the wilderness:

> The Lord went in front of them in a pillar of cloud by day, to lead them along the way, and in a pillar of fire by night, to give them light, so that they might travel by day and by night. Neither the pillar of cloud by day nor the pillar of fire by night left its place in front of the people.
> (Exod. 13.21-22)

Jesus is described as "coming in a *cloud* with power and great glory" at the end of the age (Luke 21.27). *Cloud* also relates to the Spirit through its identification with the Shekinah of Jewish tradition (Newman 1994).

When David is delivered from the hand of his enemies, including Saul, he sings a psalm: "The Lord is my *rock*, my *fortress*, and my deliverer" (2 Sam. 22.1-2). We think of fortresses being made of rock; this image and its biblical association transform *Rock* into *Fortress*. Yet even *Fortress* is not cold or distant, for Psalm 59.17 combines that image with love (foreshadowing *Love* in this text in 3:3):

> for you, O God, are my *fortress*,
> the God who shows me steadfast *love*.

Biblical references describe God as the *fountain*, source of life: "For with you is the *fountain* of life; in your light we see light" (Ps. 36.9). Notice that *Light*, which appears in this scripture verse, also appears in

Troeger's text in the same line as *Fountain; Life* will appear in the fourth line of this stanza. *Wisdom* (2:1) is also associated with *Fountain*: "*Wisdom* is a *fountain* of life to one who has it" (Prov. 16.22a).

In biblical times often a cave would be a shelter, which suggests connections between *Rock* and *Shelter* and *Fortress*, as Psalm 91 says "You who live in the *shelter* of the Most High, who abide in the shadow of the Almighty, will say to the Lord, 'My refuge and my *fortress*; my God, in whom I trust'" (Ps. 91.1-2; cf. Ps. 46.1,11). At the end of the Bible, in Revelation, the chosen 144,000 persons stand before the throne of God, worshiping because "the one who is seated on the throne will *shelter* them" (Rev. 7.15). *Light* appears with references to both the First and Second Persons of the Trinity: "O send out your *light* and your truth; let them lead me" (Ps. 43.3), and "Jesus spoke to them, saying, 'I am the *light* of the world. Whoever follows me will never walk in darkness but will have the *light of life*.'" We are pointed ahead in the text again to the repetition of *Life* in 1:4.

Judge and *Defender*, two courtroom metaphors, were mentioned earlier in the section on juxtaposition. The psalmist links God's judgment with righteousness: "The heavens declare his righteousness, for God himself is *judge*" (Ps. 50.6). The prophet Isaiah combines the sense of God defending us with being saved: "[the Lord of hosts] will send them a savior, and will *defend* and deliver them" (Isa. 19.20). *Mercy* is often our plea before a *judge*:

> Have *mercy* on me, O God,
>   according to your steadfast love;
>   according to your *abundant mercy*
>   blot out my transgressions. (Ps. 51.1)

Likewise the blind man by the side of the Jericho road cried to Jesus: "Jesus, Son of David, have *mercy* on me!" (Luke 18.38). Again we have the combination of names associated with both Second and First Persons of the Trinity.

The psalmist sings of God's *Might*:

> I will sing of your *might*,
>   I will sing aloud of your steadfast love in the morning.
> For you have been a *fortress* for me
>   and a refuge in the day of my distress. (Ps. 59.16)

(We have already sung of *Fortress* in 1:2 and *Love* will appear in 3:3.) Turning to the New Testament for *Might*, we find a hint of *Wisdom*, which will appear in 2:1 and *Lamb* in 2:2: "Worthy is the *Lamb* . . . to receive power and wealth and *wisdom* and *might* and honor and glory and blessing!" (Rev. 5.12).

The life of God has endowed all of creation with *life*, just as God breathed the breath of life into Adam in the account in Genesis 2.7. To *endow* is to furnish with a living, without involving a return benefit, in a gracious and generous manner (*Webster's*). This fits perfectly with the words of Jesus, "I came that they may have *life*, and have it abundantly" (John 10.10). The *Life* we have been given is one of great possibilities, and it has its *Source* in God, thereby bringing this stanza full circle.

Stanza Two

The second stanza begins with a metaphor basic to Judeo-Christian tradition: *Word*. The *word* of God enables creation (Gen. 1), and inspires prophets like Jeremiah (1.1-2). The opening words of the Gospel of John present Jesus as the *Word*: "In the beginning was the *Word*, and the *Word* was with God, and the *Word* was God." The annotation to John's prologue explains: The *Word* (Greek *logos*) of God is more than speech; it is God in action, creating (Gen. 1.3; Ps. 33.6), revealing (Amos 3.7-8), redeeming (Ps. 107.19-20). Jesus is this *Word* (John 1.14).[8] In using *Word* to identify Jesus as God creating, revealing, and redeeming, John placed Jesus in line with the understanding of *Wisdom* described in Proverbs:

> The Lord created me at the beginning of his work,
>   the first of his acts of long ago.
> Ages ago I was set up,
>   at the first, before the beginning of the earth.
> Then I was beside him, like a master worker;
> and I was daily his delight,
>   rejoicing before him always,
> rejoicing in his inhabited world
>   and delighting in the human race. (Prov. 8.22-23, 30-31)

---

8. Elsewhere, Troeger has said,
by 'Word' . . . I mean the Word who forges your bones and hinges your hands and crochets the net of capillaries that feeds your body . . . There is a flame that must illumine the eye and a whisper that must flutter against the ear to make our faith dance inside us, to animate our preaching with energy and grace, to use our fragile, fading human words as vessels of the eternal Word (1982, 11).

Root reflects the sound of *Rock* in the similar position in the first stanza and refers to prophecies about the heritage of God's chosen people, which culminated in Jesus Christ: "On that day the *root* of Jesse shall stand as a signal to the peoples" (Isa. 11.10) and "It is I, Jesus, who sent my angel to you with this testimony for the churches. I am the *root* and the descendant of David, the bright morning star" (Rev. 22.16). Keeping with this plant metaphor, Jesus also calls himself the true *Vine*: "I am the true *vine*, and my Father is the vinegrower. . . . I am the *vine*, you are the branches. Those who abide in me and I in them bear much fruit, because apart from me you can do nothing" (John 15.1, 5).

The Gospel of John is full of metaphors that can be used as names for Jesus. We have already looked at *Word* and *Vine*. When Jesus called himself *Shepherd* he was drawing on the tradition of the psalmist in identifying himself with an image of God: "The Lord is my *shepherd*, I shall not want" (Ps. 23.1). The prophet Isaiah announced the coming of God, using the image of a *shepherd*: "He will feed his flock like a *shepherd*" (Isa. 40.11a). So, when Jesus said, "I am the good *shepherd*. The good *shepherd* lays down his life for the sheep" (John 10.11), people understood the tradition of God who cares for people as a shepherd cares for sheep. The second sentence of John 10.11 will soon be transformed as the *Shepherd* becomes the *Lamb* who lays down his life in sacrifice. But first the task of the Shepherd is to save. *Savior* has, like *Shepherd*, references to both God and Jesus. Mary, the mother of Jesus, sings, "My soul magnifies the Lord, and my spirit rejoices in God my *Savior*" (Luke 1.46-47). The angels announce to ordinary human shepherds, "to you is born this day in the city of David a *Savior*, who is the Messiah" (Luke 2.11). On the night when he last ate with the disciples Jesus took the role of a *Servant* and washed their feet (John 13.12-16). Preaching after the resurrection, Peter remembered the *Servant* role of Jesus: "The God of Abraham, the God of Isaac, and the God of Jacob, the God of our ancestors has glorified his *servant* Jesus, whom you handed over and rejected in the presence of Pilate"(Acts 3.13).[9] Early in his ministry Jesus is twice called the *Lamb* of God by John the Baptist (John 1.29, 36). The Revelation to John also contains the most frequent use of *Lamb* as a name for Jesus Christ, for example in this description of the holy city: "I saw no temple in the city, for its

---

9. The following verses in Acts are another wonderful example of the Bible's use of many names for God: "But you rejected the Holy and Righteous One and asked to have a murderer given to you, and you killed the Author of life, whom God raised from the dead. To this we are witnesses" (Acts 3.14-15). Here Jesus is called the *Holy and Righteous One* as well as the *Author of life*.

temple is the Lord God the Almighty and the *Lamb*. And the city has
no need of sun or moon to shine on it, for the glory of God is its light,
and its lamp is the *Lamb*" (Rev. 21.22-23).

"With joy you will draw water from the *wells* of salvation," says the
prophet Isaiah (12.3). "Those who drink of the *water* that I will give
them will never be thirsty. The *water* that I will give will become in
them a spring of water gushing up to eternal life," said Jesus to the Samaritan woman at Jacob's well (John 4.14). The combination of *Well*
and *Water* in Troeger's text is interesting—Jesus is both the container
and the contained, more than just some water, he is the *Source* of *Water*, the *Well* of living water (John 4.10). The *well* of living water suggests the *Fountain* of 1:2, and of the description in Song of Solomon of
the beloved as "a garden *fountain*, a *well* of living *water*" (Song of Sol.
4.15). On the last day of the Festival of Booths Jesus cried out "Let
anyone who is thirsty come to me, and let the one who believes in me
drink" (John 7.37-38). Thus the metaphors *Well* and *Water* touch on
many other metaphors in Troeger's text: *Source, Rock, Cloud* (made of
evaporated *water*), and *Fountain*, with *Wine* and *Storm* yet to come.

Bread has been important as a staple food of life since the beginning of the agricultural revolution, and it figures prominently in the
Judeo-Christian tradition. Passover is an important tradition in Judaism,
and one of its markings is eating unleavened *bread* (Exod. 12.1-15).
Bread rains from heaven (Exod. 16.4), feeds the multitude (Mark 6.34-
44) and identifies the risen Christ (Luke 24.28-35). On the day after the
feeding of the five thousand, according to John's gospel, the crowd
asked Jesus for a sign like the manna given in the wilderness. He re-
plied, "I am the *bread* of life. Whoever comes to me will never be hungry, and whoever believes in me will never be thirsty" (John 6.35). The
last meal of Jesus became the model for the Christian celebration of
Eucharist for "on the night when he was betrayed took a loaf of bread,"
bread that became the symbol for the body of Christ (1 Cor. 11.24).
Bread and *Wine* go together in Eucharist (1 Cor. 11.23-26) and are recognized as gifts of God in Jewish tradition as well: "*wine* to gladden the
human heart, and *bread* to strengthen the human heart" (Ps. 104, 15a
and c). The first miracle of Jesus was to turn *water* into *wine* at a wed-
ding in Cana (John 2.2-11). In Eucharist *Wine* represents both the blood
of Jesus and the cup of the new covenant that God has made with humanity (cf. 1 Cor. 11.25).

Way who leads us reflects the prophet Isaiah who speaks God's
words, beginning with several names for God:

Thus says the LORD,
  your Redeemer, the Holy One of Israel:
I am the LORD your God,
  who teaches you for your own good,
  who leads you in the way you should go. (Isa. 48.17)

In his farewell discourse in John's gospel, Jesus answers a question from Thomas saying, "I am the *way*, and the truth, and the life. No one comes to the Father except through me" (14.6). I am the way to the Father, says Jesus, I am the way to I AM (Exod. 3.14), the one who spoke to Moses from the burning bush, the one who led you out of Egypt. *Way who leads us to I AM* draws the thread through Jesus Christ back to the God of Moses and the Hebrew children, reminding us that Jesus and God are one.

Stanza Three

God is *Storm* and *Stillness*, begins the final stanza of Troeger's text. In the Bible the images of *storm* include several that appear in this stanza: *Storm, Thunder, Tempest, Whirlwind*, as well as *Cloud* (1:1) and *Water* (2:3). "His way is in *whirlwind* and *storm*, and the *clouds* are the dust of his feet" (Nah. 1.3b). Jeremiah has two identical verses about *Storm* as God's righteous anger:

Look, the *storm* of the Lord!
  Wrath has gone forth,
a whirling tempest,
  it will burst upon the head of the wicked. (Jer. 23.19, 30.23)

The coming of the Holy Spirit is also marked by storm-like events: "When the day of Pentecost had come, they were all together in one place. And *suddenly* from heaven there came a sound like the *rush of a violent wind*, and it filled the entire house where they were sitting" (Acts 2.1-2). *Stillness* comes after a storm, as the psalmist says, "[God] made the storm be *still*, and the waves of the sea were hushed" (Ps. 107.29). This is echoed by the gospel story of Jesus saying to a stormy sea, "Peace! Be *still*! Then the wind ceased, and there was a dead calm" (Mark 4.39).
     In the second account of creation God "breathed into [Adam's] nostrils the *breath of life*; and the man became a living being" (Gen. 2.7). The *breath* of God appears again in Isaiah, "The grass withers, the flower fades, when the *breath* of the Lord blows upon it" (40.7). In the Wisdom of Solomon, the breath of God is identified with Wisdom,

"For *she* [*Wisdom*] is a *breath* of the power of God, and a pure emana-
tion of the glory of the Almighty" (7.25a). The association of Wisdom
points us to Jesus Christ and the *Dove* representing the Spirit of God
that descended at his baptism, "And just as he was coming up out of the
water, he saw the heavens torn apart and *the Spirit descending like a
dove on him*" (Mark 1.10, compare in all the Gospels). Visual artists,
drawing from this scripture, have used the *Dove* to symbolize the Spirit
throughout tradition.

At Mount Sinai the Hebrew people met God, and Moses would
speak and "God would answer him in *thunder*" (Exod. 19.19). When
Jesus spoke of his death in the twelfth chapter of John the crowd heard
God's voice and "said that it was *thunder*" (29). Revelation gives us a
picture of God's throne in heaven: "Coming from the throne are flashes
of lightning, and rumblings and peals of thunder" (4.5a). The *Tempest*
whirled in Jeremiah 23.19, as seen above, and was seen also by the
psalmist and Isaiah:

> Our God comes and does not keep silence,
>   before him is a devouring *fire*,
>   and a mighty *tempest* all around him. (Ps. 50. 3)

> You will be visited by the Lord of hosts
>   with *thunder* and earthquake and great noise,
>   with *whirlwind* and *tempest*,
>   and the flame of a devouring *fire*. (Isa. 29. 6)

The *Whirlwind* appears in many of the scriptures mentioned above, and
it carries God's voice in Job, "Then the Lord answered Job out of the
whirlwind" (38.1). *Fire* appears in Psalm 50.3 and Isaiah 29.6. The
strongest association of the metaphor *Fire* with God, however, for
Christians, is that of the appearance of the Holy Spirit on the day of
Pentecost, "Divided tongues as of *fire*, appeared among them" (Acts
2.3). Flames of fire, coming from the day of Pentecost, and the dove, as
mentioned above, have traditionally been the most frequent visual
symbols of the Holy Spirit.

From powerful and energetic metaphors of *Storm, Thunder, Tempest, Whirlwind,* and *Fire,* Troeger moves in the next line to gentler
images. From the well-loved Psalm 23 come words of comfort:

> Even though I walk through the darkest valley,
>   I fear no evil;
>   for you are with me;

your rod and your staff—
   they comfort me. (Ps. 23.4)

Comfort also describes the Third Person of the Trinity: "Living in the fear of the Lord and in the *comfort* of the Holy Spirit, [the church] increased in numbers" (Acts 9.31b). Equally, *comfort* comes through the Second Person, " Now may our Lord Jesus Christ . . . *comfort* your hearts and strengthen them in every good work and word" (2 Thess. 2.16-17).

Counselor originally meant one who gives advice; in modern times that has been limited often to lawyers, camp chaperones, and now also therapists. The Bible uses the original meaning of one giving guidance: "You guide me with your *counsel*" (Ps. 73.24). Speaking of the Messiah to come, Isaiah included *Counselor* in the list of the Messiah's titles:

For a child has been born for us,
   a son given to us;
authority rests upon his shoulders;
   and he is named
Wonderful *Counselor*, Mighty *God*,
   Everlasting *Father*, *Prince* of Peace. (Isa. 9.6)

When Jesus speaks of sending the Holy Spirit, the Paraclete, the Revised Standard Version of the Bible uses the word *Counselor* (John 14.16, 25, RSV).

The Judeo-Christian God is a God of nearness and *presence* with creation, as well as a God of transcendence and distance. Adam and Eve hide themselves from the *presence* of The Holy One after eating the forbidden fruit (Gen. 3.8). In the wilderness God speaks with Moses "face to face, as one speaks to a friend" and promises, "My *presence* will go with you, and I will give you rest" (Exod. 33. 11, 14).

Christians sometimes claim that a unique message of Jesus Christ is that "*love* is from *God*; everyone who loves is born of God and knows God" (1 John 4.7), yet the Hebrew people knew God as love also: "For the LORD is good, for his steadfast *love* endures forever" (Chron. 5.13). Paul drew on these traditions of God's enduring *love* in his letter to the Romans:

Who will separate us from the love of Christ? . . . For I am convinced
that neither death, nor life, nor angels, nor rulers, nor things present,
nor things to come, nor powers, nor height, nor depth, nor anything else

in all creation, will be able to separate us from the *love of God in Christ Jesus our Lord.* (Rom. 8.35, 38-39)

Troeger recaptures the enduring nature of God and also gives these last four metaphors (*Comfort, Counselor, Presence, Love*) vitality with the next phrase, *Energies that never tire.* *Energy* appears in the letter to the Colossians as the writer claims, "I struggle with all the *energy* that [Christ] powerfully inspires within me" (1.29). *That never tires* reflects the psalmist "[The One] who keeps Israel will neither slumber nor sleep" (Ps. 121.4), and the meeting of Elijah with the 450 prophets of Baal on Mount Carmel, as he taunts them saying, "Perhaps your god is asleep!" (1 Kings 18.27), implying that the God of Israel never sleeps. Once again the refrain gathers up these names and points us to the "truth that feeds them all."

OTHER ASPECTS OF EMANCIPATORY LANGUAGE

"Source and Sovereign, Rock and Cloud" opens the "fan of language" for God, containing many names and a variety of metaphors in the stanzas, while pointing to the unity of God in the refrain. The intense focus on the Holy in the stanzas means that the reflexive character of metaphor has little space in that to work, keeping us God-focused rather than humanity-focused. When humanity is mentioned it is with the collective noun *the church* in the refrain. Yet the variety of metaphors encompasses a wide emotional range rather than being merely objective. Thus, the text's emancipatory focus is on God-language, beginning with the characteristics of unity and diversity, shown in many names and through the trinitarian pattern of the stanzas and repeated refrain.

One emancipatory characteristic of the text that might not be particularly noticeable on first reading is the absence in the stanza about Jesus Christ of emphasis on male-identified metaphors. The use of "natural, impersonal images" such as *word, wisdom, root, vine, lamb, well, water, bread, wine,* and *way* all describe the character of Jesus without stressing his maleness. Of the three "relational, personal images," two clearly encompass females as well as males, *servant* and *shepherd* (Gen. 29.6: "Rachel, coming with the sheep"). That leaves only *savior,* that is slowly losing some of its secular fairy-tale associations with princes saving damsels in distress (see for example Munsch, *The Paper Bag Princess*; on the religious side, see Brock, *Journeys by Heart*). Altogether, the description of Jesus Christ in this hymn focuses on character and actions that go far beyond gender.

Equally important is the revelatory nature of the text, presenting for our use in prayer metaphors resonating with scripture and tradition, with nature and with theology. McFague's theology is framed in hymnic language, appropriate to her belief that "The *primary* context, then, for any discussion of religious language is worship" (1984, 2). The revelation of these metaphors for God occurs not simply by their presence and their traditional meaning but equally by their juxtaposition with each other, within a trinitarian pattern, and with the refrain. It is a bit like looking through a kaleidoscope, where the bits of colored glass and mirrors show new patterns and beautiful new designs each time you look. This text has endless possibilities of revelation as we look again and again at the marvel that is God and are constantly reminded that though our words are "little more than the babble of infants," (McFague 1984, 131) the truth that feeds them is the God whom we proclaim.

Chapter 10
Bring Many Names
A Multidimensional Reading

Bring many names, beautiful and good,
celebrate, in parable and story,
    holiness in glory,
    living, loving God.
Hail and Hosanna,
bring many names!

Strong mother God, working night and day,
planning all the wonders of creation,
    setting each equation,
    genius at play:
Hail and Hosanna,
strong mother God!

Warm father God, hugging every child,
feeling all the strains of human living,
    caring and forgiving
    till we're reconciled:
Hail and Hosanna,
warm father God!

Old, aching God, grey with endless care,
calmly piercing evil's new disguises,
    glad of good surprises,
    wiser than despair:
Hail and Hosanna,
old, aching God!   141

Young, growing God, eager, on the move,
saying no to falsehood and unkindness,
    crying out for justice,
    giving all you have:
Hail and Hosanna,
young, growing God.

Great, living God, never fully known,
joyful darkness far beyond our seeing,
    closer yet than breathing,
    everlasting home:
Hail and Hosanna,
great, living God!

Brian Wren, 1986, rev.
© 1989 Hope Publishing Co., Carol Stream, IL 60188
All rights reserved. Used by permission

Bring Many Names 1989, #9
Chalice Hymnal 1995, #10
The New Century Hymnal 1995, #11
Voices United 1997, #268

If the human race is created in the image and likeness of God (Gen.
1.27), it follows that both femaleness and maleness reveal the divine,
and (since we are not static but have a changing life cycle), both youth
and age give glimpses of God.

                                        Brian Wren, *Bring Many Names*

INTRODUCTION

Background

Brian Wren, British-born and educated (Ph.D. in theology), Reformed
pastor, poet, theologian, and teacher, is one of the most living popular
hymnwriters. Now living in the United States, Wren has been represented in every major denominational hymnal here since *Lutheran
Book of Worship* (1978). He has taken considerable care to be sensitive
to the nuances of language, particularly as he has been influenced by
concerns for justice and by feminist theology. As early as 1977, in his
book *Education for Justice*, he included these closing words in the "Introductory Note": "Finally, as a small step towards justice in our lan-

guage, feminine pronouns include the masculine sense, and vice-versa, except when a particular gender is specified." His 1989 book, *What Language Shall I Borrow?* and the videocassette released the same year, *How Shall I Sing to God?* both focused on the power of language, issues of inclusiveness, and the understanding that every naming of God is a borrowing of language.

Fourteen of Wren's texts appear in *The United Methodist Hymnal* (1989) and he served as a consultant to that Hymnal Revision Committee. In discussion of the language and committee process, Carlton R. Young, editor of that hymnal, cited Wren's "How Can We Name a Love" (#111), written in 1973, as one of "several new hymns [offering] the freshness of female imagery and metaphor" (Young 1993, 141). That hymn includes these lines in speaking of God: "we can, with parents' names, describe, and thus adore,/Love unconfined, a father kind, a mother strong and sure." Notice the reversal of stereotypes, as it is the mother who is *strong* and *sure*, words usually attributed to males and fathers. "God of many names" (#105), written in 1985 and included in this hymnal, contains female images in its first stanza: "God of hovering wings, womb and birth of time."

Another of Wren's texts that was being considered for inclusion in *UMH* was "Strong mother God" (stanzas two through six of the hymn above—without the current first stanza), that had been completed in February 1986. Wren wrote the first stanza in mid-1987 (dates from Wren 1989b, "Notes on the Hymns") in an attempt to gain wider acceptance for the text. Because hymns are usually titled and indexed by their opening lines, "Bring many names" was more likely to find acceptance as the remembered line than "Strong mother God." Hymnal editor, Carlton R. Young, wrote a tune, WESTCHASE, for it. In spite of this combination, the controversy raged on (about this and other new hymns), and the hymn failed to win acceptance by one vote.

The text has been set as an anthem by both Donna B. Kasbohm and Richard Proulx, and used at the Re-Imagining Conference with several new stanzas by Theresa Cotter (*Re-Imagining* 1993, 12-14). Published in Great Britain with a tune by Veronica Bennetts, the text has appeared in the United States with Young's tune in two 1995 hymnals and in the 1997 hymnal of the United Church of Canada.

The Shape of the Text

A cursory glance at "Bring Many Names" might suggest that it is an "inclusive" hymn (Procter-Smith 1990, 63-67), seeking to balance gender references (*mother/father*) and age references (*old/young*). This balancing might be seen by lifting out some of the correlated terms in the text:

strong	*warm*	*old*	*young*
mother	*father*	*aching*	*growing*
working	*hugging*	*grey*	*eager*
planning	*feeling*	*piercing*	*saying no*
setting	*forgiving*		

The terms are somewhat evenly matched, but that is due as much to poetic form as to a concern for evenhandedness. What moves the text from inclusive to emancipatory language is the way in that Wren has used the balanced form of the hymn to break open some of our stereotypes about God and their reflection on human beings, "challenging our colonized imaginations" (Procter-Smith 1990, 112). The diversity of images in this text, through adjectives and metaphors, is vital to challenging our imaginations (Procter-Smith 1990, 112; Duck 1995, 33-44).

The hymn form itself, as found in Wren's poetic setting in *Bring Many Names* #9, breaks open tradition by its unusual meter. Like traditional hymns, this text continues the pattern set in the first stanza with four lines in each stanza plus a two-line variable refrain, and a regular pattern of stresses. Each stanza contains several clauses, shaped into one sentence, except for the first stanza, which makes the first four lines one sentence while the refrain has two exclamations.

Taking their cue from the tune WESTCHASE, the sources with Young's tune list the meter as 9.10.11.9, an irregular meter. The suggested four-phrase meter fits the melody scheme of ABAC, with the stanza being three progressively longer lines (combining lines three and four in the setting of the text at the head of this section) and C being the refrain.[27] That is,

---

1. Interestingly, Veronica Bennetts' tune with that this text appears in *New Songs of Praise 3* has neither tune name nor meter listed. Of the twelve tunes in that collection, only seven list tune name and meter, and of those only one was a new tune. Bennetts' tune is basically five phrases, three for each stanza with the refrain comprising two lines of music, repeating the text. Its meter would be listed then as 9.10.11.9.9. Like Young's it sets the stanzas in three lines or phrases, but unlike Young's, as discussed in the following paragraph, the inner BB rhyme is less prominent, more easily lost.

Bring many names, beautiful and good,
celebrate, in parable and story,
holiness in glory, living, loving God.
Hail and hosanna! bring many names!

Yet Wren's rhyme scheme demands a four-line stanza plus the refrain, so that the ABBA rhyme of the first lines may be felt (the first
stanza having the weakest rhyme: *good/God, story/glory*; and the others stronger, such as stanza two: *day/play, creation/equation*). This
means the poetic, text-based meter would be 9.10.6.5.5.4, an unusual
meter.[28] Even though set in four phrases (instead of six), Young's tune
allows for the rhyme scheme by setting the first and similar third
phrases with two subphrases: 4 syllables + 5 syllables in the first
phrase, 6 syllables (by repeating notes where longer beats were) + 5
syllables in the third. This phrasing allows the repetition of the phrase
after the second line to be heard as well as two short phrases, bringing
out the rhyming words *story/glory*, thus

> *celebrate in parable and story,*
> *holiness in glory,*
> *living, loving God.* rather than
> *holiness in glory, living, loving God.*

Thus, my decision is to follow the poetic setting in *Bring Many Names*
and to suggest that the hymnal designation of the meter does not tell the
whole story about this text.

This is not a hymn that depends on rhyme, but its presence gives the
singer the ease of a comfortable form from which new ideas might be
explored. Along with the presence of rhyme, the repetition of the variable refrain "Hail and Hosanna" helps to give cohesion to the text. The
refrain is *variable* because its first line remains constant, *Hail and Hosanna*, while its second line is taken from the first phrase of each
stanza (that remains constant with four syllables each time).

The challenge of the unusual meter of the text is mediated in part by
the rhyme scheme and by the tune with that it is associated. Yet the
meter also prepares the singer to hear new truths, by its irregularity
suggesting that something new is happening here. The text relies primarily on short words; one-syllable words predominate, with a minimum of three-syllable and only one four-syllable word in the text. In

---

2. Irregular meters, however, are not actually as unusual or rare as one
might think. "*The United Methodist Hymnal* has over 500 tunes in 340 meters,
including 115 in irregular meters" (Young 1993, 60).

accordance with the intent of the text to *bring many names*, nouns and adjectives are used more often than verbs.

One other interesting facet of the text is its reliance on the participle form of verbs to describe the actions of God,[29] and the inner rhyming that results between the repetition of *bring* and the *-ing* of the participles:

stanza 2	*stanza 3*	*stanza 4*	*stanza 5*	*stanza 6*
working	hugging	aching	growing	living
planning	feeling	piercing	saying	seeing
setting	caring	crying	breathing	
	forgiving		giving	

The only four-syllable word in the text, not a participle but an adjective, also contains the *-ing* sense of rhyme, *everlasting*, in the final stanza.

STANZAS

Stanza One

Upon first appearance, the opening line, *Bring many names, beautiful and good,* might suggest the bringing of human names, much like the traditional practice of reading diptychs, the lists of names of the dead and living Christians for whom special prayer was made in worship in the early church (*Cross and Livingstone, s.v.* diptych). The sense of the richness of diversity is apparent from the opening line. Yet these opening lines might seem misleading to an outsider, for it is not until the fourth line that it is clear we are singing about God.[30] Wren has depended on the context of Christian worship for the understanding of the opening lines, and on our "reading back" into them the rest of the hymn.

The first stanza introduces the reader/singer to the attitude of the text: God's diversity and our understanding of that diversity are *beau-*

---

3. Wren says, "I like the participle form: it suggests ongoing action" (Wren 1996).

4. Wren points out that the rewriting process (adding the opening stanza) led to this ambiguity, as "Strong mother God," the original opening line, was unambiguous (Wren 1996).

+

tiful and *good*, and flow from the tradition of *parable, story, holiness,* and *glory.* This stanza does not present specifically new information but calls us to honor God who is alive and who loves us. The *many names* of God are a strong part of the Judeo-Christian heritage, but a part often forgotten or slighted when orthodoxy feels the need to proclaim the unity of the Judeo-Christian God over and against other gods. The diversity of God's names is seen when Moses encounters God's voice coming from a burning bush that is not consumed on Mount Horeb:

> But Moses said to God, "If I come to the Israelites and say to them, 'The God of your ancestors has sent me to you,' and they ask me, 'What is his name?' what shall I say to them?" God said to Moses, "I AM WHO I AM." [God] said further, "Thus you shall say to the Israelites, 'I AM has sent me to you.'" God also said to Moses, "Thus you shall say to the Israelites, 'The LORD, the God of your ancestors, the God of Abraham, the God of Isaac, and the God of Jacob, has sent me to you': This is my name forever, and this my title for all generations."
>
> (Exod. 3.13-15)

The annotation for this passage in the *New Oxford Annotated Bible* says:

> I AM WHO I AM is an etymology of the cultic name for the God of Israel, YHWH, probably pronounced Yahweh. YHWH is treated as a verbal form derived from "to be" and formulated in the first person because God is the speaker. Actually YHWH is a third person form and may mean "He causes to be." The name does not indicate God's eternal being but God's action and presence in historical affairs.

Several things can be seen in this scripture reference and its annotation.[31] First, from the annotation we hear that this naming of God refers to God's action and presence in historical affairs, that is to say, God relating to human beings and creation. Second, YHWH or I AM WHO I AM can be translated several different ways, suggesting that there is no one "magic word" for God's name. Third, the scripture reference itself contains several names for God:

---

5. It should be noted here that the story in Exodus is not the first appearance in scripture of naming God. In Genesis 4.26b we read, "At that time people began to invoke the name of the LORD (YHWH)," speaking of the time of Adam's grandson Enosh. Yet the Exodus naming is the one that points out most clearly the diversity of God's names.

```
I AM WHO I AM
I AM
The LORD
God of your ancestors
God of Abraham
God of Isaac
God of Jacob
```

All of the texts we have considered thus far—"God of the Sparrow," "Source and Sovereign," and now "Bring Many Names"—use the biblical principle of many names for God. This text follows the example of Psalm 52.9, "In the presence of the faithful I will proclaim your *name*, for it is *good*." *Beautiful* is related to several Hebrew scriptures: "Worship the Lord in the *beauty* of holiness"(Ps. 29.2b, KJV) and Psalm 27.4:

> One thing have I asked of the Lord
>   that will I seek after:
> to live in the house of the Lord
>   all the days of my life,
> to behold the *beauty* of the Lord,
>   and to inquire in [God's] temple.

Bible *stories* are told to young children, and Jesus became famous in his walk on earth in part for his telling of *parables*, recounted throughout the Synoptic Gospels. (See for example, Matthew 13, with parables of the sower, of weeds among the wheat, of the mustard seed, and of the yeast.)

Holiness and *glory* are words associated with God from the time of Moses. "Who is like you, O Lord, among the gods? Who is like you, majestic in *holiness*, awesome in splendor, doing wonders?" proclaims Moses after God delivers the Israelites from Egypt (Exod. 15.11). As the Israelites wander in the wilderness the *glory* of God appears in a cloud and then as fire (Exod. 16.10, 24.17). These terms with their biblical tradition add to the grounding of the text in the tradition of *parable* and *story* and lead us into the next line, *living, loving God.* "My soul thirsts for God," says the Psalmist, "for the *living God*" (42.2). "Beloved, let us love one another, because *love is from God*; everyone who loves is born of God and knows God. Whoever does not love does not know God, for *God is love*" (1 John 4.7). The alliteration of *living* and *loving* captures the essence of God while hinting at the repeated *h* sounds of *Hail* and *Hosanna* to come in the refrain.

Refrain

Hail and *Hosanna* are not common words, but both exclamations appear in the life of Jesus at crucial moments. *"Hail*, O favored one, the Lord is with you!" says the angel Gabriel to Mary of Nazareth, when he comes to tell her that she will become pregnant with the child of God (Luke 1.28, RSV). During the eleventh century a devotional prayer known as the *Hail Mary* came into common usage, which continued until 1955 in the Roman Catholic Church both as a devotional form and as a penitential one (Cross and Livingstone, *s.v., Hail Mary*).

"Hail, King of the Jews" (Mark 15.18) mock the soldiers as they torture Jesus immediately before the crucifixion. The cross is the most recognizable symbol of Christianity, and placed here in Wren's text, *Hail* brings Christ's passion to mind. Not only did he suffer indignation unjustly, thus identifying with the outcasts of society, but, says Christian tradition, Jesus' death freed us from sin and death. As we greet the everliving God in Wren's text, we revert to the ancient greeting *Hail*, given to Mary in honor and to Jesus in derision, remaking it into a salutation worthy of honor for the One who is *holiness in glory*.

"Hosanna to the Son of David!" cried the crowd as Jesus entered Jerusalem riding on a donkey's colt (Matt. 21.9, Mark 11.9, John 12.13). *"Hosanna* was originally a Hebrew invocation addressed to God, meaning, 'O save!;' later it was used as a cry of joyous acclamation" (*Bible*, note to Matt. 21.9). Like the Hail Mary, *Hosanna* is part of the common prayer of the church, as it appears in the eucharistic prayer, following the Sanctus:

> Holy, holy, holy Lord, God of power and might,
> heaven and earth are full of your glory.
>   *Hosanna* in the highest.
> Blessed is he [Christ] who comes in the name of the Lord.
>   *Hosanna* in the highest. (*UMH*, 9, italics mine)

The use of the two terms *Hail* and *Hosanna* together adds several possible dimensions of meaning to the text: the combination of private and public prayer (*Hail Mary* being a private prayer, *Hosanna* part of public worship), representations of female and male in relation to God (Mary and Jesus), and recognition of Palm Sunday (*Hosanna*) and salvation of Good Friday (*Hail*, King of the Jews)—as we hail God with many names, God comes to us to save us. Both words are exclamations—we greet God and proclaim our salvation with joy and energy.

Introduction to Middle Stanzas

In the four middle stanzas we move to what is unique to this text—its use of human terms to describe God in nonstereotypical ways, exemplifying emancipatory language.

The Bible itself uses parental terms to describe God. *Father* is the most common, used extensively in the New Testament, particularly in the Gospel of John. Yet it appears first in the Psalms:

> *Father* of orphans and protector of widows
> is God in his holy habitation. (Ps. 68.5)

> He [David] shall cry to me, "You are my *Father*,
> my God, and the Rock of my salvation!" (Ps. 89.26)

The use of *Father* in the telling of the story of Jesus Christ begins with the opening chapter of the Gospel of John: "No one has ever seen God. It is God the only Son, who is close to the *Father's* heart, who has made him known" (1.18). The young Jesus, presumed by his parents to be lost in Jerusalem, says to them, 'Why were you searching for me? Did you not know that I must be in my *Father's* house?" (Luke 2.49, referring to the temple of God). And in the most familiar prayer of Christian faith, Jesus taught his followers to pray: "Our *Father* in heaven, / hallowed be your name" (Matt. 6.9). *Father* has long been an accepted name for God, well loved by many.

In order to balance the maleness of *Father*, feminist theologians, biblical scholars and others have tried to recapture images of female divinity from biblical and traditional sources (Duck 1991; Johnson 1993; McFague 1987; Mollenkott 1983; Wren 1989b). The analogy of Isaiah 49.15 suggests that God is analogous to a birthing and nursing *mother*:[32]

> Can a woman forget her nursing child,
>   or show no compassion for the child of her womb?
> Even these may forget,
>   yet I will not forget you.

---

6. As a mother, a difficult while admittedly also joyful task, I found maternal images of God particularly helpful during the stressful times of pregnancy, delivery, and early motherhood. Other mothers who are open to these images have shared their stories of empowerment with me as well.

God speaks through the prophet Hosea about her relationship with Israel in terms reminiscent of mothers:

> Yet it was I who taught Ephraim to walk,
> I took them up in my arms;
> but they did not know that I healed them.
> I led them with cords of human kindness,
> with bands of love.
> I was to them like those
> who lift infants to their cheeks.
> I bent down to them and fed them. (Hos. 11.3-4)

God is likened to animal mothers several times in scripture: a *mother* bear avenging her cubs (Hos. 13.8), a *mother* eagle caring for its young (Deut. 32.11, KJV), and a *mother* hen gathering her chicks under her wings (2 Esd. 1.30, Matt. 23.37, Luke 13.34). The reference to the apocryphal book of 2 Esdras is particularly interesting for the verses preceding the reference to a mother hen: "Thus says the Lord Almighty: Have I not entreated you as a *father* entreats his sons or a *mother* her daughters or a *nurse* her children, so that you should be my people and I should be your God" (1.28-29a). This trio of images includes both *father* and *mother* and adds a female *nurse*, one who also cares for children.

In the late fourteenth century, Julian, an anchoress (one withdrawn from the world to live a life of silence and prayer, whose cell was attached to a parish church) in Norwich, England, received sixteen revelations of God's love in a series of visions. In these revelations Julian experienced God as *mother* as well as *father*: "God almighty is our *loving* Father, and God all wisdom is our loving *Mother*, with the love and the goodness of the Holy Spirit, that is all one God, one Lord" (Julian of Norwich 1978, 293, italics mine). A hymn based on Julian's writings by Jean Janzen, one of the hymnwriters represented in this study, "Mothering God, You Gave Me Birth," appears in four recent hymnals (*Hymnal: A Worshipbook* 1992, #482; *CH* #83; *NCH* #467; *Voices United* #320). Though not as widely used as *father*, the image of *mother* God is rooted in Christian tradition and is being brought to life again in our time.

Stanza Two

Mother comes first in Wren's text (though the common order in English has been *male* and then *female*), and her neverending work is acknowledged. "The God who keeps Israel," sings the Psalmist, "will neither slumber nor sleep." (121.4) *Mother God's* strength shows not only in her perseverance but in her mental capabilities as well, *planning the wonders of creation, setting the equations* for galaxies to revolve and life to evolve. Here are echoes of this description of God, speaking to Job out of the whirlwind:

> Where were you when I laid the foundation of the earth?
> Tell me, if you have understanding.
> Who determined its measurements—surely you know!
> Or who stretched the line upon it?
> On what were its bases sunk,
> or who laid its cornerstone
> when the morning stars sang together
> and all the heavenly beings shouted for joy? (Job 38.4-7)

Yet this *mother God* is not a drudge,[33] for we see her *genius at play* in both senses of *play*—her genius is engaged in planning and working, yet her creativity is also playful and lighthearted. This *genius* is akin to Wisdom whose joy we hear in Proverbs 8.30-31:

> then I was beside him, like a master worker;
> and I was daily his delight,
> rejoicing before him always,
> rejoicing in his inhabited world
> and delighting in the human race.

Metaphors move in several directions (Duck 1991, 16; following Black 1962), and this movement can be seen in Wren's text. We understand God, the unknown, through things that we know. Yet any metaphor or naming of God needs to acknowledge that God is still a mystery. We may understand in part, but we cannot understand fully. When we name God with human metaphors that metaphor carries its human connotations (that when solidified are called *stereotypes*) to God and also reflects godliness back to humanity. One of the problems with the overuse of *father* as a metaphor for God is that, by the movement of the metaphor, human fathers receive a sense of godliness that has been denied for human mothers.

---

7. Because of the reflexive nature of metaphors, some persons have objected that the "Superwoman" image of an endlessly working God is not a helpful portrayal of a mother.

This second stanza of Wren's text breaks through the familiar stereotypes related to *mother*: always hugging or nagging, her only work to bake chocolate chip cookies or apple pie, a woman with math anxiety, passively accepting the plans of others. Through Wren's portrayal, women in the twentieth century can see themselves, in creative work inside and outside the home, reflecting the image of God in positive ways. Likewise the next stanza shatters the stereotypes that consider *father* as the distant uncaring breadwinner, untouched by the little squabbles at home, incapable of expressing emotion.

Stanza Three

The third stanza begins immediately shattering stereotypical *father* metaphors and carries that shattering throughout the stanza: *warm, hugging every child* (not just a favorite), *caring and forgiving till we're reconciled.* This *father God* is not remote from our condition but feels *all the strains of human living.* Through the Incarnation, God taking on human form in Jesus Christ, Christians believe that God has felt and understands the strains of our living. The *forgiving* father echoes the parable of the prodigal son and his brother found in Luke 15.11-32, with this word picture of the father's actions as the lost son finds his way home: "But while he was still far off, his father saw him and was filled with compassion; [his father] ran and put his arms around him and kissed him" (Luke 15.20). This scriptural sentence is reflected in this stanza by Wren, showing a loving, caring, *warm father God.*

Reconciling is an important word for Christians in interpreting the work of Jesus Christ, as the letters to the Colossians and Corinthians attest: "through him God was pleased to *reconcile* to [Godself] all things" (Col. 1.20a); "God who *reconciled* us to [Godself] through Christ, and has given us the ministry of *reconciliation*; that is, in Christ God was *reconciling* the world to [Godself]" (2 Cor. 5.18-19a).

It should be noted that in setting *mother* and *father* images of God, Wren has not set complete opposites. He has not moved *mother* to a remote spot in order to move *father* closer. Rather he has pivoted between equally positive terms: *strong* and *warm*, and built images that show creativity and flexibility together with loving concern. This follows the intent, stated in the opening line of the text to *bring many names, beautiful and good.* In the following two stanzas (four and five), advanced age and youth will be attributed to God in order to show us more of God and more of ourselves.

Stanza Four

Old, aching God begins the fourth stanza, recalling a familiar, scriptural (Daniel 7) image—the ancient, long white-bearded male-God, sitting on the throne of judgment—and juxtaposing it immediately with an unfamiliar image—God *aching*, like human beings ache with age, with rheumatism and arthritis, with worn muscles and fragile bones. God is *grey with endless care* (endless care working to dispel the myth of a remote, uncaring God), aging but much like *mother God* who worked *night and day*, and *father God feeling the strains of human living and caring*. Yet this aging God is not senile but *calmly piercing evil's new disguises*. This second line recalls the question in the United Methodist Baptismal Covenant service:

> Do you accept the freedom and power God gives you
> to resist evil, injustice, and oppression
> in whatever forms they present themselves? (*UMH*, 34)

Does God need to "live longer" in order to pierce evil's disguises? No, God's goodness is always more powerful than evil. Rather, two points may be made by this stanza: First, God is not immobile before the changing face of evil; the Holy One of the ages is vigorous in unmasking evil and overcoming despair. Second, the text by its reflection is suggesting a better way for humanity to live in God's light. This stanza lifts up how human aging can carry out God's vision. Years of living can give one the experience to recognize the various forms of evil and the way evil disguises itself. Those years can also give the grounding needed to *calmly pierce* those *disguises*, the assurance that comes from knowing that God is in control and will triumph in the end. Yet age brings not only the ability to see through evil but also the ability to see the good, and rejoice in it. *Wiser than despair* follows the thought of the second line; part of the ability to proceed *calmly* and yet *piercingly* around evil is the wisdom that is greater than despair, an optimism that is realistic yet ever hopeful.

Stanza Five

Age preceded *youth* in Wren's text, a reminder that these *many names* are only hints about God's nature, not the nature itself, or to use the words of Sallie McFague: "the negative theological tradition has always insisted: God is unlike as well as like our metaphors" (McFague

1987, 97). Positing metaphors in unfamiliar sequences, female/male, aged/youth, can remind us of the metaphoric nature of our language.

This fifth stanza has undergone several changes. It appears first in Wren's *What Language Shall I Borrow* (1989a) in a chapter called "Bring Many Names," in a discussion of the infinite possibilities offered by God's perfect love, as follows:

> Young, growing God, eager still to know,
> willing to be changed by what you've started,
>   quick to be delighted,
>   singing as you go:
> Hail and Hosanna,
> young, growing God!

By the publication of *Bring Many Names: 35 New Hymns by Brian Wren* later that same year, the stanza had been revised after conversations with the Mennonite-Brethren Hymnal Council.[34] Wren states in this collection in his "Notes on the Hymns," "I stand by the theology [of the original], but believe the revision better suggests God's 'youthfulness'":

> Young, growing God, eager, on the move,
> seeing all, and fretting at our blindness,
>   crying out for justice,
>   giving all you have:
> Hail and Hosanna,
> young, growing God!

From the simple delight and singing on the go reflected by preschoolers, the text has moved to adolescence, energetically questioning the injustice of the adult world, with the agitation of knowing and seeing adult inadequacies. Yet the text was to undergo still another change, in the second line, with the author's preference being this latest version, (Wren 1995a), that appears in each hymnal where it is contained as well as at the head of this section:

---

8. Ironically, even with the revised stanza, this text does not appear in the hymnal published by this council, *Hymnal: A Worshipbook* (1992). (Just as the addition of the first stanza did not gain acceptance for the text in *The United Methodist Hymnal*.)

Young, growing God, eager, on the move,
saying no to falsehood and unkindness,
    crying out for justice,
    giving all you have:
Hail and Hosanna,
young, growing God.

In this final revision, the adolescence has been retained, the unhelpful
reference to *blindness* and the agitation of *fretting* lost, and the clarity
and strength of *saying no* (a popular slogan for teens in regard to sex
and drug education) spelled out to *falsehood* and *unkindness*. Notice
that the line *giving all you have* reflects back to the second stanza
where God is described as *working night and day*.

The sense of "youthfulness" in the fifth stanza as well as the sense
of God aging in stanza four echo the understanding of process theology. Classical understandings of God are based on God's absoluteness
or unchangeability, making God devoid of relativity and becoming
(Surin 1993, 105). In contrast, process theology believes that just as
everything in creation is endowed with an internal process of becoming, called *concrescence*, so God by interacting with the universe also
is in the process of becoming.

Hartshorne argued for understanding God in terms of two kinds of
perfection. The first kind of perfection is that God's abstract essence is
unchanging. Hartshorne uses as an example the concept of God's omniscience, God's all-knowing. Process theology understands this to
mean that God always knows everything knowable. The second kind of
perfection is a relative perfection, formed out of God's own becoming
and therefore changing. This kind of perfection can also be related to
God's omniscience as part of God's becoming: "To say that God grows
is not to say that God becomes wiser or more loving; it means only
that, as new creatures arise and new experiences occur, the objects of
the divine love have increased and therefore the divine experience has
been enriched" (Griffin in Musser and Price, 1992, 387). This understanding is essential to the ability to grasp Wren's descriptions of a God
who is *old* and *aching* and who is *young* and *growing*.

For process theology it is important to hold both kinds of God's
perfection in tension with each other, just as in this text it is important
to hold in tension images of God as *mother, father, old,* and *young*.
Emancipatory language is not based on freeing our lives from tension.
Rather it depends on our growing in faith and understanding so that we
can hold God's own nature as well as our own contradictory natures in

tension so that the fullness and richness of our life and God's mystery can be appreciated.

Comparison/Contrast of Stanzas Four and Five

To return to stanza five of Wren's text: the energy lost in the *aches* and *calm*ness of stanza four are recaptured here beginning with the shorter phrases of the end of the first line, *eager, on the move* (e.g., like the cloud and pillar in Exod. 13 and 14). Participles begin each of the following three phrases: *saying, crying, giving*. Like the fourth stanza the fifth deals also with resistance to evil, reflecting the baptismal question cited above. *Old God* is *calm* yet *piercing*, giving a picture of one stabbing a balloon with a pin to let the air out and expose the evil lurking therein. *Young God* is more energetically verbal, *saying no, crying out, giving all*, suggestive of protest marches. This stanza reflects the God who rails against the children of Israel who have fallen away from God's ways into *injustice, falsehood,* and *unkindness,* God as heard speaking through the prophets of Hebrew scriptures:

> They [the people] know no limits in deeds of wickedness;
> *they do not judge with justice*
> the cause of the orphan, to make it prosper,
> and they do not defend the rights of the needy.
> Shall I not punish them for these things? says the Lord.
>
> (Jer. 5.28b-29a)

> Therefore thus says the Lord God: Because you have uttered *falsehood and envisioned lies,* I am against you, says the Lord God.
>
> (Ezek. 13. 8)

> [God] has told you, O mortal, what is good;
> and what does the Lord require of you
> but to *do justice, and to love kindness,*
> and to walk humbly with your God?   (Mic. 6.8)

This is the God called "Mighty King, *lover of justice*" in Psalm 99.4, the God portrayed in stanzas four and five, both *old* and *young,* who steadfastly loves justice amid all changes.

Stanza Six

The sixth and final stanza begins with an echo of Psalm 99.3, "Let them praise your *great* and awesome name!" and sums up the *many names* considered in the text. *Living* refers us back to the first stanza, line four.

Paul's famous chapter to the Corinthians about love contains the sentence "For now we see in a mirror, dimly, but then we will see face to face. Now I know only in part; then I will know fully, even as I have been fully known" (1 Cor. 13.12). These words form the basis for the phrase of Wren's text, *never fully known*, referring to our human inability to know God fully in this earthly life.

The image of *light* as reflective of those who live in Christ has suggested that the opposite is equally true, *dark* equals *sin* (cf. Ephesians 6.12 "For our struggle is not against enemies of blood and flesh, but against the rulers, against the authorities, against the cosmic powers of this present *darkness*, against the spiritual forces of evil in the heavenly places."). Some contemporary theologians are suggesting that caution be taken regarding the association of darkness with sin in the context of racism and therefore with blackness or dark-skinned persons.[35]   To recast the image of *darkness*, theologians reach back to Gregory of Nyssa in the fourth century whose *Life of Moses* included a section on *darkness* as the presence of God, where we understand God as invisible and incomprehensible (1978, 94-97). So, using images from the story of Moses and the Israelites wandering in the wilderness and receiving the Ten Commandments, Wren reminds us that God is present in the joyful darkness: "Then the people stood at a distance, while Moses drew near to the thick *darkness* where God was" (Exod. 20.18); "These words the Lord spoke with a loud voice to your whole assembly at the mountain, out of the fire, the cloud, and the thick *darkness*" (Deut. 5.22a).

Because God can *never be fully known*, God is *far beyond our seeing*, both physically and in the sense of understanding. Yet this sense of remoteness, of being *beyond*, is quickly balanced by another truth: God is *closer yet than breathing*. Again we are asked to hold in tension the diversity of God, experienced in nearness and wholly otherness.

Everlasting home suggests somewhat of a resolution of the tension—*home* is a place of rest, not devoid of tension, but a settling in place, where, as Augustine says, "our hearts are restless until they find

---

9. Wren himself has written a text entitled "Joyful Is the Dark," found in *Bring Many Names* #23, with the title repeated as the opening phrase of each of the five stanzas.

rest in thee." Similar in tone are the words of Jesus, "Come to me, all you that are weary and are carrying heavy burdens, and I will give you rest" (Matt. 11.28). This *home*, like God, is from *everlasting to everlasting* (1 Chron. 16.36), a promise of eternal life (cf. John 3.16). The juxtaposition of *everlasting* and *home* suggests an eschatological meaning of *home* as eternal life. The background of process theology resonates with the use of the plural *our*, as it suggests that eternal life is not an individual thing but rather communal; we return to the matrix that is everlasting (Ruether 1983, 257-278). As the text has pushed the boundaries of our understanding of God, so the closing images of *home* and *great, living God* remind us that we dwell within this marvelous space of God now and always.

OTHER ASPECTS OF EMANCIPATORY LANGUAGE

We have already discussed the emancipatory nature of the meter, rhyme and shattering of stereotypes for *mother* and *father*. This text has broadened the register of hymnic language to include *equation* (mathematics), as well as broadening God-language to include *mother* and *father*, *old* and *young*. Making these metaphors vital to the text, by the reflexive nature of metaphors, makes visible *mothers*, the elderly (*old/aching*) and children (*young/growing*), all of them persons on the margins. The use of *youth/aging* metaphors brings understandings from process theology into hymnic language; broadening both our understanding of God, and by reflection, our understanding of ourselves within God.

Truthfulness in this text includes the embodiment of *genius, hugging, feeling, aching, grey,* and *eager*. A sense of God's justice may be seen in lines such as *calmly piercing evil's new disguises, saying no to falsehood and unkindness, crying out for justice.*

The diversity of God drawn out in the central four stanzas is unified by the opening and closing stanzas as well as the refrain. By employing four different metaphors in the center of the text, Wren has reminded us that God is beyond our metaphors, beyond gender and age, greater than our imagining (Wren 1989, 219). A hymnologist has suggested that this hymn is "reason enough that old and new words should be allowed to coexist in vital tension in our hymns, prayers, and liturgies" (Young 1995b, 134). It is this "vital tension" that enlivens emancipatory language.

Chapter 11
Lead on, O cloud of Presence
A Multidimensional Reading

Lead on, O cloud of Presence;
the exodus is come;
in wilderness and desert
our tribe shall make its home.
Our bondage left behind us,
new hopes within us grow.
We seek the land of promise
where milk and honey flow.

Lead on, O fiery pillar;
we follow yet with fears,
but we shall come rejoicing,
though joy be born of tears.
We are not lost, though wand'ring,
for by your light we come,
and we are still God's people.
The journey is our home.

Lead on, O God of freedom,
and guide us on our way,
and help us trust the promise
through struggle and delay.

We pray our sons and daughters
may journey to that land
where justice dwells with mercy
and love is law's demand.

Ruth Duck, 1974, rev. 1989

Because We Are One People 1974, #32
Everflowing Streams 1981, #77
The Song Goes On 1990, #74
Hymnal: A Worshipbook 1992, #419
Duck, *Dancing in the Universe* 1992, #50
Chalice Hymnal 1995, #633
Voices United 1997, #421
Covenant Hymnal 1997 #419

On the day the tabernacle was set up, the cloud covered the tabernacle, the tent of the covenant; and from evening until morning it was over the tabernacle, having the appearance of fire. It was always so: the cloud covered it by day and the appearance of fire by night. Whenever the cloud lifted from over the tent, then the Israelites would set out; and in the place where the cloud settled down, there the Israelites would camp. At the command of the LORD the Israelites would set out, and at the command of the LORD they would camp. As long as the cloud rested over the tabernacle, they would remain in camp. Even when the cloud continued over the tabernacle many days, the Israelites would keep the charge of the LORD, and would not set out. Sometimes the cloud would remain a few days over the tabernacle, and according to the command of the LORD they would remain in camp; then according to the command of the LORD they would set out. Sometimes the cloud would remain from evening until morning; and when the cloud lifted in the morning, they would set out, or if it continued for a day and a night, when the cloud lifted they would set out. Whether it was two days, or a month, or a longer time, that the cloud continued over the tabernacle, resting upon it, the Israelites would remain in camp and would not set out; but when it lifted they would set out. At the command of the LORD they would camp, and at the command of the LORD they would set out. They kept the charge of the LORD, at the command of the LORD by Moses.   (Numbers 9:15-23)

Lead on, O King eternal,
the day of march has come;
henceforth in fields of conquest
thy tents shall be our home;
through days of preparation
thy grace has made us strong,
and now, O King eternal,
we lift our battle song.

Lead on, O King eternal,
till sin's fierce war shall cease,
and holiness shall whisper
the sweet amen of peace;
for not with swords loud clashing,
nor roll of stirring drums;
with deeds of love and mercy,
the heavenly kingdom comes.

Lead on, O King eternal:
we follow, not with fears,
for gladness breaks like morning
where'er thy face appears;
thy cross is lifted o'er us;
we journey in its light;
the crown awaits the conquest;
lead on, O God of might.

Ernest W. Shurtleff, 1887

This favorite dedication hymn ["Lead on, O King Eternal"] was written for the all-male 1887 graduating class of Andover Theological Seminary, of that the author was a member. . . . This hymn, not unlike "Onward, Christian Soldiers," calls the faithful to fight in a war against sin to establish God's kingdom of peace and love. The conclusion of worship in the social gospel tradition replaces graduation as "the day of march" that follows "days of preparation" into "fields of conquest."

Carlton R. Young, *Companion to The United Methodist Hymnal*

INTRODUCTION

"Lead on, O Cloud of Presence" emerged while I was trying to adapt "Lead on, O King Eternal" for *Because We Are One People* (an inclusive-language hymnal). Both texts used Exodus imagery (Numbers 9:15-23). The old hymn uses triumphalist military language, while the

new hymn grows out of liberation movements. The cloud and fiery
pillar are symbols of God's presence, guiding people in uncertain times
as they journey toward freedom.

Ruth Duck, *Dancing in the Universe*

Background

Soon after she received her M.Div. degree in 1973, Ruth Duck em-
barked on work that would bring her to prominence in the area of
theological revision of language, that of writing and editing inclusive
language worship resources. Collections of hymns, *Because We Are
One People* and *Everflowing Streams*, were followed by books of worship resources—prayers, calls to worship, and litanies—*Bread for the
Journey, Flames of the Spirit*, and *Touch Holiness*). Her recent publications include two books on the development, theory, and practice of
language for worship that I consider emancipatory, *Gender and the
Name of God* and *Finding Words for Worship*. Duck's second collection of her own hymns, *Circles of Care*, was published in 1998.

Beginning with the appearance of a single text in denominational
hymnals in 1985, 1989, and 1991, two texts in 1990, and three in 1992,
Duck was "discovered" by a 1994 (*Gather II*) and two 1995 hymnals.
New Century Hymnal contains thirteen of her original texts and some
adaptations, and *Chalice Hymnal* (whose committee Duck served on)
contains eleven original texts, three translations, five adaptations, and a
new doxological stanza for "Rejoice, Ye Pure in Heart." Similar numbers of her texts appear in the hymnals of the United Church of Canada
(*Voices United*, 10 texts) and the Anglican Church of Canada. Ordained
by the United Church of Christ, Duck is associate professor of worship
at Garrett-Evangelical Theological Seminary in Evanston, Illinois.

"Lead on, O Cloud of Presence" was one of Ruth Duck's first hymn
texts, and grew out of her "attempts to revise hymns that had much
masculine imagery" (Duck 1992, Preface). It draws on Rosemary
Ruether's prophetic principle, "the tradition by that Biblical faith constantly criticizes and renews itself and its own vision" (Ruether 1983,
24), to renew for our time and in light of contemporary liberation theologies the popular text, "Lead on, O King Eternal."[1] In trying to adapt

---

1. It should perhaps be noted here that *The New Century Hymnal* has also
included a rewriting of "Lead on, O King Eternal," with the opening line "Lead
on eternal Sovereign," that they call an "alteration" (#573). This "alteration"
contains changes in twenty-two of the twenty-four lines of the text. The two
lines that are not changed are switched between the second and third stanzas.

Shurtleff's text, Duck found that it needed more than simply adapting, and her text emerged. As such it was one of the first texts written in the twentieth century with the intent of avoiding gender-naming of God (Duck 1995c).

The text we consider here is a revision of Duck's original 1974 text, completed in 1989, prompted in part by the critique of Willis Elliot, a retired United Church of Christ pastor and teacher at New York Theological Seminary. His critique prompted the change from "cloud of Yahweh" (1:1) to "cloud of Presence," in concern for Jewish-Christian dialogue, because Jews do not pronounce *Yahweh* in reverence for this most holy name of God.[2] The second stanza remained unchanged, with changes appearing in the first and third stanzas, not in thought or essence, but in nuance and wording, as may be seen by the italics. *Slavery* was removed because of African-American objections to its use as metaphor; *rules* was changed to *dwells* in 3:7 to avoid the *ruling* metaphor. Other changes were poetic, to avoid inversions and an incorrect verb form.

(1989)	(1974)
Lead on, *O cloud of Presence*;	Lead on, *O cloud of Yahweh*,
the exodus is come;	The exodus is come;
in wilderness and desert	in wilderness and desert
our tribe shall make its home.	our tribe shall make its home.
Our *bondage* left behind us,	Our *slav'ry* left behind us,
new hopes within us grow.	*a vision in us grows,*
We seek the land of promise	We seek the land of promise
where milk and honey flow.	Where milk and honey flows.
Lead on, O God of freedom,	Lead on, O God of freedom,
and guide us on our way,	*Our guiding spirit be;*
and help us trust the promise	*Though those who start the journey*
through struggle and delay.	*The promise may not see,*
We pray our sons and daughters	We pray our sons and daughters
may journey to that land	*may live to see that land*
where justice *dwells* with mercy	Where justice *rules* with mercy
and love is law's demand.	And love is law's demand.

And the essence of Shurtleff's text is changed, to fit the section of this hymnal entitled, "Justice and Peace."

2. This change enables the hymn to reach both Christians and Jews, as evidenced by comments that appear in Chapter 14.

Introductory Comments on Duck's Text

In addition to the lively metaphors focused on the theme of journey, Duck keeps the text moving forward with a heavy reliance on one-syllable words (that appear four times as frequently as two-syllable words) and on nouns and verbs. God is addressed with imperatives, but imperatives that show our dependence on God's leading rather than our commanding God. God is called *cloud of Presence, fiery pillar, your* (2:6), *God of freedom.* In one place God is spoken of in third person, *we are still God's people* (3:7), that seems odd considering that 3:6 says *by your light we come,* referring to God's light. Duck says this is an error, which might be corrected in future publication, albeit a common mistake, because church and Israel are called the people of God (Duck 1995c). The speakers of the text are consistently *we/our/us,* with the only reference to "others" being *sons and daughters* in 3:5 who are still *ours,* so that there is a sense of including everyone present, past (*tribe* and the biblical story) and future.

Comparison of Shurtleff's and Duck's Texts

Duck maintained the form of Shurtleff's text: three stanzas of 7.6.7.6.D meter, using the iambic foot (u /), and with a rhyme scheme of ABCBDEFE. The first and third lines are understressed due to four stressed syllables and three unstressed syllables. This form helps Duck's version maintain its sense of movement in a more fluid manner than Shurtleff's text, that was at cross purposes, with its sense of *march,* yet an uneven number of stresses. Another imitation that Duck makes, and that is essential in maintaining the connection between the two texts, is the opening phrase, "Lead on," that in other settings might be a trochaic foot (/ u). The use by both Shurtleff and Duck of this phrase in what is clearly an iambic text (and an iambic tune) puts stress on the word *on,* and gives the sense of movement, that helps to establish the *journey* motif in each text.

Duck has also maintained the sense of time and the motif of *journey* found in Shurtleff. The first stanza of her text is the most clearly imitative of his text, maintaining the *come/home* rhyme of the first four lines, replacing *day of march* with *exodus,* and *fields of conquest* with *wilderness and desert.* Both speak of what has gone before, *days of preparation* and *bondage left behind us.* The second stanza of both texts deals with variety: Shurtleff with *sin's fierce war/sweet amen of peace,* Duck with *fears/rejoicing, joy/tears.* The third stanzas both look toward the future: Shurtleff to the *conquest* and Duck to the hope of *justice, mercy* and *love*. Here in Duck's text we see the emancipatory quality of *justice* and the free gifts of *mercy* and *love*, as opposed to the *conquest* and the bonds placed on the conquered of Shurtleff's text.

Scriptural Grounding of the Texts

The scriptural basis of Shurtleff's text was followed by Duck, who cites Numbers 9.15-23 as the basis of both texts (Duck 1992, #50 notes). Although this scripture does not appear in the three-year lectionary followed by many Protestant and Roman Catholic denominations, it is odd that *Scriptural and Seasonal Indexes of The United Methodist Hymnal* does not list "Lead on, O King Eternal" with any of the Exodus story scriptures (Exodus 13-40, Numbers and Deuteronomy), although other hymns about leading are cited—"Lead Me, Lord," "Dear Lord, Lead Me Day by Day," and "He Leadeth Me."[3] In three hymnals that include scripture references where "Lead on, O King Eternal" appears, it is also not associated with the Exodus story but rather with 2 Timothy 4.8, 1 Timothy 6.12, and Isaiah 48.17b (*The Singing Church, The Worshiping Church*, and *Baptist Hymnal*). The scriptural index and the reference to the Timothy scriptures show the move from understanding the *leading* of God, *march*, and *preparation* no longer in terms of the biblical story but rather as an allegory of the Christian life, and the struggle to travel to salvation. When this occurs, the original meaning and life of the biblical story can be lost.

The last two verses, 22-23, from Numbers 9 show the absolute reliance of the Israelites on the leading of God:

> Whether it was two days, or a month, or a longer time, that the cloud continued over the tabernacle, resting upon it, the Israelites would remain in camp and would not set out; but when it lifted they would set out. At the command of the LORD they would camp, and at the command of the LORD they would set out. They kept the charge of the LORD, at the command of the LORD by Moses.

This is crucial to the meaning of Duck's text, for it suggests: We make our home in *wilderness* and *desert* at the command of God, and we follow at God's command; it is in this following, in the *journey*, that we are God's people. In this scripture what matters is not so much the

---

3. Duck notes that her text was originally used frequently at women's ordinations as well as during the lectionary usage of the Exodus story (Duck 1995c).

goal of the promised land as the everyday acknowledgment that God is with us and we follow as God leads.

Shurtleff's text, although related to the Exodus scriptures for its journey motif and images of God leading the people, tents, and the cross as our light (reflecting the fiery pillar), takes its tone from 1 Timothy 6.12a, "Fight the good fight of the faith." The battle motifs are vivid: *the day of march, fields of conquest, days of preparation, made us strong, battle song, sin's fierce war, swords loud clashing, roll of stirring drums, follow without fears, cross lifted o'er us* (like a battle standard), *the crown awaits the conquest.* The *not* of *swords loud clashing* and the *nor* of *stirring drums*, the *whisper* of *the sweet amen of peace*, often lose their meaning as congregations triumphantly and vigorously sing this second stanza in the same manner as the first and third. Young's suggestion (in the quote at the beginning of this chapter) that this hymn fits the Social Gospel is confirmed by the ending lines of the second stanza: *with deeds of love and mercy, / the heavenly kingdom comes.* The Social Gospel was greatly concerned with bringing the kingdom of God to fruition on earth. To accomplish this they promoted strength of character and moral life, holding rallies around the country, particularly for men, and saw themselves in battle with sin and the evils of society. The first person plural fits the sense of community of the Social Gospel movement too, as opposed to a strictly individual "I-me" salvation, often found in other hymns of this period.

One of the criticisms of both the Social Gospel movement and liberation theology has been that they consider humanity capable of accomplishing much of the work of bringing God's vision to reality on earth. Duck is concerned for the vision of the Social Gospel and liberation theologies, and she ends her text with that vision: *that land / where justice dwells with mercy / and love is law's demand.* Yet she recognizes the actual predicament of humanity with its varying emotions and tendency to wander. One way she does this is to take Shurtleff's line, *we follow, not with fears* (3:2) and modify it, *we follow yet with fears* (2:2). The point is not that we are filled with superhuman courage and thus can follow easily, but that following God may mean acknowledging our fears, for we are not superhuman or even in charge, God is. Central to Duck's text is that God is leading and we are following in the midst of our fears, joys, and sorrows. Both texts continue with *gladness* (Shurtleff 3:3) and *rejoicing* (Duck 2:3), but Duck stays with the reality of human ups and downs as she continues, *though joy be born of tears* (2:4).

Another way Duck develops the journey motif is to divide each stanza into more than one sentence. Shurtleff's text marches through eight lines for each sentence, with phrases but no real stopping places. Duck's text contains two four-line sentences in the first and third stanzas, and three sentences in the second stanza, four-line, three-line, and one-line. Thus she models for us the stopping and starting of the Israelites as the cloud of Presence stopped and started.

Shurtleff's text builds to a climax, moving from acknowledging that *the day* to *march has come* (suggesting a previous time of preparation) through consideration of how the kingdom comes (contrasting in tone with the other two stanzas) to the awaiting future, certain, and final victory—*the crown awaits the conquest*. Duck's text tells of the journey in its opening two stanzas and gives validation to the journey of life at the close of the second stanza. The third stanza opens with the clearest definition of God in this text, *O God of freedom*. This is an important contrast to Shurtleff's text with his reiterations of *O King eternal* (four times) and ending with *O God of might*. Duck has given us images for God—*cloud of Presence* and *fiery pillar*—but this singular use of God in the address that begins the third stanza gives the phrase *God of freedom* added weight. The text has already shown God's presence with us, now as we *struggle* toward the *promise* of *justice, mercy,* and *love*, the God who has freed us goes with us. Like the Hebrew people in the Exodus story, in Duck's text we too are freed from bondage and set on our way toward a better land.

STANZAS

Stanza One

"Lead on, O Cloud of Presence" draws its imagery directly from the biblical story. The cloud and fire appear as early as Exodus 13.21, described as *a pillar of cloud* and *a pillar of fire,* which enable the Hebrew children to travel *by day and by night.* The annotation to this scripture says that "cloud and fire have become traditional ways of expressing God's presence and guidance" (*Bible*). The *cloud* of God's presence is an important part of the Exodus story, as Moses speaks to God in the *cloud* (Exod. 34.5, Num. 11.25a) and the *cloud* leads the people through the wilderness (Num. 9.15-23). A *cloud* comes and overshadows Jesus, Moses, Elijah, and the disciples at the transfiguration, and God speaks to them from the *cloud* (Luke 9.34-35). Jesus tells his disciples that at the end of the age the Son of Man will come in a *cloud* (Luke 21.27). The letter to the Hebrews describes the great *cloud* of witnesses (12.1), the people of faith who have gone before and are now in God's presence continually.

The *cloud* is also a hidden feminine image, as it is the description of the *Shekinah*. *Shekinah* comes from the Hebrew word for *dwelling* and was used to describe God's dwelling among humanity (Cross and Livingstone, *s.v., Shekinah*). Shekinah is an important concept in Jewish mysticism, as she represents the true soul of God, the glory of God, associated with the cloud in the sanctuary of the Temple as well as in the Exodus. After the first century B.C.E., Shekinah took the place of Sophia and Wisdom in Jewish mysticism, and thus its feminine character was reinforced (Newman 1994).

The *Exodus* (1:2) of the Hebrew people from their bondage in slavery through the Red Sea to the Promised Land is one of the basic stories of Judaism and thus Christianity. For liberation theology the Exodus was claimed as a primary event, one that clearly showed that God was on the side of the oppressed, working to improve their social conditions first and foremost. African-Americans have equally claimed the Exodus, seen in Martin Luther King Jr.'s famous "Mountain-top" sermon, with its lines "I've been to the mountain-top! I've seen the promised land!" (3 April 1968).[4] It is appropriate that as women struggled for ordination, inclusive language and theology, they also claimed the Exodus story, thus the frequent use of Duck's text at women's ordinations.

During his time in the flesh, Jesus embodied the journeying nature of the Exodus event as he said, "Foxes have holes, and birds of the air have nests; but the Son of Man has nowhere to lay his head" (Luke 9.58), through his own travels around Galilee and Samaria accompanied by men and women (Luke 8.1-3), and in his sending out of his followers (Luke 10.1-20). The early church also linked Jesus' resurrection and the Exodus, as may be seen in the hymns of John of Damascus (c.675-c.749), "Come, Ye Faithful, Raise the Strain" and "The Day of Resurrection!"

The phrase *milk and honey* (1:8) not only refers to the abundance of the promised land (promised first to Moses when God spoke in the burning bush, Exod. 3.8) but in more recent times (after the writing of Duck's text) has been reclaimed by feminists as a sign of the fullness of

---

4. Because Duck lived in Memphis during the time of King's leadership and assassination there, this sermon had a particular influence on her (Duck 1995c).

God's grace. In one of the earliest accounts of the Eucharist, Hippolytus describes the three cups offered to the newly baptized: water as a sign of inner washing, wine as a sign of the new covenant, and *milk mixed with honey* offered "to the children of God for the healing of the bitterness of the human heart with the sweetness of His word" (Elkins 1994, 59; Thompson 1961, 22). At the Re-Imagining Conference in Minneapolis in 1993 a ritual using milk and honey was used that became extremely controversial, because it was condemned as replacing Eucharist with a pagan ritual. This is a sign of how we have forgotten and lost our history, lost the wonderful imagery of Hippolytus's cup of milk mixed with honey. Thus Duck's text can provide an anamnesis, a remembering of both the *milk and honey* of the land of promise and the promise of God's healing and sweetness given at Eucharist with *milk and honey*.

The metaphors that use words specific to the context of Christian worship—*cloud of Presence, exodus, milk and honey*—along with *tribe* all occur within the first stanza of the text. *Tribe* is an important word for describing the social organization of Judaism (the twelve tribes of Israel descended from Jacob, the grandson of Abraham, Genesis 29-30). In attempting to mediate worship in our time, a recent book on worship used *tribe* to enable its discussion (*Trouble at the Table: Gathering the Tribes for Worship*). In "Lead on, O Cloud of Presence" *tribe* would probably mean the specific group constituted for worship, with the sense that the entire church, denomination, and Christendom are the tribes to that this tribe also belongs.

Journey metaphors are prominent throughout this text, set in the midst of verbs suggesting movement: *lead* and *come* (each three times), *left, grow, seek, follow, guide, journey*. Making our home *in wilderness and desert* (1:3-4) is reminiscent of the pioneers in this country as well as other migrants. Leaving *bondage* behind (1:5) suggests the emancipation of slaves or prisoners, who then travel to new places physically as well as emotionally.

Stanza Two

We have seen that the *pillar of cloud* and *pillar of fire* enabled the journey of the Hebrew children to travel and signified God's presence and guidance. The *fire* (Num. 9.15-23) of God's presence is seen again when Elijah calls down *fire* from heaven as a sign of God's presence against the 450 prophets of Baal (1 Kings 18.24). On the day of Pentecost, the Spirit of God descends as tongues of *fire*, resting on the heads of the gathered congregation of Jesus' followers (Acts 2.3).

We have already pointed out the embodiment of human experience in this stanza. Following God does not always make our fears disappear, still we follow with faith and hope. Two of the metaphors in this stanza attribute living qualities to inanimate concepts: *hopes grow within us* and *joy is born of tears. We shall come rejoicing* echoes the refrain of the gospel song, "Bringing in the sheaves," based on Psalm 126.5-6:

> May those who sow in *tears*,
>   reap with shouts of *joy*.
> Those who go out weeping,
>   bearing the seed for sowing,
> shall come home with shouts of *joy*,
>   carrying their sheaves.

The mixture of *rejoicing, joy,* and *tears* in intense experiences is very human, and reflects the prayer of the Psalmist, with its mixture of emotions.

In the sixth line of this stanza the image of the pillar of fire appears again, *by your light we come*, giving a picture of torches or flashlights lighting the way for travel in the dark or at night. With God's light we are not lost, though we may still *wander* (cf. "prone to *wander*, Lord, I feel it" in the hymn, "Come, Thou Fount of Every Blessing" by Robert Robinson, 1758). The penultimate line of this stanza claims our heritage as God's people even in the midst of life. It echoes 1 Peter 1.9, that also carries the image of light: "But you are a chosen race, a royal priesthood, a holy nation, *God's own people*, in order that you may proclaim the mighty acts of him who called you out of darkness into his marvelous *light*."

The journey is our home was briefly mentioned above in discussing the progression of the text. Duck says,

> It was inspired by a quotation from Joseph Pintauro, "Nowadays to be on your way is to be home" (1968, 11). This reflects the sense that life is in the process not in achievement or a settled, unchanging life particularly as one is faithful to the unpredictable leading of God's Spirit (Duck 1995c).

This phrase and the following stanza also reflects the eschatology of feminist theologian Rosemary Radford Ruether, as human life is constantly in the process of moving, ideally moving toward justice, peace, and reconciliation (1983, 235-258, esp. 258).

The journey is our home is a fresh metaphor because the common understanding is that the journey is *to* home, home is the goal of travels at Thanksgiving and Christmas, our usually joyful destination after school or work. The understanding of the Hebrew people about the Exodus was equally freedom from Pharaoh and the promise of a *home* in an abundant land. Historically for forty years, their *home* was in their wandering. Through the prophet Zephaniah God promised *home* to the Israelites: "At that time I will bring you *home*, at the time when I gather you" (3.20a). Jesus promised his followers that they had a *home* with God (John 14.2-3). Slaves in this country sang "Steal away *home* . . . My *home* is over Jordan." Yet Duck changes our thinking with five words . . . *the journey is our home*. Our *home* is where we are, where God is, and God is right here, right now, with us on this *journey* of life. If we claim the promise and tradition of Numbers 9.15-23 and recognize that it is God who leads us, if we submit ourselves to go and come as God wills, then we are at *home*. The profoundness of this truth caused Nelle Morton to claim this phrase as the title of her book, *The Journey Is Home* (1985, xvii).

Stanza Three

Whereas the first two stanzas of this text tell the story of the Exodus and our own journey, the third stanza is more clearly one of prayer, with imperative verbs asking the *God of freedom* to *lead, guide,* and *help* us. Then we literally pray that our children *may journey to that land* where *justice dwells with mercy* and *love* is the *law*. This pattern is similar to the three-step spiritual meditation discussed by Doran and Troeger: *memory* (recalling the biblical story), *understanding* (the contemporary meaning of the story), and *will* (a prayer to live God's will in accordance with the story) (1986, vi). In Duck's text, memory and understanding are combined in the opening two stanzas, as we are placed into the biblical story in the first stanza with the introduction of *our* in the third line. With its imperative verbs and address of God, the third stanza is clearly "a prayer to live God's will."

This stanza particularly draws on the Psalms for its inspiration. *Lead* and *guide* in the opening two lines echo Ps. 31.3b, "for your name's sake *lead* me and *guide* me." Psalm 119 speaks of the *promises* of God fifteen times, promises made to those who treasure God's word and laws, promises of salvation. *God's mercy* and *justice* are praised and prayed for in Ps. 119.156: "Great is your *mercy*, O LORD; give me life according to your *justice*."

Through struggle and delay (3:4) refers to the struggle for liberation that forms the basis of liberation theology. This theology is concerned with bringing God's vision (sometimes called *the project of God*) to life on earth, with justice for all. Although liberation theology is hopeful about the fulfillment of the project of God, it is also realistic about the nature of human sin and limitations and acknowledges the struggle and delay involved. This fact of struggle and delay points in part to the next generation, *our sons and daughters.* The continuation of the journey by future generations is anticipated in 3:5, echoing the biblical story whose original generation did not all live to see the promised land. It also presents a view of history that takes the long perspective, rather than the short, in effecting change.

The final two lines echo the last two lines of the first stanza as they describe the land of promise. Here, however, the qualities of the promised land are embodied, attributing living qualities to inanimate concepts: Justice *dwells* with mercy and love is the *demand* of law. This description of the promised land is in line with the vision of liberation theology and with the Hebrew prophets, where God's justice is tempered with mercy and humanity is called "to do justice, and to love mercy, and to walk humbly with thy God" (Mic. 6.8, KJV). These lines also affirm the law, the Great Commandment, to love God and neighbor given by Jesus (Mark 12.28-31). Likewise, Paul reminds us, "for the one who loves another has fulfilled the law" (Rom. 13.8b).

OTHER ASPECTS OF EMANCIPATORY LANGUAGE

We have seen how this text presents the realities of human life, with its *tears, fears, rejoicing,* and *wandering.* In this text, those on the margins of society leave their bondage behind and find new hopes. *Sons and daughters* are both mentioned. Thus the language about humanity is inclusive and truthful.

God is presented with three images—*cloud, fire,* and *freedom*—a diversity in unity. Imaginative construction has been used, creatively drawing upon scripture, Shurtleff's text, and current revelation to produce a fresh text that re-members the Exodus story, making it alive for us. The promises of God are recounted and offered afresh to those who would make the journey their home.

Chapter 12
Of Women, and of Women's Hopes We Sing
A Multidimensional Reading

Of women, and of women's hopes we sing:
of sharing in creation's nurturing,
of bearing and of birthing new belief,
of passion for the promises of life.

We praise the God whose image is our own,
the mystery within our flesh and bone,
the womanspirit moving through all time
in prophecy, Magnificat and dream.

We labor for the commonwealth of God,
and equal as disciples, walk the road,
in work and status, asking what is just,
for sisters of the family of Christ.

Forgiving what is past, we seek the new:
a finer justice, and a peace more true,
the promise of empowering for our day
when men and women roll the stone away.

Shirley Erena Murray, written in 1988
© 1992 Hope Publishing Co., Carol Stream, IL 60188
All rights reserved. Used by permission

Murray, *In Every Corner Sing* 1992, #56
I Will Pour out My Spirit 1992, pp. 54-55
One Hundred Hymns of Hope 1992, #45
New Songs of Rejoicing 1994, #130
Chalice Hymnal 1995, #686

. . . The reason is that the female is as it were a deformed male. . . . The male is by nature superior, and the female inferior
Aristotle, quoted in Ruether, *Womanguides*

You [woman] are the Devil's gateway; you are the unsealer of that tree; you are the first foresaker of the divine; you are the one who persuaded him whom the Devil was not brave enough to approach; you so lightly crushed the image of God, the man Adam; because of your punishment, that is, death, even the Son of God had to die.
Tertullian, quoted in Clark, *Women in the Early Church*

Rise up, O men of God!
The kingdom tarries long.
Bring in the day of brotherhood
and end the night of wrong.   William P. Merrill, *UMH* #576

The critical principle of feminist theology is the promotion of the full humanity of women.
Rosemary Ruether, *Sexism and God-Talk*

INTRODUCTION

Background

Shirley Erena Murray's hymn, "Of Women, and of Women's Hopes We Sing," is an epideictic text, one that celebrates women and their empowerment. It is an attempt to promote the full humanity of women, to reverse the words of Aristotle and Tertullian, and to balance hymns like that of Merrill that have dominated hymnals for two hundred years. Where Merrill excluded women, Murray has intentionally included women (J. Wallace 1995).

A former teacher of languages, Murray has been writing hymns since 1979, working with themes of ecumenicity, human rights, justice, peace, the integrity of creation, and women (Murray 1992, "Notes on the Hymns"). "I write out of controlled desperation with the Church for its inability to deal seriously with new theological insight. I write with an awareness of what we are not yet saying to one another" (Murray 1996c, 16).

Alleluia Aotearoa,[40] published in 1993 by the New Zealand Hymnbook Trust, contains sixty-one of Murray's texts (Clarkson 1994, 45). In the United States, the *Presbyterian Hymnal* contains five of her texts, *Chalice Hymnal*, ten, and *The New Century Hymnal*, eleven. The Canadian *Voices United* includes twelve of her texts. Murray's texts have been published in two collections, *In Every Corner Sing* (1992) and *Every Day in Your Spirit* (1996). This second collection contains two texts focused on women: "Woman's Song," based on Mark 14.3-9, and "Roll the Stone Away" based on the Easter story and themes similar to "Of Women, and of Women's Hopes We Sing."

Murray wrote "Of Women, and of Women's Hopes We Sing" for the Ecumenical Decade of the Churches in Solidarity with Women, that was launched on Easter 1988, and sponsored by the World Council of Churches (Murray 1992, "Notes on the Hymns"). The text was first sung, to the tune CHILTON FOLIAT, on Easter 1988 in Murray's church, St. Andrew's on the Terrace, Presbyterian, in the heart of Wellington, the capital of New Zealand. Subsequent publication in a resource for the Decade enabled its use in 1993 at the National Service of Celebration for the centenary of women's suffrage in New Zealand, and "it was at this point that it became better known and sung" (Murray 1995).[41]

The purpose and aims of the Ecumenical Decade are:

1. Empowering women to challenge oppressive structures in the global community, their country and their Church.
2. Affirming—through shared leadership and decision-making, theology and spirituality—the decisive contributions of women in churches and communities.
3. Giving visibility to women's perspectives and actions in the work and struggle for justice, peace and the integrity of creation.
4. Enabling the churches to free themselves from racism, sexism and classism; from teachings and practices that discriminate against women.

---

1. Aeotearoa, meaning "long white cloud," is the Maori name for the land also called New Zealand.

2. Murray notes, however, that at this service the text was paired with the tune ELLERS, which did not fit the stresses of the text. (Hymnwriters have no control over the tunes matched with their texts after initial publication.)

5. Encouraging the churches to take actions in solidarity with women.
    (The World Council of Churches 1992, back cover)

Following these aims, "Of Women, and of Women's Hopes We Sing" not only makes women visible but, as we shall see, attempts to empower and affirm women while inviting men to act in solidarity with women.

Biblical Background of the Text

Murray says in her notes on the text that the reference in the last line is to the theme of the Decade, "Who will roll the stone away?" This is the question Mary Magdalene, Mary the mother of James, and Salome asked each other on their way to embalm Jesus on the first day of the week as he lay in the tomb after his crucifixion (Mark 16:3). When they arrived the stone had already been rolled away and Jesus had been resurrected from the dead. The Easter message, which marked the beginning of the Decade, included these words:

> At this Easter season the churches set out on a journey of faith in solidarity with women. We will encounter many stones—obstacles that will have to be rolled out of the way so that we may become a new and living community. We today ask each other: "Who will roll the stone away?"
>
> There are practices and teachings in the churches that are obstacles to women's creative theological, spiritual and decision-making contribution in church and society. There are structures and patterns of leadership and ministry that block partnership between women and men. We ask ourselves: "Who will roll the stone away?" (Oduyoye 1990, 13)

It may be argued by biblical scholars that Murray's answer to the question of the Decade's theme is not true to the biblical text. In three of the gospels the stone is already rolled away or removed (Mark 16.4, Luke 24.1, and John 20.1) and in the fourth gospel there is an earthquake and an angel comes to roll the stone away (Matt. 28.2). It is not the task of this book to argue the theme of the Decade and its implied answer, which was picked up by Murray for this text. However, it is important to acknowledge that *when men and women roll the stone away* takes poetic license with the biblical story and suggests in part a human solution. Surely Murray and I would be in agreement that apart from God any effort of human cooperation is doomed to failure. Therefore to suggest that men and women can effect this task of emancipating ourselves from the tombs of inequality and degradation, is to say that God has initiated the emancipation (and has already in fact rolled some stones away), and now it is up to human beings to join God's cause.[42]

This line of thought resonates with the biblical understanding that while Jesus' resurrection happened through "divine intervention," all Christians participate in death and resurrection as well (cf. Rom. 6 and 2 Cor. 4.13-18). One might question whether biblical references can be other than quoted in hymns, yet there is some precedent set by the African-American spiritual, "There is a balm in Gilead" that answers the question of Jer. 8.22, "Is there no balm in Gilead?" Similarly, Murray has taken the question "Who will roll the stone away?" and posed a hymnic answer.

Emancipatory Focus

This text was chosen, in part, because it fits Procter-Smith's second focus of emancipatory language: "the use of language to create collective identity for a group that has lacked such an identity and may be divided against itself" (Procter-Smith 1990, 66).[43] The collective identification of women through the text comes in part by naming in each stanza—*women/women's, womanspirit, sisters, women.* This naming is very important in making women visible. The text also fits with Karlyn Kohrs Campbell's description of feminine style: It invites audience participation (by the use of *we* and *our*, and by the very nature of hymn singing); it addresses the congregation as peers; it identifies with the audience's experience; its goal is empowerment, aided by the use of the first person plural (*we* sing, *we* praise, *we* labor, *we* seek) (Campbell 1989a, 13). The sequence of the text also aids in creating collective identity as the first stanza gathers women's hopes together, the second stanza places women in God's image, the third stanza reaches out for

---

3. A later text by Murray builds on this theme, "praise the power that made the stone roll away," the refrain of "Christ is alive, and the universe must celebrate" (*Alleluia Aotearoa!* #15).

4. An interesting coincidence is that a tune was composed for Murray's text by composer Jane Marshall, who named the tune PROCTER after Marjorie Procter-Smith, a colleague of hers at Southern Methodist University in Dallas (*One Hundred Hymns of Hope* 1992, "Notes on the Hymns" #45). In *Chalice Hymnal* this text is paired with a more immediately accessible tune, SURSUM CORDA, used in research for this book, to enable focus on the text rather than the tune.

women's concerns in society, and the fourth stanza looks forward to a better future for women.

A word might be said here regarding the identification of the congregation with the text: The hymn was premiered in a worship service that included both men and women, and it has been included in collections that are aimed at the general market, not solely a women's market. When the hymn premiered in the United States at Perkins School of Theology at Southern Methodist University it was sung with a tune by a beloved campus professor for a Women's Week worship service and was well received (Procter-Smith, 1995). The praxis groups in that it was tested for this study included both genders. In Chapter 14 we look in detail at the degree to that people identified with the text. Suffice it to say here that the singer is only being asked to sing *of women* (about women) and *of women's hopes*, not to become a woman in order to sing the text. In the first stanza, both genders are called (in God's plan) to nurture creation, and both genders can share in *passion for the promises of life*. In the third stanza *we labor* and *walk equal as disciples*, both of that include men. The final line of the text breaks open the meaning of gender cooperation.

Shape of the Text

Sequence. The theme of the Ecumenical Decade gives weight to the last line of Murray's text, as does the debut of the hymn on Easter. One might consider the text as a climactic arrangement (Leech and Short 1981, 222-225, 236), where the final line breaks open the entire text, *as men and women roll the stone away*. The word *men* stands out both by its lone appearance at the end of the text and by its prominence as the first of the two terms. The metaphor suggests that together women and men, led by God, will effect the changes envisioned in the text: *new belief, the commonwealth of God*, justice *in work and status, a finer justice, a peace more true, the promise of empowering*.

Yet the use of the word *women* twice in the first line of the text suggests a psychological arrangement, where what is said first is most important (Leech and Short 1981, 231-233).The rest of the text might be seen as describing what *women's hopes* are and why we are singing about *women* and *women's hopes*. Given the Christian tradition that drew heavily on Aristotle and theologians like Tertullian, to sing *of women* and *women's hopes* is startling, making the first line the most important.

The experience of singing this text with several groups (see Chapter 14) suggests that most persons hear the first line as most important and then hear the final line as a balance to the first line. Each of these experiences has been with a mixed-gender grouping. Perhaps in a women-only setting the final line would have less weight than the first, providing more of a satisfying metaphoric closing than a counterweight to the strength of the opening line.

Meter and Rhyme. The text is set in iambic pentameter (10.10. 10.10), a meter often used in the nineteenth century. It can be a troublesome meter for hymns as "the lines are long, the thought process becomes too involved, and the mind has wandered long before it arrives at the end of a stanza" (Lovelace 1982, 59). The couplet rhyme scheme, AABB, is vital to keep one from losing the sense of rhyme. The couplet rhymes are most true in the fourth stanza of this text, as each of the other stanzas contain near rhyme: *belief/life* (stanza 1), *time/dream* (stanza 2), *God/road* and *just/Christ* (stanza 3).

A study of the words and their length in this text bears out Lovelace's concerns. Of the one hundred and fourteen words in the text, forty-three of the one-syllable words are relatively unimportant, primarily prepositions and conjunctions. The effect of using so many prepositions appears immediately in the first stanza with the use of the word *of* six times in four lines, producing a more formal rather than active stanza. This predominance of relatively unimportant words causes the lines of poetry to be understressed, that means that in singing (or reading) the text "bumps" against the melody or rhythmic pattern.

Each sentence of the text takes an entire stanza, or forty syllables. Murray's use of two-, three-, and four-syllable words has integrity in these long lines and sentences. Yet the length of line and sentence is particularly problematic in the middle lines of stanza three. Here the two phrases in each line are reversed for rhyme rather than sense:

| and equal as disciples, walk the road, | *and walk the road equal as disciples,* |
| in work and status, asking what is just, | *asking what is just in work and status* |

In another sense, these shorter phrases, along with two action verbs in each of stanzas three and four (as opposed to one active verb each in stanzas one and two), give these stanzas a sense of motion appropriate to their subjects: working and actively seeking a better way.

Register. Given the problems with the meter of the text, Murray has created a hymn that is relatively free of the code words that denote

Christian hymnody. The first stanza might be sung by women (and men) in any situation of solidarity with women, sacred or secular. In the entire text the word *God* appears only twice and *Christ* only once, although the noun phrases in stanza two also point to the Divine. The use of *we* four times and *our* three times suggest that the focus of the text is human solidarity in the light of God. The second stanza incorporates the most abstract thoughts and most "religious" concepts. Interestingly, it fits the meter most naturally of the four stanzas. The third stanza contains three phrases of religious metaphors, whereas the fourth is straightforward until the final line and vital metaphor.

STANZAS

Stanza One

One of the controversial elements about this hymn text centers on this issue of how women are empowered in it. Obviously naming and making women visible (*Of women, and of women's hopes we sing*) is one way that women can be empowered. Another way of empowering women that has been used in a variety of circumstances is that of describing some of the actions of women. Words to this effect appear in the first stanza of Murray's text: *nurturing, bearing, birthing*. Yet many women contend that limiting female images to maternal ones is to exclude the many women who do not and cannot have children. One of the concerns of feminist theology is that of being as inclusive as possible, particularly in representing the varieties of women's experiences. Is there room for a multiplicity of images? *Yes*, affirms the concept of emancipatory language—a multiplicity of images is essential.

Murray's text does include a multiplicity of images: Women's roles in the text are not limited to nurturing and birthing, as we *labor, walk, work*, and *seek justice* in the third stanza, and in the fourth move toward exploring *finer justice* and *truer peace*. In addition, the suggestion of maternal images can stretch to include men, as Gail Ramshaw has said,

> A mother is undeniably a female image. However, to nurture, to guide, to feed, to embrace, to comfort, to midwife: these are not in any way explicitly gender-specific activities. Women do them, men do them, and some men do them better than some women (1995, 126).

The final line of the text also reflects back to this opening stanza, and subsequent singing may contain the understanding that all Christians are called upon to share in the nurturing of creation, to bring new belief to birth, to have a passion for the promises that God has made for life. Notice the holistic nature of the concerns of this first stanza: for the whole creation (ecological), for growth of new belief or understanding (mental), and passion for the promises of life (emotional). That we sing not only of *women's hopes* (abstract) but also of *women* themselves gives a sense of embodiment to the text, along with its other concerns.

The formal nature of this first stanza with its reliance on prepositions was mentioned above. One element that aids in its flow is the use of repetition of sounds: the antanaclasis of *of women/of women's hopes*, the alliteration of *bearing/birthing/belief* and *passion/promises*, the repeated *r*-sound in each multisyllabic word in the second line, *sharing/creation's/nurturing*, and the repetition of *-ing* in *sing/sharing/nurturing/bearing/birthing*. The use of anaphora, beginning each line with *of*, also guides the flow of this opening stanza.

Stanza Two

For hymns, code words are important, because they are the words that define the faith and draw from scripture and tradition. The second stanza of this text is full of words and metaphors that define and express Christian faith in new ways rooted in the tradition. *God whose image is our own* refers to the creation story in Genesis 1.26: "Then God said, 'Let us make humankind in our *image*, according to our likeness.'" Human beings are made in the *image of God*, a claim that has been acceptable for males, but with the use of Aristotelian concepts and theologians' interpretations of the story of Eve, the apple, and the Fall, women have not fully realized that they also carry God's image. It is important when reading/singing this phrase of the hymn to translate it as *God whose image we bear* rather than the easily implied reverse, *God who bears our image*.[5] Scripture and tradition are clear that it is not God who is made in our image—that would be idolatry. But, made in the image of God, we are "a little lower than God, and crowned with glory and honor" (Ps. 8.5). Women have not always taken or been allowed to take these empowering thoughts to heart and life.

The mystery within our flesh and bone might be considered outside a religious context as the mystery of human life—the wonder of life, the mystery of growth, individuality, and sexuality. Yet in a Christian context it has several additional meanings. One comes from the crea-

---

5. Murray says it even more clearly in the title line of another of her hymns, "O God, we bear the imprint of your face" (*In Every Corner Sing* #54).

tion story in the second chapter of Genesis when Adam greets Eve with the words, "This at last is bone of my bones and flesh of my flesh; this one shall be called Woman." (Gen. 2.23). In the Hebrew scriptures *flesh and bone* is used to refer to kinship, both physical and spiritual (cf. Gen. 29.14, 2 Sam. 5.1, 1 Chron. 11.1).

Another meaning of *the mystery within our flesh and bone* comes from its placement as the second of three line-long phrases in this stanza. This second stanza is made up of three line-long phrases naming whom we are praising; each has a noun followed by an adjectival phrase. The number *three* is important in Christianity as it represents our understanding of the unity of God in three "persons," known as the Trinity: the Creator, Jesus Christ-Savior, and Holy Spirit-Comforter. Imposing a trinitarian pattern on the second stanza of Murray's text reveals that this second line, *the mystery within our flesh and bone*, is related to the Incarnation, when God took on flesh and bone in the person of Jesus of Nazareth. Therefore in this second line of this stanza we praise the God who comes in flesh and bone, a God whose image women bear in their very bodies, a God who comes to live among us, a God who is in relationship with us. For women to claim themselves and their bodies as such is to claim holiness, in direct contrast to Tertullian's "You are the Devil's gateway."

The womanspirit moving through all time completes the Trinity, with the Holy Spirit infusing all time with her presence. *Womanspirit* is not a traditional word in Christianity, but it has precedence in the Hebrew word *ruach*, which means *spirit* and carries both grammatical feminine gender and female imagery of the mother bird brooding to bring forth life, associated with the Spirit of God in creation (Gen. 1.2) and at the conception and baptism of Jesus (Luke 1.35, 3.22) (Johnson 1993, 50). Thus, the *womanspirit* links together the God of creation and the incarnational Jesus Christ. One of the early anthologies of feminist theological readings was entitled *Womanspirit Rising*, by Carol Christ and Judith Plaskow. Other feminist theologians and liturgical scholars have also linked *woman* with different words in their attempts to redefine terms, such as *Womanguides* (Ruether 1985, title) and Miriam Therese Winter's titles: *WomanPrayer/WomanSong, WomanWisdom, WomanWord.*

As the *womanspirit* moves through time it is revealed, says our text through the use of enjambment, which adds emphasis, in *prophecy, Magnificat, and dream. Prophecy,* according to the dictionary, is the function or vocation of a prophet, specifically the inspired declaration of divine will and purpose (*Webster's*). The scriptures are full of the stories of prophets—Moses, Elijah, Elisha, Isaiah, Jeremiah—to name but a few. Jesus himself was called a prophet, as when he entered Jerusalem on the day we now call Palm Sunday (Matt. 21.10). Women are also named as prophets in scripture—Miriam, Deborah, Huldah, and Anna. According to the prophet Joel, quoted by Peter on the day of Pentecost when the Holy Spirit descended on the church, God says, "I will pour out my spirit on all flesh; your sons and your daughters shall prophesy, your old men shall dream dreams, and your young men shall see visions" (Joel 2.28; Acts 2.17). Throughout history women have appealed to these two scriptures to claim authority to speak the word of God.

The *Magnificat* is the song sung by Mary, the mother of Jesus, when she finds out that she is to bear a child, the son of God. Found in the book of Luke (1.46-55), it is based on the song of Hannah (1 Sam. 2.1-11) and praises the God who turns the world upside down, exalting the lowly and humbling the proud. The use of *Magnificat* reflects us back to the incarnational *mystery within our flesh and bone*, as Mary celebrates God who comes among us.

Dream, the last word in stanza two, in the scriptural tradition is another way God reveals herself to humankind. One of the best-known dreams from the biblical tradition is when Jacob dreams of a ladder reaching to heaven with the angels of God ascending and descending on it (Gen. 28.12-13). Joseph, the son of Jacob and Rachel, becomes famous in Egypt for his interpretation of dreams (Gen. 37 and 40). His namesake in the book of Matthew has three dreams, telling him to take Mary as his wife, then with the infant Jesus to go to Egypt and finally to return to Israel (Matt. 1 and 2). *Dreams* and visions appear throughout the scriptures, and the Joel/Acts scripture reminds us that dreams, like *prophecy*, are gifts of the *spirit*, in this case, the *womanspirit*.

Stanza Three

The code words in stanza three relate to the social nature of humanity. First is the phrase *commonwealth of God.* The gospel of Mark begins Jesus' ministry with the words "Jesus came to Galilee, proclaiming the good news of God, and saying, 'The time is fulfilled, and the kingdom of God has come near; repent, and believe in the good news'" (Mark 1.14-15). The annotation says that this summarizes Jesus' message; the whole gospel of Mark is an expansion of this verse (*Bible*). The *kingdom* of God is an important concept in Christianity, representing the rule of God and the fulfillment of God's promises and hopes for creation.

In moving away from *king* as gendered language for God, theologians have suggested phrases such as *the reign of God, the vision of God, the project of God* or *the commonwealth of God*. To many in the United States *commonwealth* connotes the remoteness of the British *Commonwealth*, that contained countries around the globe in a common allegiance to the British crown.[45] Yet *commonwealth* has the additional meaning of a government where supreme authority is rested in the people, with a stress on the common good (*Webster's*). The *common good* is an important concept for theologies that grow out of the Social Gospel and liberation theology movements.[46] These theologies point to the scripture imperatives to give others more than is asked (Matt. 5.40-42) and the model of the church in Acts that shared all that it had in common (Acts 2.44-47).[47] For its simple meaning of *sharing the common wealth*, this phrase (*commonwealth of God*) works well here, as the stanza follows with *equal as disciples* and *asking what is just in work and status*. If nothing else, it is a plea for the justice of equal pay for equal work, a sharing of the common wealth.

Disciples are followers of a teacher who spread their teachings; originally a more general word, it has come to be used almost exclusively in religious contexts. The gospels refer to both the inner circle of Jesus' twelve male disciples and to the wider circle of disciples, which included other men and women (Luke 8.1-3 and 10.1, 17). *The family of Christ* draws on kinship terms—*sisters* and *family*—and takes its biblical reference from the words of Jesus: "whoever does the will of my Father in heaven is my brother and sister and mother" (Matt. 12.50, cf. Mark 3.35, Lk. 8.21). Notice how this third stanza of Murray's text draws on several groupings from human society: *commonwealth*—gov-

---

6. Although for Murray, living in New Zealand, "'Commonwealth of God' is certainly a personal choice, maybe, because my country is still part of a Commonwealth . . . and it feels a richer word now than 'kingdom,' that is strongly hierarchical, and does not contain the idea of 'shared good' as in the old English 'common weal'" (Murray 1995).

7. Concerned that "common good" did not adequately express their intentions, Latin American liberation theologians have relied more on the concept of "the logic of the majority," the majority reflecting the majority poor.

8. "All who believed were together and had all things in common; they would sell their possessions and goods and distribute the proceeds to all, as any had need. Day by day, as they spent much time together in the temple, they broke bread at home and ate their food with glad and generous hearts, praising God and having the goodwill of all the people. And day by day the Lord added to their number those who were being saved." (Acts 2.44-47)

ernment, *disciples*—educational and spiritual, *work*—vocational, *status*—social (class), and *sisters/family*—kinship.

Stanza Four

The fourth stanza of this text takes the social needs presented in the third stanza and frames them again as God's commonwealth: *the new, a finer justice, a peace more true.* This is more than just equal pay for equal work—it is something human beings cannot even envision without God's help.

Forgiving what is past is an important phrase in keeping with the tone of this text. Murray is not suggesting in this text that women trade places with men, that women become the power brokers, or that women seek revenge for all that has gone before. Following the model Jesus gave us of forgiving—in the Lord's Prayer, in the suggestion to Peter to forgive seventy-seven times (Matt. 18.21-22), and from the cross himself forgiving his killers (Luke 23.34)—we forgive the past and look forward.

The comparative *finer* and *more true* point to *the new, the promise of empowering for our day.* The *empowering* will be here and now, *for our day,* and will happen simultaneously *when* and as *men and women roll the stone away.* (The empowerment is both to be able to move the stone and the empowerment of being freed from the tomb. We are both inside and outside the tomb.) *The stone* refers biblically to the stone placed at the opening to the tomb of Jesus, placed there by Joseph of Arimathea (Matt. 27.60). When the stone is rolled away—by women and men working together and through God's promise of empowering—the metaphor suggests that we are freed from our tombs of inequality and degradation, freed to claim and live out the promises of the first three stanzas of this hymn.

OTHER ASPECTS OF EMANCIPATORY LANGUAGE

We have discussed how this text creates a collective identity for women within the context of Christianity by its focus on making *women* visible, by the use of *we* and *our*, and by the text's focus on women's empowering and equality. We have also discussed how *men* are included through the final metaphor and in other parts of the text. Concern for truth and justice for women, for the family of Christ, and for creation all appear in this text, framed by the idea of God's commonwealth.

Likewise the work and status of women are held up to the light of the commonwealth of God. Feminist theology is given voice in this text, following Procter-Smith's emancipatory focus (1990, 66) and Ruether's critical principle of God's identification with women and the promotion of the full humanity of women (1983, 19).

The text is creative in its naming of the Holy One as *mystery within our flesh and bone* and *womanspirit moving through all time*, and it presents various facets of God as incarnational, empowering, creative, concerned with work and status, familial, visionary as well as practical (commonwealth of God). Using the practical purposes of the Ecumenical Decade, Murray has provided a poetic setting, imaginative in its identification of God with women, acknowledging both the mystery of God and the hopes God plants in women as well as the daily needs of women (and men) in their lives here on earth.

"Of Women, and of Women's Hopes We Sing" challenges singers to take women seriously as equal creations of God and active participants in life on this planet. This challenge is part of the emancipatory character of the text. Perhaps centuries from now things will be so different in church and society that this text will seem superfluous rather than startling (see Chapter 15). But for now, Murray's text stretches hymnic register by its focus on women, its subsequent descriptions of God, and its stress on equality. It is particularly important that *decorum*, a sense of appropriate use, be exercised in using the text, both so that women do not feel exposed by the text and that men can deal with it. The challenge of the text does not have to be eased by use of decorum, rather the exercise of decorum in using the text helps to assure that challenge will be given a context in that to be understood and faced.

The use of decorum with this text helps to assure that message: that one group long kept on the margins of church and society, women, may be upheld as those whom God holds dear, who carry God's image within them. Then, having acknowledged their worth, women can join with each other and with men to work for the commonwealth of God, when all persons will be valued and the gifts of God within each person will be freed.

Chapter 13
O Holy Spirit, Root of Life
A Multidimensional Reading

O Holy Spirit, Root of life,
Creator, cleanser of all things,
anoint our wounds, awaken us
with lustrous movement of your wings.

Eternal Vigor, Saving One,
you free us by your living Word,
becoming flesh to wear our pain,
and all creation is restored.

O Holy Wisdom, Soaring Power,
encompass us with wings unfurled,
and carry us, encircling all,
above, below, and through the world.

based on the writings of Hildegard of Bingen
Jean Janzen, 1991

Hymnal: A Worshipbook 1992,#123
Chalice Hymnal 1995, #251
The New Century Hymnal 1995, #57
Voices United 1997, #379

Spiritus Sanctus Vivificans Vita
Antiphon for the Holy Spirit
The Holy Spirit is a life-giving life,
moving all things,
and a root in every creature,
and cleanses all things from impurity,
scrubbing out guilt,
and anoints wounds,
and is therefore a gleaming and praiseworthy life,
arousing and resurrecting all.

(Hildegard in Newman 1988, 141)

O Vis Eternitatis
Responsory for the Creator
O strength of eternity,
you who ordered all things in your heart
by your Word all were created
as you wished,
and your Word himself
put on flesh
in that form
that was taken from Adam.

And thus his garments
were cleansed
from the greatest pain.

O how great is the kindness of the Savior
who set all things free
through his incarnation,
that divinity breathed forth
without chain of sin.

And thus his garments
were cleansed
from the greatest pain.

(Hildegard in Newman 1988, 99)

O Virtus Sapientie
Antiphon for Divine Wisdom
O energy of Wisdom,
you who circled circling,
encompassing all
in one path that possesses life,

having three wings,
of which one flies on high
and the second distils from the earth,
and the third flies everywhere.
Praise be to you, as befits you,
O Wisdom.

(Hildegard in Newman 1988, 101)

De Spiritu Sancto
To the Holy Spirit
Holy Spirit, making life alive,
moving in all things, root of all created being,
cleansing the cosmos of every impurity, effacing guilt,
anointing wounds.
You are lustrous and praiseworthy life,
You waken and re-awaken everything that is.

(Hildegard in Fox 1987, 373)

O Vis Aeternitatis
O Eternal Vigor,
all of creation is arranged and in order in your very heart.
Through your Word, all things are created just as you wish.
Your very own word even took on flesh in the same form
        that derived from Adam,
and removes heart-breaking from that very garment
        humanity wears.
O how magnificent is the compassion of the Saving One,
who frees all things by his becoming one with human life.
Divinity breathes into compassion without the chains of sin,
And so removes heart-breaking pain from that very garment
        humanity wears.
Glory to the Father and to the Son and to the Holy Spirit.
And so removes heart-breaking pain from that very garment
        humanity wears.   (Hildegard in Fox 1987, 384)

O Virtus Sapientiae
O moving force of Wisdom, encircling the wheel of the cosmos,
Encompassing all that is, all that has life,
        in one vast circle.
You have three wings: The first unfurls aloft
        in the highest heights.
The second dips its way dripping sweat on the Earth.
Over, under, and through all things whirls the third.
Praise to you, O Wisdom, worthy of praise!

(Hildegard in Fox 1987, 368)

INTRODUCTION

Background

"Constructing feminist liturgical tradition requires two things: a feminist reconstruction of our common liturgical memory, and a feminist enlargement of our common liturgical imagination" (Procter-Smith 1990, 36). Jean Janzen's hymn based on the liturgical songs of Hildegard of Bingen (1098-1179) moves between these two things, bringing Hildegard to consciousness from our collective memory and enlarging our imagination by re-presenting Hildegard's imagery for our day. The liturgical term, *anamnesis*, has "the sense of 're-calling' or 're-presenting' before God an event in the past, so that it becomes *here and now operative by its effects*" (Dix's italics 1978, 161). Thus, Janzen searches Hildegard's thoughts and brings them to consciousness so that they become real again for us, over eight hundred years after they were originally written; the text is an anamnesis.

Hildegard was an incredible woman for both her time and ours. At an early age she evidenced her uniqueness through a *visio*, a radiance that she called "the reflection of the living Light" (Newman 1988, 2). Given as a tithe (as one of ten children) to God at age eight, she was raised by Jutta, a recluse associated with a monastery of St. Disibod, in present-day Germany. Hildegard became a nun and upon Jutta's death was elected abbess of the growing community of women that had gathered there. She eventually moved her community to Rupertsberg, near Bingen, and founded a second house at Eibingen. In addition to being the spiritual leader and administrator of these two communities, Hildegard wrote of her visions (*Scivias*), natural science, herbs and medicine, lives of saints, and a collection of over seventy liturgical songs (*Symphonia*). Her letters spread her influence wider than her convents, including correspondence with kings and leaders of the church. During all this time, Hildegard suffered attacks of illness as well as battling the restrictions set on women in her day. Translations of Hildegard's works, biographies about her, and recordings of her music have flourished in the last ten years.

Jean Wiebe Janzen is a poet, who teaches poetry writing at Fresno Pacific College, in Fresno public schools, and at Eastern Mennonite College in Virginia. Her primary work has been with free verse, and she is the recipient of a National Endowment for the Arts Creative Writing Fellowship in Poetry, 1995 (Janzen 1995b). Janzen wrote her first hymns in meter at the request of the Mennonite Church. Eight of her hymns were published in *Hymnal: A Worshipbook* in 1992. These included three texts based on the writings of medieval mystics—Hildegard, Mechtild of Magdeburg, and Julian of Norwich—in addition to two psalm-based texts, a chorus, an alteration of an early nineteenth-century text, and an original text. "O Holy Spirit, Root of Life," based on Hildegard's writings has been included in several hymnals published since 1995, *Chalice Hymnal, The New Century Hymnal,* and *Voices United.*

"Feminist liturgical anamnesis," says Procter-Smith, "is the active remembrance of our collective past as seen through women's eyes and experienced in women's bodies" (1990, 53). As we consider this hymn text, we explore how it presents one woman's vision and how the text conveys that vision as an embodied experience.

Shape of the Text

Three stanzas of four lines each shape this text, the shortest of the six considered in this book. Each stanza consists of one sentence, made up of two names for God in the opening line, followed by a variety of phrases describing God's actions. The rhyme scheme throughout is ABCB.

The lines are set in the rising meter of iambs (u /), in the traditional Long Meter of hymn texts: 88.88. Long Meter was the classic Latin hymn meter, standardized by Ambrose of Milan (Eskew and McElrath 1995, 86); although Hildegard's texts were not written in Long Meter, they were written in Latin, so the use of Long Meter is a nice touch as well as an effective vehicle for this hymn. The rising iambic foot echoes the sense of flight in the text: *Wings* appears in the first and third stanza. In the third stanzas the middle two lines are understressed, which when read, glides the text onward to the stresses.[48] The text is rooted in rhyme and meter while soaring with the iambic foot.

---

1. When hymns are sung, the same tune is used for each stanza regardless of differing poetic stresses, which tends to force the text into regular rhythmic patterns. "O Holy Spirit, Root of Life" appears in *Hymnal: A Worshipbook* with the tune HEALER by Leonard Enns, 1989. HEALER is set in 4/4 and 6/4 (with alternating divisions of three and two beats a measure). The second line of the tune rushes ahead, while the third and fourth lines include long notes that add extra stress conflicting with the natural stresses of the text. The other three hymnals all use the tune PUER NOBIS NASCITUR for this text, set in 3/4 with the rhythm fitting an iambic pattern, and giving a dance-like motion to the text; yet, not deviating, for the understressed lines it loses some of the motion of the text in the final stanza. HEALER has the advantage of being a contemporary

Lovelace suggests that this meter is particularly suitable for majestic subjects and stately treatment (1982, 25). The "majestic subject" is God, and, relying on Hildegard, Janzen has built the text on a variety of metaphors for the Holy One and her actions. The text is unified by its focus on its subject and the *perichoresis* of the Trinity. Perichoresis is an understanding of the Trinity as movement or dance between the Three Persons, rather than understanding them as static points of a triangle.

The Subject of the Text

Each stanza begins with two names for God, and, using imperative verbs, the first and third stanza directly address the Holy One with names associated with the Third Person of the Trinity—*Spirit* and *Wisdom*. The middle stanza has a sense of stepping back for a moment as we sing *you free us* rather than the imperatives of stanzas one and three.[49] Yet this second stanza contains a strong sense of incarnation and identification of God with us, and thus it continues the mode of prayer begun in the first stanza and completed in the third stanza.

Although the opening line of this hymn is directed to the Spirit, and it appears in the sections about the Holy Spirit in *Chalice Hymnal*, *The New Century Hymnal*, and *Voices United*, I feel that *Hymnal: A Worshipbook* is more correct about its interpretation by placing it between two trinitarian hymns ("All Glory Be to God on High" #122 and "O Worship the Lord" #124 both contain a stanza for each of the Persons of the Trinity.) *The New Century Hymnal* (#57) cites three liturgical songs that served as the source of the text—two of these appear in Hildegard's schema for *Symphonia* under the heading "Father and Son" ("O vis eternitatis" and " O virtus Sapientie," Newman 1988, 98-101), and only one under the section "The Holy Spirit" ("Spiritu sanctus,"

---

tune with freer rhythms, while PUER NOBIS NASCITUR has the advantage of coming from the fifteenth century, closer historically to Hildegard's time. (Although its step-wise movement is very unlike the musical compositions of Hildegard herself, that contain wide melodic leaps. See Newman 1988, 29.)

2. It is interesting to consider the use of imperatives in hymnic language, if one considers them as "commanding" God. Yet this is the language of "asking with assurance of answer" used in the psalms and the language of prayer; for example, "Protect me, O God" (Ps. 16.1), "Hear my prayer, O Lord" (Ps. 102.1), "Give us this day our daily bread" (Matt. 6.11).

Newman 1988, 140-141). All of the stanzas draw on characteristics and actions traditionally associated with different Persons of the Trinity.

Hildegard's writing is marked by its unusual imagery and sheer immediacy (Newman 1988, 41, 43). Janzen has captured that immediacy in the briefness and directness of her text, including her use of imperative verbs, a majority of one-syllable words, and a minimum of prepositions and articles. She has also based the text on Hildegard's metaphors, and through the variety of metaphors and their juxtaposition, has created a text unusual in its own way.

Hildegard's Texts as the Basis for Janzen's Text

"O Holy Spirit, Root of Life" is drawn, almost line for line from three of Hildegard's liturgical songs found in her *Symphonia*, using the paraphrases by Rev. Jerry Dybdal and Matthew Fox, as can be seen by juxtaposing the texts (confirmed by Janzen 1995c). The first stanza is drawn primarily from "De Spiritu Sancto/To the Holy Spirit;" the second depends on "O vis Aeternitatis/O Eternal Vigor;" the third relies on "O virtus Sapientiae/O Moving Force of Wisdom." Dybdal's and Fox's entire translations appear at the beginning of this section, following the text of Janzen's hymn and the translations of medieval scholar Barbara Newman.[50]

Janzen's text	Hildegard's songs (trans. Fox and Dybdal)
O Holy Spirit, Root of life,	root of all created being
Creator, cleanser of all things,	making all life alive . . . cleansing the cosmos
anoint our wounds, awaken us	anointing wounds. . . you waken everything
with lustrous movement of your wings.	You are lustrous . . . You have three wings
Eternal Vigor, Saving One,	O Eternal Vigor . . . Saving One
you free us by your living Word,	who frees all things . . . Your very own word
becoming flesh to wear our pain,	took on flesh . . removes heart-breaking
and all creation is restored.	all things are created just as you wish.
O Holy Wisdom, Moving Force,[51]	O moving force of Wisdom
encompass us with wings unfurled,	encompassing all . . . the first [wing] unfurls
and carry us, encircling all,	encircling the wheel of the cosmos
above, below, and through the world.	over, under, and through all things

3. In this book both Newman's scholarly literal translations and those of Fox and Dybal, which inspired Janzen's text, will be used, as each illumines the hymn text.

4. Note *Moving Force* was Janzen's original text, following Fox and Dybdal, now changed to *Soaring Power*, see below, under Stanza Three.

Is it necessary to know Hildegard's songs and theology to understand and appreciate Janzen's hymn text? No, but knowing something about Hildegard's thought can spark our interest in the text and add to our understanding and appreciation, much the way understanding the Bible and theology gives us a deeper understanding of other hymn texts. The first time "O Holy Spirit, Root of Life" is sung by a congregation, it will be helpful to place it in context—involving study of Hildegard's thought, singing or reading her songs or other writings, or using some of her images in preaching.

STANZAS

Stanza One

The first stanza begins with a catalogue of names for the divine: *Holy Spirit, Root of life, Creator, cleanser of all things.* Although the catalogue might be interpreted as deriving from the first name, *Holy Spirit,* the other three names also may be interpreted as referring to the other persons of the Trinity. Thus the richness of many names for God is immediately present in the text, through the clear use of metaphor.

Holy Spirit is the most frequent name for the Third Person of the Trinity. The Spirit is present in the Hebrew scriptures, as God speaks through the prophet Joel, "I will pour out my *spirit* on all flesh; your sons and your daughters shall prophesy" (Joel 2.28a), and is promised by Jesus in John 14. 6, "But the Advocate, the *Holy Spirit,* whom [God] will send in my name, will teach you everything, and remind you of all that I have said to you." The preceding *O* is one of the grand gestures, the solemn apostrophe, mentioned by Newman as a salient feature of Hildegard's style. Newman suggests that this may come in part from the great "O" antiphons (sung responses) of Advent, forerunner of the present-day hymn "O come, O come, Emmanuel," that were in use as early as the ninth century during Advent vespers and probably known to Hildegard (Newman 1988, 40; Young 1993, 505).

Root of life is an image reflecting Hildegard's interest in medicinal plants and herbs.[52] The original Latin reads "et radix est in omni creatura" (Newman 1988, 240). It is translated variously as "root of all created being" (Fox 1987, 373), "root of the world tree," "root in every

---

5. Flanagan suggests that the combination of root, cleansing, and anointing wounds is related to the connection of roots with healing, examples of that are found in Hildegard's medical writings (1989, 110).

creature" (Newman 1988, 141, both),[6] "root stock of every creature"
(Flanagan 1989, 220). Newman suggests that for Hildegard, words like
the Latin *radix* "almost always have a metaphysical sense; the literal
meanings of 'root' . . . suggests something very like the Tillichian
'ground of being'" (Newman 1988, 39). *Root of life* then suggests the
source of our life, its grounding, that that enables all creatures to grow
and thrive (related to the First Person of the Trinity). The sustaining
character of *Root of life* is a metaphor for the nurturing of the Holy
Spirit in the lives of Christians. *Root* also refers to prophecies about
Jesus Christ (the Second Person of the Trinity): "On that day the root of
Jesse shall stand as a signal to the peoples" (Isa. 11.10) and "It is I,
Jesus, who sent my angel to you with this testimony for the churches. I
am the *root* and the descendant of David, the bright morning star"
(Rev. 22.16).

The meanings of *Root of life* as the Source of our life points to the
next word in the text, *Creator*, traditionally the term used for the First
Person of the Trinity, the Godhead present and active in creation. The
Holy Spirit, through her identification with Wisdom (Prov. 8.22-31),
was present also, like Jesus Christ (John 1.1-4), at creation. Again we
see the reflection of the entire Trinity in one metaphor. The theme of
Creator God is followed in the third line with the words *awaken us*.
The second account of Genesis speaks of God breathing life into Adam,
thus *awakening* him to life, and then putting Adam to sleep and, after
creating Eve, *waking* them both from sleep (Gen. 2, especially 7 and
21).

Cleanser of all things has many echoes in biblical and traditional
Christianity. God *cleanses* the world of evil with a flood (Gen. 6 and
7), *cleanses* the land for the chosen people (Deut. 32:43, the Song of
Moses), and *cleanses* individuals from their sin (Ps. 51.2). One aspect
of Christian baptism is *cleansing* from sin by God through water (compare Ruth Duck's hymn, "Wash, O God, Our Sons and Daughters") and
through the blood of Jesus Christ (1 John 1.7). Thus we have a sense in
this catalog not only of the Creator God but the Savior Christ as well as
the Holy Spirit.

Anoint our wounds: In biblical tradition oil was used to anoint
prophets, priests, and kings (Luke 7.46, Exod. 29.7, 1 Sam. 15.1). Material things such as altars were *anointed* in order to consecrate them,

---

6. Newman provides two translations for each of Hildegard's liturgical
songs in her edition of *Symphonia*: a literal prose translation and her own verse
translations. Thus when quoting her translations there will generally be two
slightly different readings.

make them holy (Cross and Livingstone, *s.v. anoint*). *Anointing* is still done today in some Christian traditions as part of baptism and as part of healing rituals, for physical, mental, or emotional wounds. (It is akin in the everyday world to putting ointment on a cut or abrasion, though the anointing of God is able to heal more quickly and to heal wounds that are unseen.) There is a relationship here also between *anoint* and *Root of life*, for Hildegard was very interested in the use of plant roots in healing (Flanagan 1989, 110). The vowels in an*oi*nt and w*ou*nd, along with the repetition of the *n*-sound slow us down to take a healing moment. The healing described in this phrase has echoes in the healing work of Jesus Christ and in the comforting power of the Holy Spirit (John 14.26, KJV).

Awaken us with lustrous movement of your wings: In each Gospel account of the baptism of Jesus, the Holy Spirit is present in the form of a dove (Matt. 3.16, Mark 1.10, Luke 3.22, John 1.32). This association of the Spirit with *wings* is in line with the vision of a winged God found in the Hebrew scriptures: "I bore you on eagles' *wings*" (Exod. 19.4), "in the shadow of your *wings* I will take refuge" (Ps. 57.1b, cf. Ps. 17.8, 36.7, 61.4 and 63.7). Jesus used the image of a mother hen gathering her brood under her *wings* when he lamented over Jerusalem (Matt. 23.37, Luke 13.34). *Lustrous* is taken from Hildegard's "De Spiritu Sancto," "You are lustrous," and relates also to her sense of *visio*, of light. *Webster's* defines *lustrous* as "reflecting light evenly and efficiently without glitter or sparkle; radiant in character or reputation." *Lustrous* is an apt word choice for one who saw visions of light reflecting God.

Before leaving this first stanza of the hymn, two things should be noted. First, as has been pointed out, this stanza includes a sense not only of the Holy Spirit but also a strong sense of God the Creator and sustainer of life and reference to Jesus Christ's cleansing powers as well as description of him as *Root*. Second, notice the grounding of the images in embodiment: *Root of life* who provides nourishment for life, *cleanser of all things* who touches and scrubs everything, *anoint our wounds*—touch and heal us, *awaken us* by touching us with the air and light, which moves as you move your *wings* around us. These images assume bodily creatures and a God who nourishes and touches our bodies, much like a nursing mother, a housewife, a medical nurse, and a mother waking her children for school, to take seriously Procter-Smith's comments about liturgical anamnesis (1990, 53). These are experiences of women's collective past, experienced in women's bodies, though not outside the realm of men's experience.

Stanza Two

The second stanza, like the first, begins with several names for the Holy: *Eternal Vigor, Saving One,* and *living Word.* The address of God is followed by a recounting of God's actions on our behalf: freeing us, becoming flesh and sharing human suffering, and the restoration of creation. Hildegard's original text gives the added meaning here of understanding that restoration as restoration of all things ordered in God's heart (Newman and Fox/Dybdal translations, above).

The sense of movement begun by *the movement of God's wings* in the first stanza is continued by the activities of God toward creation through this second stanza. Yet in contrast to the shorter phrases of the first and third stanzas (phrases varying from two syllables and various combinations of three, four, and five syllables up to eight), this second stanza contains consistent eight-syllable phrases. Therefore, although this stanza maintains vigor and a sense of movement, it is more of a sustained embodied movement, rather than soaring.

Eternal Vigor is Dybdal and Fox's translation of "vis aeternitatis" (Fox 1987, 384). *Eternal* is one of the characteristics of God and of Jesus Christ (John 1.1, Rom. 1.20, Eph. 3.11). It is also related to *Wisdom* (looking ahead to the first line of stanza three), as Wisdom is a reflection of *eternal* light (Wisd. of Sol. 7.26). *Vigor* reflects Hildegard's interest in plants and in the healthy growth of human beings,[7] as *Webster's* defines it: "active bodily or mental strength or force; active healthy well-balanced growth, especially of plants." Thus, it refers back to *Root of life* and also forward to *Moving Force*, Janzen's original first line for the third stanza, as well as the energy of *awakening* and *wings* from the first stanza.

The active sense of *vigor* is carried forward with the phrase *Saving One*, suggesting the activity of God. Both the God of Israel and Jesus Christ are referred to as *saving*: "The Lord is the strength of his people; [God] is the *saving* refuge of his anointed" (Ps. 28.8), and "The saying is sure and worthy of full acceptance, that Christ Jesus came into the world to *save* sinners" (1 Tim. 1.15). Here again, we see in this stanza the perichoresis of the Trinity, as the juxtaposed names for the Holy One reflect the movement of the divine between different Persons of the Trinity.

---

7. In suggesting that Hildegard was probably the first German scientist and medical doctor, Fierro includes Hildegard's teachings of four principles of good health: rest (freedom from stress), a balanced diet, exercise, and a moral life (1994, 21).

In Hildegard's text it is clear that the *Saving One* is the one who became incarnate, one with human life, Jesus Christ, who set all things free. Janzen's text goes on to suggest the same identification with the phrase *living Word* (*Word* being the Gospel of John's first name for Jesus).[8] The use of the adjective *living* fits with *vigor* and *Root*, and prepares for the incarnational phrase *becoming flesh*. Because of its position in the poetic line, *living One* also reflects the rhythm of *Saving Word*; the *-ing* gives a sense of rhyme to these two long, unrhymed phrases.

From what does the *living Word* of Jesus Christ *free* us? Scriptures suggest three things we are *freed* from: our ailments (Luke 13.12, Jesus' words to the bent-over woman as she is healed), from sin (Acts 13.39, Paul's sermon at Antioch in Pisidia), and from the law of death (Rom. 8.1). The first two, ailments and sins, hearken back to the *wounds* and *cleansing* of the first stanza of this text. Freedom from the law of death is particularly a Christological concept—through the resurrection Jesus Christ overcame the law of death, so that it may no longer have hold over human lives, that is his *saving* work (reference back to line one of this stanza).

The third and fourth lines of this stanza draw on Colossians 1.19-20, "For in [Jesus Christ] all the fullness of God was pleased to dwell, and through him God was pleased to reconcile to [God's]self all things, whether on earth or in heaven, by making peace through the blood of the cross." The dwelling of God in Jesus Christ is the doctrine of incarnation, God *becoming flesh*, that sets Christianity apart from other religions by its claim that Jesus was fully divine as well as fully human. In Hildegard's text, identification is made with Adam relating not only to Adam as the "first" person with flesh but also in the understanding of Christ as the Second Adam, "for as all die in Adam, so all will be made alive in Christ" (1 Cor. 15.22).

Becoming flesh is followed by the metaphor *to wear our pain*. In Hildegard's original text, "O Vis Aeternitatis," this metaphor is placed as a repeated refrain: "And thus his [Adam's] garments / were cleansed / from the greatest pain" in Newman's translation (1988, 99) and "and removes heart-breaking from that very garment / humanity wears" in the translation by Fox and Dybdal (Fox 1987, 384). This metaphor

---

8. The use of *Word* in this text also ties together the studies that show the linkage between the concepts of *Word—Logos—Wisdom*. Newman has used the writings of Hildegard and others to begin to trace the lines of the presence of a sense of female divinity throughout history (1994.)

suggests that as in Jesus Christ God "puts on" flesh, God also "puts on" our pain as we would put on clothes. Jesus Christ/God had the choice of any garment at all, and yet chose *to wear our pain* as the ultimate act of solidarity, bearing the pain of rejection and death, walking the way of agony and loneliness. The realities of human pain and suffering were taken onto God's self in the person of Jesus Christ in his earthly life and particularly in what is called his Passion, his torture and crucifixion, on the day called "Good Friday" not for his suffering but for the good for humanity of his redemptive act. Thus this metaphor reflects the scriptural phrase, "through the blood of the cross."

Restoration is both a promise of God to humanity and a human longing and prayer to God. Three times in Psalm 80 (verses 3, 7, and 19) the congregation pleads, *"Restore us, O God; let your face shine, that we may be saved."* The promise of God, written in 1 Peter 5.10, moves from the *pain* of humanity to our *restoration*: "And after you have suffered for a little while, the God of all grace, who has called you to eternal glory in Christ, will himself *restore*, support, strengthen, and establish you." In wearing our pain, the pains of sin and death, even a gruesome death, Jesus Christ, *restored* the bonds between God and humanity that had been broken in the fall of Adam and Eve. And *all creation is restored* suggests not simply a personal restoration as that in the well-loved words of the psalmist: "[God] *restores* my soul" (Ps. 23.2c), but the restoration of *all creation*. Hildegard's text states that all things are ordered in God's heart, as God wished (Newman 1988, 99). Added to Hildegard's love of plants and the natural world, this final line is clear that everything in creation has been restored through Jesus Christ. This echoes Colossians 1.20a, "and through [Jesus Christ] God was pleased to reconcile to [God's]self all things, whether on earth or in heaven" wherein all creation is restored to the heart of God.

Stanza Three

The third stanza opens with the apostrophe *O Holy Wisdom* (translation of *Sapientie*), drawing again on the solemn apostrophe *O*, mentioned by Newman as a salient feature of Hildegard's style (Newman 1988, 40). As an attribute of God, *Wisdom* is described in the book of Proverbs, chapters 1, 8, 9, 14, and 16, and in The Wisdom of Solomon, chapters 7 and 9. In these places *Wisdom* is described as *she*, as present at creation with God (Prov. 8.22-31), as holy (Wisd. of Sol. 7.22), as coming from God (Wisd. of Sol. 9.6), and, important for the sense of motion in this text, as "more mobile than any motion" (Wisd. of Sol 7.24). *Wisdom* is currently enjoying a revival of interest under her Greek name, *Sophia*, due in part to biblical studies that have uncovered her tradition and her connections with Jesus as the *Wisdom* of God (1 Cor. 1.30, "Christ Jesus, who became for us *wisdom* from God" and others) and women who claim this example of female divinity as part of our Judeo-Christian heritage.

As first printed in *Hymnal: A Worshipbook*, the second phrase of this third stanza was *Moving Force*, taken directly from the Dybdal/Fox translation of Hildegard's "O virtus Sapientiae." This is related to *Eternal Vigor* in stanza two and to both usages of *wings* (stanzas one and three).

In the hymnals since *Hymnal: A Worshipbook* this phrase has been changed to *Soaring Power*. The change "came as a request from the committee for *The New Century Hymnal*, to avoid questions of new age connotations. And I like the revised phrase" (Janzen 1995c). The *Chalice Hymnal* committee saw the text in its revised version in a sampler published by *The New Century Hymnal* and copied the change (Duck 1995b). The revised phrase is an appropriate translation of the Latin word *virtus*. *Soaring* carries both the sense of flight and also a sense of lightness (through the multivalence of language carrying the meanings of physical weight and of visual brightness), reflecting the *lustrous movement* mentioned in the final line of the first stanza. *Power* relates to the *energy* of God in the preceding stanzas, creating, cleansing, saving, freeing, restoring, while maintaining the sense of vigor and movement without the coercive connotations of *Force*.

The sense of *Soaring* is expanded as the next line of this stanza moves into the *unfurling* of the *wings* of the Holy God of *Wisdom* that then *encompass us*. Three-syllable words are generally used judiciously in hymnwriting, and Janzen has been particularly careful in this third stanza to use two three-syllable words that express the vital nature of this text: *encompass* and *encircling*. *Encompass* means to form a circle about, to envelop and include (*Webster's*); *encircle* means to form a circle around and to pass completely around (*Webster's*). Thus the stretched-out wings of Holy Wisdom first form a circle about us and then move to form circles around all of creation, soaring *above, below, and through the world*. Throughout the text, we and all of creation have been assured of God's activity on our behalf, creating, cleansing, anointing, awakening, saving, freeing, becoming flesh, taking on our pain, restoring creation. Now all creation is held in the very wings of God and taken soaring to God's very heart in loving freedom. The perichoresis of the Trinity encompasses us and encircles us.

The final line of the text draws on Hildegard's images of *wings* associated with each of the Three Persons of the Trinity, from her song "O virtus Sapientiae" to present a vivid picture of the energy of God:

> You have three wings: The first unfurls aloft
>   in the highest heights.
> The second dips its way dripping sweat on the Earth.
> Over, under, and through all things whirls the third (Fox 1987, 368).

Newman translated these lines: "One wing soars in heaven, / one wing sweeps the earth, / and the third flies all around us" (1988, 101). Three wings might represent the Trinity, or perhaps the number is a condensation of the vision of the prophet Isaiah :

> In the year that King Uzziah died, I saw the Lord sitting on a throne, high and lofty; and the hem of his robe filled the temple. Seraphs were in attendance above him; each had six wings: with two they covered their faces, and with two they covered their feet, and with two they flew. (Isa. 6.1-2)

Notice that there are three pairs, one pair associated with the face (higher, like heavens), one pair associated with the feet (lower, like earth), and one pair to fly (all around). The text becomes iconic as these three wings are given flight in the short, moving phrases of the final two lines of the text: *and carry us, /encircling all, / above, / below, / and through the world.*

Consider the word-picture Janzen has drawn from Hildegard's texts: The Holy God of Wisdom has unfurled her wings and we are encompassed by them and carried, circling the world, cleansed and awakened, set free and restored, to enjoy all of creation. We have been invited to join in the dance of all creation, the dance begun in and nurtured by the Trinity. The nurturing and protecting wings of God shelter us, lovingly carry us. There is a sense of embodiment both of us and of God. Beyond that, no matter where in the world we may go, God is already there.

OTHER ASPECTS OF EMANCIPATORY LANGUAGE

Our discussion of this text began by drawing on Procter-Smith's suggestion for feminist liturgical anamnesis and suggesting that this hymn, based on the liturgical songs of Hildegard of Bingen, brings this spiritual woman to consciousness from our collective history and enlarges our imagination by re-presenting her spiritual understandings for our day. Although Hildegard is not mentioned in the text itself, it has been shown how the hymn was drawn from three of her texts in her *Symphonia*, and it has been suggested that understanding Hildegard and her work, however briefly, will aid in understanding and appreciating this hymn text.

The many names for the Holy, their freshness, and the movement between the Persons of the Trinity through the images of the text help give the text its emancipatory character. Equally important is the sense of embodiment discussed, based on the metaphors of touching and sustaining life, of root, cleansing, anointing, wings, wounds, becoming flesh, pain, restoration, being carried. Janzen has managed the sense of embodiment without relying on gender, leaving our minds free to produce our own ideas of how these varied images might be pictured. It is this freedom that invites us into this text to be encircled by its images and to be encompassed by the One to whom it prays.

PART IV
PRAXIS

To understand the importance of praxis for this study, we return first to our discussion of revelation in Chapter 5. There it was pointed out how revelation begins in individual consciousness and then must be translated into communal consciousness to become socially meaningful (Ruether 1983, 13). Hymnwriters particularly feel the need of community to both call forth and support their individual revelations. Christianity understands the power of community as that promised by Jesus Christ, "For where two or three are gathered in my name, I am there among them" (Matt. 18.20). When gathered Christians sing hymns, Jesus Christ is present, and the power of the Holy Spirit works in and through the music and text to both enable worship and to enable God to move in the lives of the singers.

It has been demonstrated how close readings enrich our understanding of individual hymn texts. Yet even the methodology of close reading acknowledges the limitations of one person's understanding and interpretation. One individual's close reading can be tested and enriched by considering the insights of others. Again, individual consciousness is translated into communal consciousness.

Chapter 14
Praxis:
Seeking Communal Affirmation

PRAXIS RESEARCH

The research for this text has taken two approaches to praxis. First, after being introduced as part of a search for emancipatory hymnic language, these hymns were sung and discussed with several groups, totaling 113 persons, primarily laity. Second, the texts were sent to fourteen pastors and worship leaders for comments and discussion of their usability with their current congregations. This provides some variety within the praxis itself. Obviously these are not large samples and they are focused on United Methodists. Larger studies and those focused on other denominations might yield different results. Yet, one advantage of using United Methodists is the wide spectrum of theological beliefs held within the denomination, which is reflected to some extent in this text.

Group Discussions

Three group discussions took place in United Methodist churches, chosen for their accessibility to me, their differing locations (state and city size), the contrast of multicultural and monocultural, the differences in their self-understandings, and the knowledge that each group was interested in hymn singing.

After being introduced briefly to the focus on hymn texts and the characteristics of emancipatory language, the groups sang the hymns in the order presented in the multidimensional readings. Brief comments were made about the author, the situation for that the text was written, and any changes made in the text. Because "God of the Sparrow" was the most familiar of the six texts, it was a good place to start. Whereas "Bring Many Names" began the consideration of gender made explicit in hymns about God, "Of Women, and of Women's Hopes" engendered the most emotional responses and thus was well placed later in the discussion. "O Holy Spirit, Root of Life," suggested by several worship leaders as a hymn for healing services, seemed to regather the group after their divisions on the previous text. The whole process took around one hour.

The Church of the Good Hope, United Methodist, is a multicultural church of about 175 members, primarily middle class, in northwest Milwaukee, where I served as Director of Music until 1996. The discussion was open to the entire congregation and held on Trinity Sunday (11 June 1995) immediately after worship. Sixteen people participated: nine women, five men, and two girls, including African-Americans and European-Americans, a wide spectrum of ages, and two differently abled persons.

Trinity United Methodist Church, in the heart of Atlanta, is also a multicultural church, with about 230 members, with a wide spectrum of incomes. Trinity has long been involved in issues of social justice and draws both from its neighborhood, from persons committed to social justice, and from professors and students of Candler School of Theology at Emory University. The discussion was held with a Sunday evening lectionary study group on 20 August 1995, with sixteen persons, ages thirty and up, all European-American.

Christ United Methodist Church is a European-American church of around 260 members, located in Bay City, a lower-to-middle-class small city on Saginaw Bay in Michigan. The discussion was open to the congregation and took place on 23 August 1995, a Wednesday evening (their regular choir rehearsal night), with eleven choir members, the pastor, and the worship chairperson, ages thirty and up, participating.

On 11 July 1995 I was given the opportunity to present my research at a Faculty Forum during the summer school session at Garrett-Evangelical Theological Seminary in Evanston, Illinois. I used the event as another group discussion, to gain more feedback on the hymn texts. Nineteen people participated, ages thirty to sixty, primarily United Methodists, many who were involved in worship planning (including students training for ordained ministry, some of whom were serving churches at that time).

Some additional comments will be shared from two other groups. The first was composed of two United Methodist young women (then ages ten and eleven), their pastor father, and a visiting Presbyterian musician, who participated in a discussion about these hymn texts on 27 June 1995. These persons are ardent hymn singers and accustomed to paying close attention to the words of worship. The second was a group of about forty-five church musicians and clergy gathered for a two-day workshop entitled "Futures Forum in Christian Worship: Teamwork 2020 A.D." held in Ann Arbor, Michigan. On the second day of the conference, 26 February 1996, I presented a paper on eman- cipatory language and hymnody that included singing the six texts used in this study. Because there was only time for brief comments, this dis- cussion lacked the comprehensiveness of the three discussions held in churches. Yet several important comments came out of this workshop.

Individual Comments

Worship leaders are responsible for picking the hymns for congrega- tional worship and thus influence the hymnic repertoire of a congrega- tion. In order to receive feedback on the usability of these hymns, cop- ies were sent to thirteen pastors and to three church musicians who have the responsibility of picking hymns weekly. Eleven pastors and all the musicians responded with comments. Six of the pastors are United Methodists from Michigan, as are two of the musicians. Four Presbyte- rian pastors responded, two from Michigan, and one each from Illinois and Wisconsin. The other two respondents are a United Methodist pastor from Wisconsin and a United Methodist musician from Mis- souri. These persons serve both large and small churches, in cities, towns, and rural areas, primarily European-American, lower-to-middle- class congregations.

Some Overall Observations

Without exception, the persons involved in the praxis research for this book were interested in talking about hymns and about their texts and tunes. One of my constant tasks was to keep the focus on texts rather than tunes.[1] People were clear about what they liked strongly or dis- liked strongly, and were able to articulate that, even the young people.

---

1. As has been noted in the close readings, several texts were sung with simpler tunes (when there was a choice) so that the focus could remain on the words, rather than on a difficult tune.

One disadvantage to this group approach was that, with some exceptions,[2] the hymns were not sung in the context of worship. The attitude of the discussions was inclined toward approaching God, because they were "church people" in a "church place" talking about "church things," yet the space provided by actual worship for reflection and heightened expectation was missing. It would be an interesting project to follow up with these congregations after the singing of these hymns in worship, a project that would need to be done in conjunction with other worship leaders.

The worship leaders, in part because they are leaders, and in part because they were given full opportunity to speak directly to each text (time constraints on the groups led to many consensus comments), spoke at some length about the texts and occasionally suggested rewrites. Several of the worship leaders are very familiar with the writings of some of these hymnwriters and reflected this in their comments, generally noting that this was a favorite writer of theirs. For the most part these comments were not used, as they were not specific to the text at hand.

The worship leaders did not have the advantage of asking questions about a text or having its background briefly explained, as did the groups. This lack of background information in looking at a text is similar to what worship leaders often experience in looking through a hymnal and picking hymns each week. Yet the contrast between the groups and individuals can occasionally be seen wherein the group is more accepting of a text knowing its background or a particularly biblical or theological reference than the individual worship leaders were.

The different understandings and responses to texts also point to the fact that what may be emancipatory for some persons is not emancipatory for others. Ultimately, an emancipatory approach to the whole use of hymns and metaphors, including a wide variety of each, will be important for emancipatory worship.

This chapter considers separately the group responses and the individual responses of worship leaders. Brackets denote explanations by

---

2. "God of the Sparrow" and "Source and Sovereign, Rock and Cloud" were sung in worship at Church of the Good Hope, and the writer had the advantage of talking to persons individually after worship about their experience with these hymns, noted in individual hymn discussions below. The "Futures Forum" group sang "Lead on, O Cloud of Presence," and "O Holy Spirit, Root of Life" in an evening prayer service, following the speech/discussion. Several comments were evoked by the worship setting.

me regarding the remarks of other persons. Along with the sharing of responses will be intermittent comments by me as they apply to my close readings. It should also be acknowledged that occasionally in both the group responses and the individual responses things were said that I wished I had said or realized.

GOD OF THE SPARROW

The lack of punctuation and rhyme along with the unanswered questions give this hymn a startling character. People appreciated its wide range of metaphors and understanding of God and its inclusion of all of creation in God's care.

Group Responses

The Church of the Good Hope. This hymn was sung twice in worship during the research time, and is a favorite text of both an eighty-four-year-old woman and an eight-year-old boy. People commented on the contrasts and how the hymn shows us that God is there through the good and the bad. "We have forgotten that all creatures are created by God and need our respect," noted one person. Most people were confused by the *pruning hook* image, though one of the group was able to explain both what it looks like and what it does. One of the United Methodist Women said it made her think of those of God's children who are homeless. The second time it was sung, three months later, someone commented that "when we sang it, it sounded like we were in a cathedral; it was louder than we could have sung."

Trinity United Methodist Church. This hymn was new to this group, although it appears in the hymnal they use. One person found the question phrases "disjunctive," whereas another liked "not knowing what word will come next." Someone suggested the creatures also need to be able to say *Anger* and *Justice*. The opening stanza reminded someone of another contemporary hymn, "Earth and All Stars" (*Presbyterian Hymnal* #458). Stanza two, with *earthquake* and *woe*, seemed "out of place" to one person. The sequence of *rainbow*, *cross*, and *empty grave* of stanza two were questioned and the suggestion was made that they are part of the story of salvation. That led into discussion of stanza four describing the need of each of us for salvation—that there is not just one story of salvation. The *pruning hook* was seen as a symbol of judgment, of who would live and who would die. *Children* in the final stanza was seen as looking to the future, and *Home* as a "landing place." The comprehensiveness of this text and its depiction of the different aspects of God were appreciated.

Christ United Methodist Church. Most of the group had sung this hymn before in worship. They were the only group to mention the unrhymed character of the text—some felt the lack of punctuation gave "no break" and made it hard to sense the direction of the text. *Creature* was perceived as negative by one person, whereas another thought it gave an interesting sense of inanimate/animate. *Pruning hook* conveyed a sense of justice to one person. One person found *Home* "a surprise, and an important reflection of love."[3] Generally, the group found this text "less egotistical" than many hymns, liking the depiction of "God not for humans only," and sensing the call of this text for "keeping an open mind."

Faculty Forum. A number of participants knew this hymn and "loved" it. They cited the variety of images, the economy of the text, its many names, and biblical themes. When one person questioned the use of *pruning hook*, another was quick to refer to a biblical passage (Joel 3.10, that sets a context of judgment). Someone lifted up the contrast of *cry* and *earthquake* with the rest of the text. Suggestions for its usage included at "children's time" in worship, during Kingdomtide (a liturgical season now subsumed in the ordinary Sundays after Pentecost), with the biblical themes, when focusing on nature. One church had used this hymn during the final worship service with its pastor of eleven years and the person who reported this use said that this hymn "gathered together the emotions of that time." One person came up after the discussion, to speak privately to say that the *rainbow* is seen as a sign of God's acceptance by gay and lesbian Christians, and that she particularly appreciated that "window." This is a prime example of how the Spirit can work through a text, speaking to persons in ways we had not planned, through language that is emancipatory.

Additional comments. "At first I didn't like this hymn," commented one person, "because it seems choppy and disconnected. This time I felt the

---

3. When this text was sung as part of my presentation of the outline for this book to my doctoral colloquium, a pastoral psychology major was quite adamant that *Home* would be a problem for many persons to sing or identify with, given the prevalence of dysfunctional homes. In all the presentations of this text that concern was never raised again.

'end-words' [*Awe, Praise*, and such] connected it." Another person felt that the answers to the questions of this text lie underneath it, like a phrase in the book/movie *A River Runs through It* that speaks of the words under the rocks of the river (Maclean 1976, 104). Others cited this hymn as "beautiful," "fresh," and "flowing."

Worship Leaders' Responses

Only one respondent said that he would not use "God of the Sparrow" in worship, as it was too allusive for the congregation he was currently serving. Many had already sung this hymn because it appears in several hymnals. The suggestions for usage varied from general praise hymn, to outdoor or Earth Day worship, use with children, when discussing creation, the nature of God, peace and justice, for Eucharist, thanksgiving, or Rural Life Sunday. Several churches found it being picked regularly by the congregation during hymn sings. One respondent mentioned that the first stanza had been sung at the family burial of a pet bird.

This hymn received many favorable overall comments:

I love it!
varied and beautiful images
one of my favorite "new" hymns, images reflect a caring and missional
    faith
our congregation loves the idea that God is the God of everyone and
    everything
it teaches us not to put God into a box
the choice of images themselves invoke a feeling of awe

One pastor who loved the hymn discovered that his congregation was uncomfortable with the vagueness of the text. Although one respondent did not like the questions (*how does*), another thought they "made the enigmatic aspects of God real." "This hymn speaks to the difficulty of putting faith into words. Many faithful people don't know how to 'say faith'," remarked another pastor. Another respondent suggested that the end words (*Awe, Praise*, and so on) are all good examples of how and why we pray.

Several comments related to individual words or phrases. One musician felt that *creature* was an "ugly word" and *prodigal* was awkward to sing. Although one respondent commented that *pruning hook* was unfamiliar, another used that phrase to talk about "God the Vinedresser who prunes the diseased and dead branches out of our lives" (John 15.1-2). One respondent said that the first stanza made her think of van

Gogh's painting, "Starry, Starry Night" (a good idea for a visual to use with the hymn).[4] The second stanza's ending with *Woe* and *Save* contrasted strongly with the fourth stanza's *Care* and *Life* for another respondent. One pastor said, "All these incredible and striking opposites are not opposites at all, but rather are part of God's intricately woven tapestry of life." "I love how the text moves from *creature* to *children/home*, demonstrating the movement of our relationship to God from appropriate awe to gracious intimacy [joy and home]," summed up one respondent.

SOURCE AND SOVEREIGN, ROCK AND CLOUD

Like "God of the Sparrow," the variety of metaphors and images in this text caught the interest of the singers. Pointing out the trinitarian pattern of the stanzas helped people to make some sense of the "many names."

Group Responses

The Church of the Good Hope. This hymn was sung in worship on the day of the discussion, Trinity Sunday. "God is everything and infinite, that's what this hymn says to me," said one person. Remarking on stanza two, another said, "the *Way who leads*, seems incomplete; it needs *Truth*" (from John 14.6). The contrast between *Storm* and *Stillness* was seen as helpful. *"Source and Sovereign* says it all."

Trinity United Methodist Church. Although the majority of the group did not know this hymn, one person had used the refrain to begin her paper on inclusive hymnody for a seminary class. Persons appreciated the "tangible, not elusive, images." The trinitarian nature of the hymn was not obvious to them and helped explain for them how the names fit together. The first stanza sounded to someone like "tough love." *Well and Water* in stanza two were lifted up as female images. The third stanza was cited for its pastoral yet strong images: *Stillness* and *Com-*

---

4. I have also had good experiences when using this hymn with children and youth by having them draw pictures of phrases or stanzas of the hymn. These pictures were then displayed for the congregation (either in the sanctuary or narthex) when the hymn was sung. Not only did this make the hymn more personal for the young people, but it gave them another outlet for their response to God.

fort cited as not passive or weak (as sometimes perceived). The final phrase of the third stanza, *Energies that never tire*, seemed Platonic to one person. Another person felt the first line of the refrain sounded a bit "politically correct." On the whole, they were interested in this hymn, suggesting it might be used as meditation, for confirmation class, as preparation for a sermon on the related texts from the Gospel of John, Genesis 1, or the I AM text from Exodus, at the Easter vigil, as an affirmation of faith, or on Trinity Sunday.

Christ United Methodist Church. "What stands out?"—"the diversities we don't think of about God." Phrases that stood out included *Energies that never tire*, *Savior*, and *Lamb*. Some persons heard all the names as nongendered, others thought *Shepherd, Judge*, and *Defender* connotated maleness. Regarding Troeger's preferred version of *but the truth that feeds them all*, one person thought that would add another, unnecessary, image to the text. The group particularly liked the way the refrain "resolved" the stanzas.

Faculty Forum. Several persons had sung this with the seminary choir for a chapel service. The trinitarian pattern eluded most persons. One person suggested that this text reminded him of the game show *Jeopardy* with the category being "What Is God?" Another felt it ought to be sung with trumpets and marching [suggesting something of the power sensed in the text]. Phrases that people particularly liked were: *Energies that never tire, Root, Way that leads us to I AM*, and the entire third stanza about the Spirit. In discussing the change in the refrain's third line, some saw *behind* as foundational, whereas others liked the sense of God as the source of *truth feeding* our naming. "This hymn puts it all together," summed up one participant.

Additional Comments. "'God is in everything,' says this hymn. I like the concreteness." "This is an all-encompassing hymn." "The refrain is essential."

Worship Leaders' Responses

Ten respondents said they would use "Source and Sovereign, Rock and Cloud" in worship; one of these would use it regularly as he preaches often on the theme of God-language. Two respondents said they would not use it, one because the images are "too scriptural" (and unknown to his congregation), the other because "it reads more like a sermon, with food for thought and study, but not connecting to the emotions."[60] One respondent would use it with her choir;[61] another suggested that it would be more useful beyond the local church, for conferences.

The respondents who would use this hymn suggest including scriptures relating to the images (particularly Exodus and the I AM passages from John). They would use it on Trinity Sunday, at baptismal services, at prayer services, as an opening hymn of praise or as *special music* (a term generally used for solos and duets). One pastor said she would use it after a tragedy like the Oklahoma City bombing as "a reminder of all God is, so that we may remain centered and focused."

Many overall comments were favorable:[62]

> great imagery of the truth that is God
> rich tapestry of Biblical allusions
> good mix of strong and tender, justice, and mercy
> it releases the boundaries surrounding "God"
> it does in the stanzas what the refrain states[63]
> a good reminder that it takes many words and perspectives to being to approach "truth"

Of the individual phrases, several persons remarked on the power of the longer phrases in fourth line of the stanzas (*Life whose life all life endowed* and so on). Several persons raised concerns about the refrain: one felt that "Troeger made an error in putting it in the negative;" another felt it would have been better "to end with praise rather than admonition;" another felt it seemed a bit "confusing and ideological (pushing a point);" and one found the first line of the refrain awkward while wishing to rewrite the third line to read *but the truth within them*

----

5. This last comment was from a musician. Many preachers today would be concerned if their sermons did not connect with the emotions as well as the mind.

6. She feels particularly frustrated that her pastor takes a "one image only of God" approach, and therefore hymns like this one would generally not be used with her congregation.

7. This text, more than the others, called forth remarks about the tune, particularly from United Methodists who found the tune in *The United Methodist Hymnal* difficult for congregations to learn quickly. As one of the musicians said, "The text is too important and too cerebral to risk losing because of frustration in singing." (See also discussion of the tune in Chapter 9.)

8. I particularly agree with this statement, which describes the iconic nature of the text in being what it is calling forth.

all.[9] One pastor felt that this text is particularly important as our imaginations and memories have been "shunted by doctrinal formulas."

BRING MANY NAMES

Given the many natural and biblical images of the preceding two hymns, people responded strongly to the human and relational images of God in this text. The middle four stanzas particularly provoked different thoughts on how we perceive God.

Group Responses

The Church of the Good Hope. The group found the order of this hymn interesting and thought it combined the contrasts well. They remarked that *warm father* is a nurturing image often omitted and that *working mother* is a reality. *Old* and *young* reminded one person of the Joel scripture used also in Acts (Joel 2.28, Acts 2.17). The phrases *calmly piercing* and *joyful darkness* were lifted up. The feelings of the group were summed up in these comments:

> God is everything, wrapped up in one; don't separate God
> eternal mystery of God
> exciting stuff of God
> this is a gift to the Church, everyone can identify with a stanza

Trinity United Methodist Church. "Marvelous" was the first comment on this hymn, immediately followed by laughter over the endlessly working *mother* image. Several persons were struck by the way this text saw God in people, in contrast to the images in the previous two hymns. One person expressed her sense of sadness that the female image of God is often considered too intimate. Another liked the sense that the stanza about *father* "challenges the impassability of God." Several men present felt it would have been better to have the *father* stanza first, although the women felt it was important to sing the *mother* stanza first. One person suggested that the order follows the relating of infants, described by Erickson and others: *mother, father,* parents (*old*),

---

9. It should be noted again that the hymnal version of this text reads *but the truth behind them all.* Troeger's preferred version is his revision that appears in *Borrowed Light—but the truth that feeds them all.* As discussed previously this was noted in the group discussions, but it was not in the individual surveys.

and other children (*young*). The fourth stanza struck several persons as "compelling, makes sense, new image," but another spoke up immediately "but this is the God I grew up with." Many thought the image was subverted, and liked the phrases of *disguises* and *surprises*. The last stanza was seen as a combination of "high" images [mysterious] and incarnational images.

Christ United Methodist Church. "Wow! It's us, we're a part of God." "I like the surprises, the nontraditional inclusion of mother and young." "It grabbed me the first time through." Other comments focused on the process theology (pointed out by the pastor) of the fifth stanza with its sense that God is still unfolding today. Several persons remarked on the comforting semi-refrain of *Hail and hosanna*, although one person saw that phrase as antiquated.

Faculty Forum. One or two persons had sung this hymn in worship previous to our discussion. The group liked the inclusion of *old/young* and *mother/father* as well as the focus on humanity. Someone suggested that the different verses would make an interesting spoken call to worship. Another person said that this hymn reminded them of "The Old Rugged Cross" because of the way they felt God related to them personally through the text.

Additional Comments. "I like the second stanza, where Jesus is strong without being masculine." "The phrase at the end of each stanza helps the list of names." Someone came up after the discussion to say that the images in the fourth stanza still seemed stereotypical, "Grandfather God" on the throne and far away.[10] Adjectives used to describe this text were: *glorious, thought-provoking, true,* and *colorful.*

Worship Leaders' Responses

"Yes, I would definitely use 'Bring Many Names'" responded seven worship leaders. "Maybe," said five persons, whereas two said, "No." Of the two "noes" one felt it was too long and still stereotypical of mothers and fathers, whereas the other said it "takes some sophistica-

---

10. This stanza invoked this response from a variety of persons of all ages, races, and genders. It seems that the opening adjectives of *old, aching,* and *grey* recall the mind-picture of the ancient, bearded, distant, man-God so strongly that it is not changed or challenged by the following phrases. Perhaps a female image here might help to challenge that memory and mind-picture.

tion to use Wren's hymns in an 'average' congregation." Those who definitely would use the hymn or who might suggested using it with "naming" themes (baptism, confirmation) or in the context of a sermon on life-passages, with family services (Grandparent's Day, Mother's Day, Father's Day, Festival of the Christian Home), at intergenerational services, with Sunday School or Vacation Bible School, for Christian Education Sunday or graduate recognition, with the parables of Jesus, during the Lenten cycle, or with stories about the saints of the church. Two persons suggested this hymn be used as special music sung by the choir or at events beyond the local church, such as conferences.

Overall favorable comments included:

interesting ideas and images
heightened everyday language
rich images that use the different ages/stages of life
a God of all ages for all ages
brings out God's dynamic movement in the world
the varied images of God are directly connected to various life situa-
    tions that should appeal to both Boomers and Survivors (Genera-
    tion X)
invitational
like the use and celebration of the different seasons of human life
love the way it affirms the spirit of God in everyone whatever their
    stage in life

One respondent commented that stanzas two and three (*Strong mother God* and *Warm father God*) "are a good balance for those who get stressed with either mother or father." Another person, commenting on these stanzas felt that although the stanza on *father* drew on rich biblical images, the stanza on *mother* drew more on the modern, secular world. Another pastor felt that the *mother* imagery "would sound strange and offensive to many in our congregation, therefore I would hesitate to use it." Lines three through five in stanza three particularly appealed to one respondent as "extremely helpful in our church at this time where a lot of hurt is causing many stresses." One respondent was thankful for the positive images of *youth* in stanza five, lines four and five, while another felt that this stanza's growing God "seems to fly in the face of God's constancy to everyone except process theologians." The closing stanza was cited as "passionate," and another person particularly liked the phrase *closer yet than breathing.* The refrain's *Hail and hosanna* reminded one pastor of Palm Sunday. Stanza four received the most specific comments, negative and positive. On the negative side: Some felt it reinforced ageist stereotypes and "Grandfather God" images and raised concern with the words *grey* and *aching*. One person suggested changing the opening line to *God of years untold*. One person felt that the use of *aching* would strike many as an infirmity of God and therefore strange. On the positive side: "Best stanza—this is instantly recognizable." Others found the opening phrase "wonderful" and also liked the phrase *wiser than despair*. The person who felt stanza four was the strongest suggested reordering the stanzas to 1, 4, 3, 2, 5, 6. Although this would move the text from the most familiar images to the least familiar, I believe the juxtaposition of *mother/father, old/young* serves as a strong reminder that our language is metaphoric.

LEAD ON, O CLOUD OF PRESENCE

Stories are an important part of life and faith, and the retelling of the Exodus story in this hymn resonated with people. They also appreciated its affirmation that life is a journey: When we wander God goes with us.

Group Responses

The Church of the Good Hope. The group loved this "story in song," remarking that it lifts up the desert experience while reminding us of the biblical images of *pillar* and *cloud*. Some read the first two stanzas as more historical and the third related most to today. *Joy be born of tears* reminded one person of the promise in the Psalms that "joy comes in the morning" (30.5b). One person commented on *The journey is our home*: "We forget that the journey itself is important." And *love is law's demand* was claimed as important "in our lawless land." The consensus of the group was that sometimes when we accept Christ we think that's all there is; this text reminds us that we're on our way; God always engages us; this text reminds us of what life is about.

Trinity United Methodist Church. Two persons had sung this hymn previously during worship at a district workshop, another recognized *The journey is our home* as the title of Nelle Morton's book, and one person (the church choir director and Ph.D. student in liturgy) recognized the changes in the text since its publication in *Everflowing Streams*. The echoes of the Exodus story were praised, with the sense of the third stanza coming into the present and pointing to the future. One person felt a similarity between this text and "Lift Every Voice and Sing" (*UMH* #519) with their themes of Exodus, *journey*, and *tears* in the middle stanza. The themes of *journey* and *home*, of being "strangers in a strange land," were given voice in this hymn in a way that gave several persons a sense of comfort when they felt they didn't fit in.

Christ United Methodist Church. "I like this," began the comments, "I can picture the Israelites." The concept of hope was helpful to several persons. People found the "contradictory" [metaphorical] images interesting: *joy born of tears, struggle of life, journey is our home.* One person thought that *the journey is our home* was used in the new United Methodist confirmation materials. Another questioned the idea of freedom while *wandering*, while praising the line, *help us trust the promise through struggle and delay.* One person saw the journey as metaphysical, with the text suggesting that we be happy where we are; still others felt that it meant when God calls us to move, Jesus says, "Don't worry."

Faculty Forum. Words and phrases that resonated with the group were: *The journey is our home, struggle and delay, pillar, vision.* They saw this as a good teaching hymn, to use with the lectionary readings on wilderness and wandering. One person thought it had been considered for *The United Methodist Hymnal* and wondered why it was not included. Another person suggested that the churches of the former Soviet Union might find this hymn useful as those people struggle to find freedom.

Additional Comments. "This hymn helps me remember this story from the Bible." "I like *We are not lost, though wandering.*" "I don't like the combination of *law* and *demand*, but *justice dwells with mercy* is beautiful." "Faithful to scripture." "Liberating." "I can see where this could be useful in bridging Jewish and Christian worship."

Worship Leaders' Responses

Only one person would hesitate to use "Lead on, O Cloud of Presence," because the images would be "meaningless for the congregation unless the scriptures or sermons mentioned the cloud and fire from the book of Exodus." The other thirteen responses were very enthusiastically, "Yes!" Times to use the hymn ranged from general use, especially as closing hymn of dedication, to peace and justice, renewal of baptism, confirmation, Human Relations emphasis, national holidays such as

July 4, Memorial Day and Martin Luther King Jr. Day, graduate recognition, Eastertide to Pentecost, "anytime the Exodus scriptures are used," to consecration of mission trip groups or elders and deacons (in the Presbyterian Church).

Overall favorable comments included:

> I wish we had more peace and justice hymns like this that are "contemporary"
>
> sings well to the head and to the heart
>
> this is it! beyond sexist/nonsexist arriving in the promised land of rich biblical imagery
>
> wonderful Exodus imagery, great words, solid liberation theology
>
> an instant revelation—association with its model deflates triumphalism and gives honest, realistic hope
>
> a good example of Ruth's gift for rewriting traditional hymns
>
> good image of seeking and following God's guidance
>
> takes a grand hymn and puts it in more inclusive language in words and images—useful in older, more traditional congregations to introduce them to new images
>
> like scriptural images, simple phrasing
>
> recognition that though not always knowing (never knowing) where we're going we can celebrate the moment of change and journey, life itself

Within the first stanza, phrases that stood out to the respondents included the final phrase, *where milk and honey flow*, that was "great to see," and *new hopes within us grow*. Although one person felt that too many conjunctions (four) in the second stanza made the movement of thought jerky,[66] several lines in this stanza came in for praise. *Joy born of tears* "is a wonderful line, so true," said one pastor. Another pastor cited that line and the preceding line as particularly poignant, and cited the final line of this stanza, *The journey is our home*, as one of genius. Another respondent concurred about that line—"What a difference this perspective would make in our churches!" Still, another respondent felt this final line did not "ring quite true" and was concerned as well about line five and six of this stanza—"I want a *home* that's not always moving around;" the third stanza's sixth line gave a "better hope for *home*" to this pastor. One pastor knew the earlier version of the third stanza of this text and preferred it to the revision. One respondent found

---

11. Although I didn't find the conjunctions problematic, if the movement is made jerky by their use, it might be an iconic feature of the text, reflecting the constant stopping and starting of the Exodus, although not intentional on the part of the author.

respondent found *help us trust the promise through struggle and delay* "a good reminder not to give up," whereas another praised the strength of the closing two lines of the text.

OF WOMEN AND OF WOMEN'S HOPES WE SING

This text seemed to raise the most emotional responses of the six texts. Sometimes responses differed by gender, and occasionally by age. On the whole women were most accepting of this text, but often felt it might best be used in a group with other women (without men).

Group Responses

The Church of the Good Hope. The opening discussion of this hymn centered on the irony of the proclamation of equality because, even though in church circles women outnumber men, the women leaders are mostly volunteer, and the men are "breadwinners." Someone said, "If we followed Paul to a conclusion, there would be no women in church." Commenting on the third stanza someone remarked that even when women are in the forefront, they are not equal with male leaders, standing down instead of in the pulpit.[67] Another person noted the second-class status of women, considered unclean after childbirth. Several persons saw this hymn as a mission song, spreading the gospel like the women at the tomb or the Samaritan woman at the well. Important phrases lifted up were *birthing new belief, Magnificat,* the equality of *commonwealth,* and the inclusivity of the final line of the text. *Forgiving what is past* rang true for some about the need to learn and then move on. Many felt that the sense of empowering that continued to the end of the text was very important. Although one or two were unsure about singing it in worship, one man suggested that "We need to give women their due."

Trinity United Methodist Church. "This is certainly emancipatory," began the comments, "claiming the empowerment of women and the use of their gifts." "It's a 'women's' hymn," remarked another, "the flip side of 'Rise up, O Men of God.'" Several women noted feeling that hymns in worship sometimes were oppressive. "['Of Women, and

---

12. This concern, although valid, is more complex than it might appear, because some women in leadership choose to "stand down" with the people, attempting to model a different kind of leadership than the "raised up" leader.

of Women's Hopes'] is exclusive language, yet important for women and there's relief at the end when men are included," said one person. One man found the first stanza images not emancipatory, while another found them "helpful." Several persons felt it would be hard for men to sing. Someone said that it was helpful to have other images of commonality between women than just motherhood and embodiment. One person felt *commonwealth* was a strictly Western term. Someone else remarked that we aren't *equal as disciples* walking the road. The final line of the hymn was cited as "beautiful but unbiblical" (see Chapter 12, regarding this theme of the Ecumenical Decade). Many of the women were enthusiastic about the possibility of using this text with women's groups and on women's retreats.

Christ United Methodist Church. Although one person liked the image of *mystery within our flesh and bone* and another mentioned the importance of "this worldly" work and status, most of this group felt this was "just for women." One woman said, "This turns me off, there's too much *bearing* and *birthing*, it's a bit superior."[13] When the pastor wondered aloud if it might be used on a Sunday morning to balance old images, most persons expressed feeling uncomfortable putting these images next to father images of God. One person conceded that it might be used on Mother's Day.

Faculty Forum. Most of this group saw this hymn as affirming women as the children of God. They liked the specificity of the opening line and of the *God whose image is our own.* Other phrases lifted up were *bearing and birthing new belief, forgiving, when men and women.* One person saw *prophecy, Magnificat* and *dream* as prophecy, praise, and vision.

Additional Comments. "I like the positive ending of this hymn and the word *womanspirit.*" Persons commented on the lack of true rhyme in stanza three and the "essay" quality. Yet another person said, "This answers a great need in my work with women religious for new images that will resonate with the heritage of faith."

---

13. What is happening when giving birth is seen as such a controversial event, dividing women, and something to be either embarrassed about or to "talk down" rather than a joyous, terrifying, creative wonder?

Worship Leaders' Responses

"Of Women, and of Women's Hopes We Sing" generated the lengthiest comments from worship leaders about its usability. Five persons said "Yes" they would use it on Sunday morning (three men and two women), six women (pastors and musicians) said they would use it only for United Methodist Women's Sunday or women's retreats or other events, two persons questioned if they would ever use it, and one person said "No, the opening line would be off-putting to my congregation and women who say 'I'm not a feminist.'" In addition to U.M.W. Sunday and women's events, the other suggestions for usage ranged from Advent (particularly "Mary's Sunday") to Easter and post-Easter, Mother's Day, with themes about women from scripture and tradition or about freedom from oppression, and in healing services, "particularly with oppressed women, possibly in a service where divorced women were seeking healing."

Overall comments reflect both the text itself and the questions it raises about women and men. Even considering this text made people think about concerns around the recognition of gender in worship.

> would males feel excluded? I recognize the overwhelming "male language" in hymns—that isn't right either! would like another stanza about females and males working together (some place for males "to go")
> represents a beautiful balance between the intentions of worship, theology, of heart and soul!
> references to justice, power, and forgiveness [stanzas 3 and 4] will appeal to many women but be threatening to men who "just don't get it" [from a male]
> I like stanzas two and four
> theme too progressive, yet still a damn good theme
> interesting
> might need to be in context where the focus is on women's faith role so not read as exclusive language
> I like the idea of seeking a finer justice and that it is together, women and men, that by God's grace we experience the freedom of stones rolled away
> important to use with contextual comments
> no reason that all, men and women, can't sing of women and women's hopes, as along as we aren't doing so as the only valid hopes
> too strong for me [from a woman]

An enthusiastic "yes" drew on the phrases *passion for the promises of life, Magnificat, and dream.* The third line of this stanza was cited by a man as a good feminine image of growth and development, whereas a woman said, "I personally do not like the birthing image that is so often a theme for women. Giving birth is a privilege but not one to brag about."

The opening line of stanza two evoked several concerned comments that the *Imago Dei* concept was reversed or presented weakly. One person (a female pastor) questioned the meaning of *womanspirit*.

The use of *commonwealth* in stanza three was questioned by several persons who felt that it would not be recognized as a substitute for kingdom.[14] One pastor felt it was good to affirm explicitly that we walk the road *equal as disciples*. Another noted "the good justice based theology" of this stanza.

"I personally love stanza four," said one respondent, as "a nice 'wipe the slate clean' and clear out the emotionalism/defensiveness of the women's movement so we can move on to better times." The closing line evoked several comments, one person asking, "What does *stone* symbolize?" and another pastor saying it was too esoteric, as his congregation is very literal.[15] Another respondent said that "the cooperative image here is the strongest line in the hymn, without it I don't think men would want to sing this." Yet another respondent felt that the closing line was "a good biblical image of new beginnings."

O HOLY SPIRIT, ROOT OF LIFE

This text was comforting to many, not only because of its nongendered images (unlike those in the preceding text) but also for the images of protecting wings and sense of embodiment. People were also delighted to know about this woman (Hildegard of Bingen) from our Christian heritage.

Group Responses

Church of the Good Hope. This hymn drew the fewest comments from this group, perhaps because of its introspective nature. They felt it

---

14. It is my experience that the substitution is a "teachable moment" wherein the concept of the kingdom of God can be expanded in people's understanding.

15. These responses point to the idea that knowing this hymn was written for Easter and based on the biblical story of rolling the stone away from Jesus' grave is an important factor for understanding it.

spoke to them similar to the way the Bible does. *Wounds* were identified as hurts, sins, and illness. *Becoming flesh to wear our pain* was understood as Christ on the cross, restoring creation.

Trinity United Methodist Church. Although one or two persons had a "hard time relating" to this text, others praised its "primitive, but not simplistic, holistic" character. One person contrasted it with "Source and Sovereign, Rock and Cloud," finding "O Holy Spirit, Root of Life" more intangible and poetic. Many liked the images of the *wings* of the Spirit encompassing and carrying us, and someone associated this text with Psalm 91. One person who was interested also in Native American spirituality saw connections between the *wings* of this text with the Native American use of *hawk* and *eagle* as Spirit indicators. Another felt *Cleanser of all things* was helpful in understanding forgiveness. *Root of life* struck one person as disconnected from the rest of the wings images, yet that person also knew about Hildegard's interest in herbs and healing. The group suggested this hymn might be used during Advent or Lent, or at healing services (not just for physical healing). One person also thought it might be used at ecumenical services, where the work of the Spirit is something we can agree on, wherever else we might disagree.

Christ United Methodist Church. This group seemed particularly relieved to sing this hymn after "Of Women, and of Women's Hopes We Sing," and responded enthusiastically to the images found here. "Everything in it reflects the Holy Spirit" said one person; "it's my favorite [of the six]." Several persons knew about Hildegard's work with herbs and healing; others found *Root of life* reminding them of springtime and harvest. *Lustrous movement* struck several persons as a very visual image, although one person, struck by that image and the wings images was reminded of Madeleine L'Engle's book, *A Wind in the Door* [that carried images of wings on some paperback covers]. Some were reminded of Advent with *becoming flesh* in stanza two, whereas another person thought about cell renewal in connection with *all creation is restored.* The freedom given (in Jesus Christ) in stanza two was seen as a "whole new way of life," "something that nonbelievers don't understand." The *wings* of stanza three were seen as trinitarian (*above, below, and through the world*). One person associated *wings* with the life-continuing activity of butterflies and bees pollinating flowers. Several persons mentioned the strong "nature" images of the texts and a sense in the text of the cycle of life.

Faculty Forum. The group found the intermixing of trinitarian images in this hymn helpful. One person suggested that the names in this text relate to the Third Person of the Trinity whereas the actions relate to the First and Second Persons. Someone pointed out the sense of *Vigor* in meaning *energies* [that they also liked in Troeger's text]. Another person knew about Hildegard's illuminations and felt that this text expresses the unity given by the Spirit, which those paintings exhibit. Some thought the hymn would be helpful in teaching, particularly using the metaphors as openings to conversations about the Spirit/God and our relationship.

Additional Comments. Although some didn't connect with this hymn and found it lacking in motivation to social action, others found this a comforting text. Someone suggested that *Soaring Power* was "more angelic" than *Moving Force* [and thus more in line with the tone of the text]. "I love the 'calmness' of this text."

Worship Leaders' Responses

Eleven worship leaders responded, "Yes, I would use 'O Holy Spirit, Root of Life,'" and the other three said, "Maybe" (two of those said they would use it with a choir). Six persons said they would use it at Pentecost, and four persons suggested healing services. Other suggestions for use were at confirmation, baptism, Trinity Sunday, St. Hildegard's Day, when focusing on nature or the restoration of creation, as preparation for a prayer of confession, as a call to worship, during Advent, during the Sundays after Christmas or during Epiphany "as we celebrate what difference the birth of Christ makes in our lives" (these seasons were particularly seen as reflected in the second stanza of the hymn), when focusing on prayer life, and in connection with texts about "eagle's wings."[16]

Overall favorable comments included:

good hymn with interesting history and strong images
wonderful text with depth
super lyrics from a wonderful saint [Hildegard]
quite nice
angel images probably a big hit these days

---

16. A recent popular hymn is "On Eagle's Wings" by Michael Joncas (*UMH* #143) based on Exodus 19:4 and Psalm 91.

great hymn from a great woman [Hildegard]—the best images of the
collection
very usable—certainly would speak to all

One respondent said, "Although the dove is a traditional image of
the Spirit, for some reason the reference to the Spirit's *wings* struck me
as innovative." Another responded, "This is a very comforting text, like
wrapping up in a warm comforter or blanket and having your faith and
energy restored."

Two persons cited *cleanser of all things* as a great image in the first
stanza, whereas a third found *anoint our wounds* and *lustrous movement* powerful. One respondent liked stanzas two and three better than
the first "because the images seemed less jumbled, more related to each
other."

Although several respondents suggested that the second stanza
made the hymn useful for Advent through Epiphany, one respondent
found that stanza elusive and allusive, commenting, "Is it the Spirit
who becomes flesh?—not according to the Prologue of John."[17] *Eternal
Vigor* received several comments: One pastor said, "What a surprising
description." Another remarked, "This is new! not common, seems
almost a bit odd" and then cited lines three and four of this stanza as
her favorites. One of the musicians loved the image, "especially after
being sick and lacking vigor for the last six months!"

One pastor mentioned that *O Holy Wisdom*, like the reference to
Wisdom in "O Come, O Come, Emmanuel" (*UMH* #211, st. 2), was a
"safe" reference to *Sophia*. Four persons found the closing two lines of
the hymn beautiful and strong.

CONSIDERATION OF EMANCIPATORY ASPECTS

Here we consider briefly the emancipatory elements that were high-
lighted in both the group and individual interactions with these texts.
Further comments appear in the conclusion to this text, in the following
chapter.

"God of the Sparrow" was appreciated for the diversity of images
presented, particularly for the images of the whole of creation. The
change from *creature* to *children* was viewed by many as an "ah-ha"

---

17. In the multidimensional reading it was pointed out that this interweav-
ing of the Spirit and Jesus Christ reflected the perichoretic nature of this text, as
the Persons of the Trinity are fluid rather than static. (See Chapter 13.)

moment, an insight about the true relationship between God and humanity and all creation. Another emancipatory aspect to this text are the many "windows" for persons to see God and be seen by God, as in the example of the *rainbow*. Most persons understood this hymn as an expression of care for the earth, as well as calling forth human responses to the Creator.

"Source and Sovereign, Rock and Cloud" was experienced as almost overwhelming in its diversity of images. Pointing out the trinitarian pattern helped many make sense of what was otherwise too chaotic. For many persons, the refrain served as a vital unifying element. Most persons were willing to hear and sing the variety of metaphors, yet clearly it is a text that takes time to absorb.

"Bring Many Names" brought immediate responses from almost everyone, as they identified with different aspects of God. The fourth stanza was the divisive stanza, with most persons seeing it either as emancipatory or as restrictive. Interestingly, the sixth stanza seemed to be the best loved, as it brought together the various images plus balanced the nearness and awesomeness of God all at the same time.

"Lead on, O Cloud of Presence" was enthusiastically received as an imaginative re-presentation of the biblical story in tune with contemporary experience. It resonated as truthful for many persons, and many saw it addressing concerns of justice. The retelling of the biblical story was important to many, who value scripture and tradition. The experience of being able to share this text across Jewish and Christian faiths was also emancipatory to some.

"Of Women, and of Women's Hopes We Sing" raised the energy level of the singers. Whether they appreciated the images or felt that they were exclusive, this text challenged many persons, that is a task of emancipatory language.

"O Holy Spirit, Root of Life" served as an anamnesis for many persons and embodied a sense of healing and welcome, both aspects of emancipatory language. The *winged* images also gave this text a sense of mysterion.

The factor of usage is a very important one regarding emancipatory language. If texts are written but not sung in worship, their language cannot emancipate. The related factor of music cannot be underrated— one of the reasons "God of the Sparrow," "Bring Many Names" and "Lead on, O Cloud of Presence" resonated with persons was that each is paired with a singable tune, in the first two cases tunes without previous associations. It helps "Lead on, O Cloud of Presence" that its tune, LANCASHIRE, has been sung to an Easter text ("The Day of Resurrection" by John of Damascus) and not solely wedded to the Shurtleff text; otherwise, it might have too much militarism associated with the tune.

The resistance of both worship leaders and congregations to new texts and the lack of time to study texts and fully uncover their meaning are other factors that will affect the use or nonuse of emancipatory language. When things are seen as "new" and are not seen as obviously resonate with scripture and tradition, they can be easily dismissed. Yet each of the six texts studied brings with it a richness of scriptural resonance as well as resonance with today's world.

Chapter 15
Conclusion

INTRODUCTION

This book has attempted to show that the language of hymns has much to commend it for study. We have considered a strand of the history of hymns and how hymns function as a genre within the context of Christian worship. In addition to the obvious poetic characteristics of rhyme and meter, we have explored the scriptural, theological, rhetorical, and linguistic aspects of hymns. We have developed a methodology that enables a multidimensional reading of the various aspects of hymnic language. We have shown not only that there is a wealth of understanding to be found within each of hymns studied but that hymns as a genre are complex.

For the laity of the church, the persons in the pews, hymns are an important means of receiving and expressing theology, what we know and believe about God. Through hymn singing, the treasures of the church—the Wesleys' understanding about grace, Luther's rock-solid faith, and the healing understood by Hildegard of Bingen—are passed down through generations. Through hymn singing, persons can feel included or feel shut out. Through hymn singing, faith can be awakened, strengthened, or challenged.

In addition to defining hymns as clearly as possible and delineating their function, this book has developed the concept of emancipatory hymnic language and applied it to the study and singing of six recent hymn texts to determine if they demonstrate elements of emancipatory language. The focus of this concluding chapter is on aspects of emancipatory language found in the six hymns studied.

EMANCIPATORY LANGUAGE IN HYMNS

Emancipatory language, as described in this text, is based on the premise that God identifies with and loves those on the margins of society,
the poor, the outcast, the differently abled, and women. The theologies
of liberation and the Social Gospel, along with feminist theology, have
emphasized that God's promises for shalom apply to this life and this
world. Our definition of emancipatory language begins with making
women and others on the margins of society visible and moves toward
language about humanity that is truthful and just. Emancipatory God-
language seeks a diversity of metaphors that are all held within the
unity of one God, revealed in scripture, in the life of Jesus Christ and
still today through the Holy Spirit, to set us free from sin and death.
The strategy for creating emancipatory language is imaginative construction, aided by anamnesis (remembering and making present again)
and mysterion (God's self-revelation). The results of singing emancipatory language may not be evident immediately, but over time
changes will be seen in the church and in the lives of those using such
language.

The six hymns were chosen for several specific reasons. First, I
chose authors who represented both genders and whose work I believe
will endure the test of time. Second, with the exception of "Of women,
and of women's hopes we sing" that only appears in one, the hymns
chosen have each been published in at least two mainline Protestant
denominational hymnals since 1989. Third, I chose hymns that I believe represented at least one or more aspects of emancipatory language. Fourth, I believed that each of these hymns included some
emancipatory aspect of three emerging theologies: liberation theology,
feminist theology, or ecological theology. Last, these hymns appealed
to me personally and were texts I was interested in studying.

God of the Sparrow

This text had several additional factors to commend it for this book,
mentioned on page 106 above. To reiterate, its lack of rhyme and its
unusual meter immediately emancipate it from the tradition of regular
metered and rhymed hymn texts. It moves beyond gendered language
for both humanity and God, giving a marvelous diversity-in-unity of
metaphors for the divine. "God of the Sparrow" is also important for its
removal of humanity from the center of creation, an important perspective in ecological theology. Jaroslav Vajda does this almost without our

notice, by beginning his text with its focus on God and then on nature: *sparrow, whale, stars, earthquake,* and *storm. The trumpet blast* and *the pruning hook* point to God's justice, judgment, and vision.

The multidimensional reading of this text displayed its deep resonance with biblical faith, as each of the metaphors related to God contained multiple scriptural references, therefore grounding the text in biblical revelation. The visibility concern of emancipatory language is answered by the phrases *the hungry, the sick, the prodigal,* and *the foe,* and each of these persons from the margins of society are held in God's care in this text. In addition, the truthfulness about life's variety is carried in the words *earthquake, storm, woe, save, grace, love.* The reiteration of *God of* maintains the unity of God, whereas the *of* phrases draw out the diversity of God. The setting of the text, without rhyme and punctuation, is evidence of imaginative construction, as is the drawing on scripture (one type of anamnesis). The variety of metaphors also suggests God's revelation to the author.

I chose this hymn in part because I knew that it was being widely used, not only appearing in many hymnals but also actually being sung in worship. The praxis section of the research on this hymn confirms the wide age span touched by this text; it is a hymn that can grow with people. Worship leaders were almost unanimous in using it and suggesting a wide variety of worship settings when it might be used; these are vital factors to the continuing use of a hymn. The fact that congregations choose this hymn during hymn sings also speaks to its continuing usage and its appeal. Equally important is the use of this hymn already outside of worship at events such as during a pet bird's funeral and on a walk for hunger.

Three other comments stand out regarding the emancipatory nature of this text: First is the turn from *creature* to *children* in the final stanza; this was commented on by many persons as a wonderful affirmation of God's love for each one of us, felt personally by many singers. Second is the comment by a lesbian that she feels included in God's care through the metaphor of the rainbow used in the third stanza; this text reached out to her in a way that many texts have not. Third is the response that came after the hymn was sung in worship at The Church of the Good Hope: "When we sang it, it sounded like we were in a cathedral; it was louder than we could have sung." I understand this response as relating a spiritual experience, wherein things are more than they seem or sound. Sometimes in worship there is a sense that one has joined the worship of "the great cloud of witnesses" (Heb. 12.1), and that is an emancipatory experience.

Source and Sovereign, Rock and Cloud

This text was chosen for its diversity of metaphors for God and the intriguing way in that they are juxtaposed. Surely this text opens up our understanding that God is more than we can imagine. The multidimensional reading of this text revealed not only the intricate pattern of the metaphors but also their deep scriptural resonance.

Although avoiding gendered pronouns for God, the text includes metaphors that, although literally nongendered may recall both female and male images (*wisdom/water, judge/defender*),[73] in addition to the many natural images that have no gender association (*rock, cloud, root, vine, bread, wine*). The second stanza is particularly important in regard to feminist theology as it describes Jesus Christ without reverting to male-identified metaphors, using instead metaphors of *word, root, vine, lamb, well, bread, wine.* Two of the metaphors used in this stanza are frequently associated with female characteristics of the divine, *wisdom* and *water.* The metaphors from the natural world lift up ecological concerns in a subtle way, reminding us of the reflection of God in *rock, cloud, root, vine, lamb, dove, thunder, whirlwind, fire.*

Clearly the focus of this text is on the diversity of metaphors for God, and for each Person of the Trinity; if that is not clear in the stanzas, it is reiterated in the refrain after each stanza. Here is a strong plea for an understanding that none of us holds the truth—God is the Truth feeding all our attempts at naming, our mere metaphors. The diversity of metaphors also points to the revelation of God throughout scripture and throughout Christian tradition to our own time. Biblical metaphors are re-presented here and the mystery that is God is proclaimed. Thomas Troeger has been very imaginative in the construction of this text, in the juxtaposition of metaphors and in his subtle use of the trinitarian pattern.

Only two-thirds of the worship leaders would choose this hymn for worship, although the rest were willing to use it in other settings. Occasionally in the group settings persons seemed overwhelmed by the diversity of metaphors and the poetic catalogue. The refrain was seen as

---

[73]As mentioned in the discussion of this text, Chapter 9, words like *judge* and *defender* may be changing in their associations as more women preside in courtrooms and we recall the image of a mother bear defending her cubs. Still, for many persons, the mind-pictures are those of male judges and knights in shining armor.

vital, as a "resting place" and also something that persons could affirm, as opposed to the "listing" of metaphors. The groups did not give strong emotional responses as they did with other texts, except perhaps to the refrain. There is some sense in mainline denominations that those who want to include many metaphors are under siege from those who would enforce "Father, Son, and Holy Spirit" as the only orthodox metaphors for God. Those persons who felt under siege took particular comfort in the refrain.

There was concern voiced with this text from those who knew the tune first published with it in *The United Methodist Hymnal*. Their concern was that that tune is difficult to sing, and therefore not usable. My personal experience with this text began with reading it and delighting in the variety of metaphors. Then one summer for three monthly hymn sings this hymn was chosen by a fourteen-year-old boy in the congregation where I served as musician. The first time my accompanying partner looked at the tune and said, "I'm sorry, I don't think I can play this," and she didn't. The congregation and I struggled through that time, with the repetitions getting easier throughout the summer. The youth who chose the text was intrigued by the many names for God and he also delighted in choosing a tune the congregation obviously was not comfortable singing. By the time this hymn was sung in worship the following Trinity Sunday (the next June) people were beginning to be able to appreciate the all-encompassing nature of the metaphors, and to have some ease with the tune. I doubt however if it will ever be a general favorite. In the praxis research for this study I was glad to follow Troeger's suggestion to use a more accessible tune for his text, choosing the tune that accompanies it in *Chalice Hymnal*, ABERYSTWYTH. This experience, however, demonstrates the complexities of text and tune and their acceptance by congregations. Can texts be emancipatory if they are not sung? Will an extraordinary text, like this one, be used for study and meditation, and thus yield its understandings and challenges in that way? Will users of *Chalice Hymnal* with the "easier" tune sing this hymn more often than United Methodists do?

Bring Many Names

This hymn was chosen for its *mother* metaphor of God and the delightful metaphors relating God to the genders and stages of human life. Although some might be concerned that the *mother* metaphor limits women's identification with this text, the stanza is God-focused, and includes other images of women's experience, *working night and day, planning*, working with *equations*, and *genius*, and *play*. Women can also see themselves in the stanzas about *young* and *old*, as those metaphors are embodied without being gendered. Truthfulness and embodiment appear also in the words *hugging, feeling, aching, grey*, and *eager*. The juxtaposition of metaphors emphasize that all aspects of human life are treasured by God.

"Bring many names" exhibits emancipatory characteristics of liberation, feminist, and process theologies. It is explicit in its inclusion of women and men through the metaphors of *mother* and *father*, and the metaphors of *young* and *old*. Placing the stanza on *mother* first exhibits a feminist understanding, as does the emphasis on *father's* nurturing possibilities. Feminist concerns for stereotypes are also affirmed by the inclusion of *equation* in the stanza on *mother*, breaking women's "math anxiety" stereotype. We have discussed how the stanza *Young, growing God* reflects and teaches an understanding of process theology. Liberation theology's emphasis on justice and truthfulness is expressed in the phrases *calmly piercing evil's new disguises, saying no to falsehood and unkindness, crying out for justice*. The inclusion of *darkness* as an important part of God in stanza six, can also be read as liberating for African-Americans, because *darkness* is often seen as negative.[74]

The God-language in this text is emancipatory in its stretch to include *mother* and *young*. The focus of the four middle stanzas and the additional metaphors in the final stanza give a wide variety of metaphors for God. Although the text is not biblical in the sense of retelling a biblical story, the metaphors used can be found in scripture as well as in human experience. Clearly human life throughout the ages is represented by the metaphors in the text. *Joyful darkness* can also be seen as an anamnesis as it reflects not only biblical understanding but was also important to the influential Gregory of Nyssa in the early church; this is something perhaps only realized by a multidimensional reading of the text. Brian Wren has been very imaginative in the construction of this text, in its metaphors and its meter. He has also clearly demonstrated testing his individual revelations with communal affirmation and correction, as this text has been revised several times since its first writing.

---

[74]As James Baldwin said, "For a black writer in this country to be born into the English language is to realize that the assumptions on that the language operates [sic] are his enemy. . . . I was forced to reconsider similes: as black as sin, as black as night, and blackhearted" ("On Language, Race and the Black Writer," Los Angeles Times, April 29, 1979, V: 1; quoted in Bolinger 1980, 89).

The praxis groups responded, for the most part, immediately and personally to this hymn. They particularly appreciated the personal images and felt that these brought God into relationship with them. Some disagreement ensued over the stanza of *Old, aching God* and whether it was stereotypical or not, therefore whether it was emancipatory or confining. The worship leaders were more mixed in their responses, with only half affirming this hymn's unqualified use in worship. They were often more conflicted about both the fourth stanza (*Old*) and the second (*mother*) and whether these were emancipatory or stereotypic. Like "God of the Sparrow" this hymn is aided by a singable and strong tune, that probably enhanced the group experience of this hymn. In one sense, this hymn meets the criteria for emancipatory language as it challenges our understanding of God not only to include *mother* but to question what we think about God as *old* and *young*, and by reflection, what we think about ourselves and others as mothers, as fathers, as young and old.

Lead On, O Cloud of Presence

This text was chosen for several reasons. First, its author has been a leader in writing and editing resources for worship that reach out to include women and others on the margins of society. Second, it retells a biblical story, an important task of hymns in my perspective; singing scripture and biblical stories is a particularly effective way to learn and memorize this wellspring of faith.

Ruth Duck was one of the first intentionally to write hymns that did not exclude women, and this is one of her earliest attempts. As we have discussed in Chapters 5 and 11, this hymn emerged as a creative ritualization as she attempted to rewrite a hymn that was full of masculine and military images. As such, it is a wonderful example of imaginative construction.

"Lead on, O Cloud of Presence" particularly reflects liberation and feminist theologies. The earliest of these six texts, it was written when liberation theology was first being taught in seminaries, when there was great excitement about the implications it had for Christians on the margins of society. Women were just beginning to see themselves on the margins of society as well, and Duck was concerned with creating hymns that praised God, included and invited women, and carried liberation concerns. As we have discussed, the Exodus event is an important focal point for liberation theology, and "Lead on, O Cloud of Presence" focuses on that story and its implications for today. The freedom and liberation promised by God as well as God's presence as we move toward that freedom form the central theme of the text. Although gendered terms are not used, the opening image of the *cloud of Presence* has increasingly been claimed by feminist theologians as an important image that reflects the feminine character of the Holy. Concern for justice, an important element of both liberation and feminist theologies, is very evident in the text, in the phrases *bondage left behind us, justice dwells with mercy, love is law's demand.*

Language for humanity includes the words *sons and daughters* and use of the first person plural throughout the text. Truthfulness about human experience appears in the honesty of *tears, fears, rejoicing,* and *wandering.* Concerns for justice form the final lines of the text, its description of the land of promise.

The language for God opens us to the metaphors of *cloud, fire,* and *freedom,* metaphors seldom used in hymnody but strongly biblical. Therefore they are an anamnesis, re-presenting God's presence anew to us. The mystery of God is captured in *cloud* and *fire,* in their connotations and in their freshness. The emancipatory characteristic of revelation was also present in the creation of this text, which was revealed in the midst of rewriting Shurtleff's text. The testing of individual revelation in community may be seen in the revision of Duck's text from 1974 to 1989.

The persons in the praxis groups and individuals were very enthusiastic about this text. There was a sense that they hunger for strong biblical texts and that this text feeds that need. Persons affirmed that the text was true to their experience of wandering, being tearful and fearful, and yet knowing God was with them. There was sometimes a sense of relief spoken as persons felt affirmed that *the journey is home.* The justice concerns and description of the land of promise not as escape but as filled with *justice, mercy,* and *love* was appreciated by many. Most persons know the Shurtleff text well and found in comparison that Duck's version has a sense of peace with justice, even though the word *peace* is not sung.

It is interesting to compare the sense of identification that persons found in this text with that of the previous text. In Wren's text, people got so involved in the middle four stanzas that they almost could not or did not differentiate the metaphors for God from their own identification with the metaphors. Here in Duck's text the identification is with the Hebrew people and with those who still *wander* (all of us!) and there is a strong sense of God's presence with us, but as different from us. That balance of God's nearness and yet separateness is captured throughout Duck's text and also in the final stanza of Wren with its contrast of *joyful darkness far beyond* and *closer yet than breathing.*

This text has the advantages of a familiar tune, strong biblical resonance, and a variety of worship settings in that leaders are able to use it. The one person who complained that it is too dependent on the biblical images may be in a "church growth" setting where the strategy is not to depend on traditional symbols and the Bible to attract those persons called "seekers." This text could be used as a "teachable moment" to introduce the congregation to these powerful images of God's presence.

One final word on the emancipatory nature of this text: At the presentation of this text in the workshop in Michigan, one woman came up very excited afterward. She is a Christian and her grandson was preparing for his bar mitzvah. It is traditional for each set of grandparents to offer something in that worship setting, and she was delighted and relieved to find a text that bridges the Jewish and Christians faiths in ways that can be strongly affirmed by each. Emancipatory language, as conceived in this text, is very interested in this building of bridges and drawing persons together in praise of God.

Of Women, and of Women's Hopes We Sing

This text was chosen specifically for its explicit mention of women throughout the text. Shirley Erena Murray has written a number of texts that exhibit emancipatory language, but this one was the most specific in making women visible. The use of the first person plural reinforces the collective identification of women and builds to *the promise of empowering for our day.* Truth and justice concerns appear in words and phrases *equal as disciples, work and status, forgiving, past/new, men and women* (together) *roll the stone away.*

"Of Women, and of Women's Hopes We Sing" is thus the most obvious expression of feminist theology in the six texts studied. Liberation theology may also be seen in the concerns for equality *in work and status* and the search for *a finer justice.* Written for an event focused on churches in solidarity with women, this text follows Ruether's critical principal, promoting full humanity for women. In making women visible, in addressing their social and spiritual concerns in a way that empowers, and in describing God in creative ways that reflect the feminine dimension of the divine, this text moves feminist theology into doxology.

The language used for God shows Murray's imaginative construction: *God whose image is our own, mystery within our flesh and bone,* and *womanspirit moving through all time in prophecy, Magnificat and dream.* There is a sense of three-in-one, diversity-in-unity, of God who creates, God who is incarnate, and God who still moves among us. This text clearly draws on the revelation of God to and through women, with the sense of past, present, and future all included in that revelation.

It has been noted that this hymn generated the most emotional responses of both the groups and individuals involved in the praxis research for this text. A number of women in particular felt it would be wonderful to use in settings focused on women and women's spirituality. Some men and some women saw it as divisive, whereas others felt it might be useful to redress past imbalances. Some worship leaders were willing to use it on Sunday morning, and an equal number felt it would be better received at women's retreats.

Although it is important that texts like this one be used, some might say that perhaps it is not necessary that they be repeated often, for part of the task of a hymn like this is to startle our imagination and to challenge our thinking. Yet there may be women's groups and women's settings and congregations that live with this hymn and are empowered to make real changes in the way they interact with each other and the world. Real change will not occur until emancipatory language takes hold in our thoughts and our actions. How will this occur if congregations that profess to value all human beings continue subconsciously to consider some human beings more worthy than others?

O Holy Spirit, Root of Life

This text was chosen for several reasons. First, it brings to life the words and vision of a woman long-forgotten in the church, Hildegard of Bingen. Second, the images are fresh and resonate with ecological theology. Third, it is a hymn focused on the Holy Spirit, the least-sung-about member of the Trinity.

"O Holy Spirit, Root of Life" reflects a feminist perspective, that of valuing the visions of a woman. This text also resonates with Elizabeth Johnson's emphasis on the *Spirit*, as a starting point for feminist theology and it includes *Wisdom* as a metaphor for God. Hildegard has been an important resource for some persons in the field of ecological theology, with her work concerning the wholeness of persons and her interest in plants and healing. The nature images, including the images of wings and the inclusion of all creation, give this text a sense of wholeness for all creation, as the place wherein God dwells. As such it also includes the feminist and ecological sense of embodiment, given voice in works such as McFague's *The Body of God*.

Like several of the texts studied, this one does not rely on explicit gender references, yet there is a strong sense of embodiment within the text, aided by words like *root, cleansing, anointing, wings, wounds, becoming flesh, pain, restored, carry, encompass*. The realities of *cleansing, wounds* and *pain* are spoken of and gathered up in *anointing* and as *all creation is restored*.

The metaphors for God seem striking in their freshness, although they are almost 900 years old—*Root of life, Eternal Vigor, Saving One, Holy Wisdom, Moving Force/Soaring Power*. These metaphors are presented as part of the diversity within God's unity, and in this text, the Persons of the Trinity dance gracefully, intertwining their steps. This text is a wonderful example of anamnesis, as Hildegard's words are brought to life anew for us today, and her revelations shared. There is also a sense of mysterion in the text, of the mystery of God, and the space it makes for us. Jean Janzen has done marvelous work in enabling these ancient words to sing once more.

In the praxis groups this hymn did what it sings about, serving to heal the discord of the previous challenging text and to recapture the sense of praising God together. Two-thirds of the worship leaders would use it in worship. Persons felt encircled and encompassed by the loving arms/wings of God as they sang this text and commended its use for healing services. As one person, recovering from a lengthy illness, shared, "This is a very comforting text, like wrapping up in a warm comforter or blanket and having your faith and energy restored." It is unusual to hear such a comment about a new hymn, and it speaks to the power of the Holy Spirit, that can reach through a Catholic abbess in medieval Germany to a Mennonite poet in the California in the twentieth century to comfort and empower a United Methodist musician in Missouri five years later. Emancipatory language can enable that kind of welcoming and empowering to happen.

LAST WORDS

When I began the research for this book, the possibilities of finding emancipatory language in hymns appeared to be a fruitful point for study. From my earlier work on the hymn texts of Fred Kaan, I knew that theological and literary analysis of hymn texts could add to their understanding. With the assistance of tools from the fields of rhetoric and linguistics, these multidimensional readings have uncovered more than I realized existed within individual hymn texts. Yet even my careful readings could not contain all the insights, as was evidenced by the varied responses obtained in the praxis research.

Each of the six texts studied has its own particular combination of emancipatory elements. There is no one text that contains all of the strands in equal amounts. It is through the singing of many hymns that we are enlightened, challenged, and inspired. Yet each of these texts can have an important place in the life of a congregation and in the life of individuals. As these final two chapters attempt to show, the concept of emancipatory language and its application to hymn texts is important study, but the final result depends on lives that are changed and converted to turn around and walk again more clearly in God's way. The purpose of emancipatory language is to deepen our praise of God and thus deepen God's activity within our lives that we may be freed to fulfill our baptismal vows "to resist evil, injustice, and oppression" and serve Jesus Christ "in union with the church that Christ has opened to people of all ages, nations, and races" (*UMH*, 34). These six texts point us along the way toward emancipatory language that can open our hearts and lives to the One who is Holy.

Sources Cited

Adey, Lionel. 1988. *Class and Idol in the English Hymn.* Vancouver: University of British Columbia Press.

Albrecht, Gloria. 1995. *The Character of Our Communities: Toward an Ethic of Liberation for the Church.* Nashville: Abingdon Press.

Aldredge-Clanton, Jann. 1995. *In Search of the Christ-Sophia: An Inclusive Christology for Liberating Christians.* Mystic, Conn.: Twenty-Third Publications.

Alleluia Aotearoa. 1993. Wellington: New Zealand Hymnbook Trust.

Baker, Frank. 1985. *Charles Wesley's Verse: An Introduction.* London: Epworth Press.

Bakhtin, M. M. 1986. *Speech Genres and Other Late Essays.* Austin: University of Texas Press.

Baron, Dennis. 1986. *Grammar and Gender.* New Haven: Yale University Press.

Batastini, Robert. 1988. "President's Message." *The Hymn.* 39:2 (April): 6.

Beall, Steven. 1994. Conversation with the author, 16 August.

Beardsley, Monroe C. 1958. *Aesthetics: Problems in the Philosophy of Criticism.* New York: Harcourt, Brace and World.

Because We Are One People. 1975. Chicago: Ecumenical Women's Center. First edition, 1974.

Beckerlegge, Oliver A. 1983. "Introduction" to *Volume 7: A Collection of Hymns for the Use of the People Called Methodist.* Eds. Franz Hildebrandt and Oliver A. Beckerlegge. *The Works of John Wesley.* New York: Oxford University Press.

Berger, Teresa. 1995. *Theology in Hymns? A Study of the Relationship of Doxology and Theology According to A Collection of Hymns for the Use of the People Called Methodists (1780).* Translated by

Timothy E. Kimbrough. Nashville: Kingswood Books/Abingdon Press. Originally published in German in 1989.

Biber, Douglas. 1989. " A Typology of English Texts." *Linguistics* 27:3-43.

_____. 1993. "The Multidimensional Approach to Linguistic Analysis of Genre Variation: An Overview of Methodology and Findings." *Computers and the Humanities.* 26:331-345.

Biber, Douglas, and Edward Finegan, eds. 1994. *Sociolinguistic Perspectives on Register.* New York: Oxford University Press.

Bible. RSV. 1952. *The Holy Bible Containing the Old and New Testaments. Revised Standard Version.* New York: Thomas Nelson & Sons.

_____, NRSV. 1991. *The New Oxford Annotated Bible with the Apocryphal/Deuterocanonical Books.* Ed. Bruce M. Metzger and Roland E. Murphy. New Revised Standard Version. New York: Oxford University Press.

Black, Edwin. 1966. *Rhetorical Criticism.* New York: The Macmillan Co. First edition, 1965.

Black, Max. 1962. *Models and Metaphors.* Ithaca, N.Y.: Cornell University Press.

Bolinger, Dwight. 1980. *Language—the Loaded Weapon.* New York: Longman.

Bower, Peter. 1994. "An Artistic Creation That 'Directs Attention to What God Has Done and to the Claim that God Makes Upon Human Life': Jaroslav Vajda's God of the Sparrow." *Reformed Liturgy and Music* 28:3 (Summer 1994): 147-150.

Brock, Rita Nakashima. 1988. *Journeys by Heart: A Christology of Erotic Power.* New York: Crossroad.

Brook, Stella. 1965. *The Language of The Book of Common Prayer.* London: Andre Deutsch.

Burke, Kenneth. 1973. *The Philosophy of Literary Form.* Berkeley: University of California Press.

Bynum, Carolyn. 1982. *Jesus as Mother: Studies in the Spirituality of the High Middle Ages.* Berkeley: University of California Press.

Cameron, Deborah. 1992. *Feminism and Linguistic Theory.* New York: St. Martin's Press.

Campbell, Karlyn Kohrs. 1982. *The Rhetorical Act.* Belmont, Cal.: Wadsworth.

_____. 1989a. *Man Cannot Speak for Her: Volume I. A Critical Study of Early Feminist Rhetoric.* New York: Praeger.

_____. 1989b. *Man Cannot Speak for Her: Volume II. Key Texts of the Early Feminists*. New York: Praeger.

Cannon, Katie G. 1988. *Black Womanist Ethics*. Atlanta: Scholars Press.

Caron, Charlotte. 1992. *To Make and Make Again: Feminist Ritual Thealogy*. New York: Crossroad.

Chalice Hymnal [Christian Church: Disciples of Christ]. 1995. Daniel B. Merrick, ed. St. Louis: Chalice Press.

Chopp, Rebecca. 1991. *The Power to Speak: Feminism, Language, God*. New York: Crossroad.

Christ, Carol P., and Judith Plaskow, eds. 1979. *Womanspirit Rising: A Feminist Reader in Religion*. San Francisco: Harper and Row, Publishers.

Clark, Elizabeth. 1983. *Women in the Early Church*. Wilmington, Del.: Michael Glazier, Inc.

Clark, Linda J. 1994. *Music in Churches: Nourishing Your Congregation's Musical Life*. Bethesda, Md.: Alban Institute.

Clarkson, Margaret. 1994. Review of *Alleluia Aotearoa: Hymns and Songs for All Churches*. *The Hymn*. 45:1 (January): 44-45.

Cobb, John B., and David Ray Griffin. 1976. *Process Theology: An Introductory Exposition*. Philadelphia: The Westminster Press.

Coffin, Henry Sloan, and Ambrose White Vernon, eds. 1910. *Hymns of the Kingdom of God*. New York: A.S. Barnes.

Cone, James H. 1972. *The Spirituals and The Blues: An Interpretation*. New York: Seabury Press.

_____. 1975. *God of the Oppressed*. New York: Seabury Press.

Crawford, Evans E. 1995. *The Hum: Call and Response in African American Preaching*. Nashville: Abingdon Press.

Cross, F. L., and E. A. Livingstone, eds. 1990. *The Oxford Dictionary of the Christian Church*. Second Edition, Revised. Oxford: Oxford University Press. First edition, 1984.

Crystal, David, and Derek Davy, 1969. *Investigating English Style*. Bloomington: Indiana University Press.

Daly, Mary. 1987. *Websters' First New Intergalactic Wickedary of the English Language*. Conjured by Mary Daly in cahoots with Jane Caputi. Boston: Beacon Press.

Dillard, Annie. 1974. *Pilgrim at Tinker Creek*. New York: Bantam Books.

_____. 1977. *Holy the Firm*. New York: Harper and Row.

Dix, Gregory. 1978. *The Shape of the Liturgy*. London: Dacre Press, Adam & Charles Black. Distributed by Westminster, Md.: Christian Classics. First edition 1945.

Doran, Carol, and Thomas H. Troeger. 1992. *Trouble at the Table: Gathering the Tribes for Worship*. Nashville: Abingdon Press.

_____. 1990. "Choosing A Hymnal: An Act of Ministry on Behalf of the Whole Church." *Reformed Liturgy and Music* 24:2 (Spring), 86-90. Reprinted from *The Hymn* 37:2 (April 1986), 21-24, 43.

Douglas, Kelly Brown. 1994. *The Black Christ*. Maryknoll, N.Y.: Orbis Books.

Douglass, Frederick. 1994. *Narrative of the Life of Frederick Douglass, An American Slave, Written by Himself, 1845*. New York: The Library of America.

Duck, Ruth C. 1991. *Gender and the Name of God: The Trinitarian Baptismal Formula*. New York: The Pilgrim Press.

_____. 1992. *Dancing in the Universe: Hymns and Songs*. 1992. Chicago: GIA Publications.

_____. 1993. "Towards a Feminist Emancipatory Hymnody." Unpublished paper written for the Feminist Liturgy Seminar, North American Academy of Liturgy, November 24, 1993.

_____. 1995a. *Finding Words for Worship: A Guide for Leaders*. Louisville: Westminster/John Knox Press.

_____. 1995b. Conversation with the writer, October.

_____. 1995c. Letter to the writer along with comments, 15 November.

_____. 1998. *Circles of Care: Hymns and Songs*. Cleveland, Ohio: The Pilgrim Press.

Eiesland, Nancy L. 1994. *The Disabled God: Toward a Liberatory Theology of Disability*. Nashville: Abingdon Press.

Elkins, Heather Murray. 1994. *Worshiping Women: Re-Forming God's People for Praise*. Nashville: Abingdon Press.

Ellis, Jeffrey, and Jean Ure. 1969. "Language Varieties: Register." In *Encyclopaedia of Linguistics, Information and Control*. Edited, A. R. Meetham and R. A. Hudson. New York: Pergamon Press.

_____, eds. 1982. "Register Range and Change." Vol. 35 of *International Journal of the Sociology of Language*. New York: Mouton Publishers.

England, Martha Winburn, and John Sparrow. 1966. *Hymns Unbidden: Donne, Herbert, Blake, Emily Dickinson and the Hymnographers*. New York: The New York Public Library: Astor, Lenox, and Tilden Foundations.

Eskew, Harry, and Hugh T. McElrath. 1995. *Sing with Understanding: An Introduction to Christian Hymnology*. Second Edition, Revised and Expanded. Nashville: Church Street Press. First edition, 1980.

Everflowing Streams: Songs for Worship. 1981. Ruth C. Duck and Michael G. Bausch. 1981. New York: The Pilgrim Press.

Fantham, Elaine. 1984. "Studies in Cicero: Orator 69-74." *Central States Speech Journal* 35 (Summer): 123-125.

Fierro, Nancy. 1994. *Hildegard of Bingen and Her Vision of the Feminine*. Kansas City, Mo.: Sheed & Ward.

Fish, Stanley E. 1974. *Self-Consuming Artifacts: The Experience of Seventeenth-Century Literature*. Berkeley: University of California Press. First edition, 1972.

Flanagan, Sabina. 1989. *Hildegard of Bingen, 1098-1179: A Visionary Life*. London: Routledge.

Fox, Matthew, ed. 1987. *Hildegard of Bingen's Book of Divine Works with Letters and Songs*. Santa Fe, N.M.: Bear and Co. Songs translated by Rev. Jerry Dybdal and Matthew Fox.

Gadamer, Hans-Georg. 1990. "The Universality of the Hermeneutical Problem." In *The Hermeneutical Tradition: From Ast to Ricoeur*. Edited by Gayle L. Ormiston and Alan D. Schrift. Albany, N.Y.: State University of New York Press.

Gealy, Fred. D., Austin C. Lovelace, and Carlton R. Young, eds. 1970. *Companion to the Hymnal: A Handbook to the 1964 Methodist Hymnal*. Nashville: Abingdon Press.

Gregory of Nyssa. 1978. *The Life of Moses*. Translation, Introduction and Notes by Abraham J. Malherbe and Everett Ferguson. Preface by John Meyendorff. New York: Paulist Press.

_____. 1979. *From Glory to Glory: Texts from Gregory of Nyssa's Mystical Writings*. Crestwood, N.Y.: St. Vladimir's Seminary Press.

Griffiss, James E. 1990. *Naming the Mystery: How Our Words Shape Prayer and Belief*. Cambridge, Mass.: Cowley Publications.

Gutiérrez, Gustavo. 1973. *A Theology of Liberation: History, Politics, and Salvation*. Translated and edited by Sister Caridad Inda and John Eagleson. Maryknoll, N.Y.: Orbis Books. Originally published in 1971 in Spanish.

Harding, Sandra. 1986. *The Science Question in Feminism*. Ithaca, N.Y.: Cornell University Press.

_____. 1991. *Whose Science? Whose Knowledge?* Ithaca, N.Y.: Cornell University Press.

Harris, Maria. 1991. *Dance of the Spirit: The Seven Steps of Women's Spirituality*. New York: Bantam Books. First published, 1989.

Harrison, Beverly Wildung. 1985. "The Power of Anger in the Work of Love: Christian Ethics for Women and Other Strangers." In *Making the Connections: Essays in Feminist Social Ethics.* Edited by Carol S. Robbs. Boston: Beacon Press.

Haugen, Marty. 1995. "God of the Sparrow" [anthem]. Chicago: GIA Publications.

Heyward, Carter. 1990. "Jesus of Nazareth/Christ of Faith." In *Lift Every Voice: Constructing Theology from the Underside.* Susan Brooks Thistlethwaite and Mary Potter Engel, eds. New York: Harper and Row.

Hollander, John. 1981. *Rhyme's Reason: A Guide to English Verse.* New Haven: Yale University Press.

Holmer, Paul L. 1978. *The Grammar of Faith.* San Francisco: Harper and Row.

Hymes, Dell, 1974. *Foundations in Sociolinguistics: An Ethnographic Approach.* Philadelphia: University of Pennsylvania Press.

Ingram, Robert D., comp. 1992. *Scriptural and Seasonal Indexes of The United Methodist Hymnal.* Nashville: Abingdon Press.

Isasi-Díaz, Ada María. 1993. *En la lucha/In the Struggle: Elaborating a Mujerista Theology.* Minneapolis: Fortress Press.

James, William. 1958. *The Varieties of Religious Experience.* New York: Mentor. Originally lectures, 1901-1902.

Janzen, Jean. 1995a. Letter to the writer, 10 July.

——. 1995b. Formal biography provided to the writer, 10 July.

——. 1995c. Letter to the writer, 5 November.

Jasper, David, and R. C. D. Jasper. 1990. *Language and the Worship of the Church.* New York: St. Martin's Press.

Johnson, Elizabeth A. 1993. *She Who Is: The Mystery of God in Feminist Theological Discourse.* New York: Crossroad.

Joos, Martin. 1967. *The Five Clocks.* New York: Harcourt, Brace & World, Inc. First edition, 1961.

Julian of Norwich. 1978. *Showings.* Translated from the Critical Text with an Introduction by Edmund Colledge, O. S. A. and James Walsh, S. J. Preface by Jean Leclercq, O. S. B. New York: Paulist Press.

Kasbohm, Donna B. 1993. "Bring Many Names" [anthem]. Schiller Park, Ill.: World Library Publications.

Kennedy, George. A. 1984. *New Testament Interpretation through Rhetorical Criticism.* Chapel Hill: The University of North Carolina Press.

Kinzie, Mary. 1994. "The Six Major Elements from which a Poem is Made." From "On Reading Poems." Handout for Gian Balsamo's "Poetry" course offered at Northwestern University, Fall 1994.

Lakoff, George, and Mark Johnson. 1980. *Metaphors We Live By.* Chicago: The University of Chicago Press.

Leaver, Robin A. 1984. "Editorial." *News of Hymnody* 10 (April 1984), 1.

_____. 1990. "The Hymnbook as a Book of Practical Theology." *Reformed Liturgy and Music.* 24:2 (Spring): 55-57.

_____. 1992. "Christian Liturgical Music in the Wake of the Protestant Reformation." In *Sacred Sound and Social Change: Liturgical Music in Jewish and Christian Experience.* Lawrence A. Hoffman and Janet R. Walton, eds. South Bend, Ind.: University of Notre Dame Press.

Leaver, Robin A., and James Litton, eds. 1985. *Duty and Delight: Routley Remembered.* Carlton R. Young, exec. ed. Carol Stream, Ill.: Hope Publishing .

Leech, Geoffrey Neil, and Michael Short. 1981. "The Rhetoric of Text." In *Style in Fiction: A Linguistic Introduction to English Fictional Prose.* New York: Longman Group Ltd.

Leff, Michael. 1990. "Decorum and Rhetorical Interpretation: The Latin Humanist Traditions and Contemporary Critical Theory." *Estratto do Vichiane 3a serie*, Anno 1, Napoli.

_____. 1995. Conversation with this writer, 18 September.

Leff, Michael, and Andrew Sachs. 1990. "Word the Most Like Things: Iconicity and the Rhetorical Text." *Western Journal of Speech Communication* 54:3 (Summer): 252-273.

L'Engle, Madeleine. 1973. *A Wind in the Door.* New York: Dell Publishing.

Lovelace, Austin C. 1982. *The Anatomy of Hymnody.* Chicago: GIA Publications. First published 1965.

_____. 1995. "The God Whom We Proclaim" [anthem]. Nashville: Abingdon Press.

Lutheran Book of Worship. 1978. Prepared by the churches participating in the Inter-Lutheran Commission on Worship. Minneapolis: Augsburg Publishing House.

Maclean, Norman. 1976. *A River Runs through It and Other Stories.* Chicago: The University of Chicago Press.

Marshall, Madeleine Forell. 1995. *Common Hymnsense.* Chicago: GIA Publications.

McDaniel, Jay. 1989. *Of God and Pelicans: A Theology of Reverence for Life*. Louisville: Westminster/John Knox Press.

McFague, Sallie. 1984. *Metaphorical Theology: Models of God in Religious Language*. Philadelphia: Fortress Press. First edition, 1982.

_____. 1987. *Models of God: Theology for an Ecological, Nuclear Age*. Philadelphia: Fortress Press.

_____. 1993. *The Body of God: An Ecological Theology*. Minneapolis: Fortress Press.

Metzger, Bruce M., ed. consult. 1991. *New Revised Standard Version Exhaustive Concordance*. Nashville: Thomas Nelson Publishers.

Miller, Casey, and Kate Swift. 1988. *The Handbook of Nonsexist Writing: For Writers, Editors and Speakers*. Second Edition. New York: Harper Perennial.

Mollenkott, Virginia Ramey. 1983. *The Divine Feminine: The Biblical Imagery of God as Female*. New York: Crossroad.

Morley, Janet. 1992. *All Desires Known: Inclusive Prayers for Worship and Meditation*. Harrisburg: Morehouse Publishing.

Morton, Nelle. 1985. *The Journey Is Home*. Boston: Beacon Press.

Munsch, Robert N. 1980. *The Paper Bag Princess*. Toronto: Annick Press Ltd.

Murphy, James J. 1990. *Rhetoric in the Middle Ages: A History of Rhetorical Theory from Saint Augustine to the Renaissance*. Berkeley: University of California Press. First edition, 1974.

Murray, Shirley Erena. 1992. *In Every Corner Sing: The Hymns of Shirley Erena Murray*. Carol Stream, Ill: Hope Publishing Co.

_____. 1995. Letter to the writer, 18 October.

_____. 1996a. *Every Day in Your Spirit*. Carol Stream, Ill.: Hope Publishing Co.

_____. 1996b. Letter to the writer, 29 February.

_____. 1996c. "Company of Clowns and Cripples: Personal Confession about Writing Hymn Texts." *Music in the Air* [New Zealand]: Summer: 16-19.

Musser, Donald W., and Joseph L. Price, eds. 1992. *A New Handbook of Christian Theology*. Nashville: Abingdon Press.

New Hymns for the Lectionary. 1986. Carol Doran and Thomas H. Troeger. New York: Oxford University Press.

New Songs of Praise 3. 1987. Oxford: Oxford University Press, BBC Publications.

Newman, Barbara. 1994. "Female Divinity in the Judeo-Christian Tradition." Course offered at Northwestern University, Winter, 22 February, lecture notes.

_____. 1995. *From Virile Woman to WomanChrist*. Philadelphia: University of Pennsylvania Press.

Newman, Barbara, trans. and ed. 1988. *Saint Hildegard of Bingen: Symphonia: A Critical Edition of the Symphonia armonie celestium revelationum [Symphony of the Harmony of Celestial Revelations]*. Ithaca, N.Y.: Cornell University Press.

Newsom, Carol A., and Sharon H. Ringe, eds. 1992. *The Women's Bible Commentary*. Louisville: Westminster/ John Knox Press.

Oduyoye, Mercy. 1990. *Who Will Roll the Stone Away? The Ecumenical Decade of the Churches in Solidarity with Women*. Geneva: WCC Publications, Risk Book Series.

One Hundred Hymns of Hope. 1992. Carol Stream, Ill: Hope Publishing Company.

Pearson, Helen Bruch. 1983. "The Battered Bartered Bride." *The Hymn* 34 (October): 216-220.

Pintauro, Joseph, and Sister Corita [Kent]. 1968. *To Believe in God*. New York: Harper and Row.

Procter-Smith, Marjorie. 1990. *In Her Own Rite: Constructing Feminist Liturgical Tradition*. Nashville: Abingdon Press.

_____. 1995. Telephone conversation with the writer, 15 September.

Procter-Smith, Marjorie, and Janet R. Walton, eds. 1993. *Women at Worship: Interpretations of North American Diversity*. Louisville: Westminster/John Knox Press.

Proulx, Richard. 1989. "Bring Many Names, Beautiful and Good" [anthem]. Chicago: GIA Publications.

Psalter Hymnal. 1988. Emily Brink, ed. Grand Rapids, Mich.: CRC Publications. First edition, 1987.

Quinn, Arthur. 1982. *Figures of Speech: 60 Ways to Turn a Phrase*. Salt Lake City, Utah: Gibbs M. Smith, Inc.

Ramshaw, Gail. 1995a. *God beyond Gender: Feminist Christian God-Language*. Minneapolis: Fortress Press.

——. 1995b. "Words Worth Singing." *The Hymn* 46:2 (April): 16-19.

——. 1986. *Christ in Sacred Speech: The Meaning of Liturgical Language*. Philadelphia: Fortress Press.

——. 1992. *Words that Sing*. Chicago: Liturgical Training Publications.

Rauschenbusch, Walter. 1911. *Christianity and the Social Crisis*. New York: Hodder and Stoughton. First edition, 1907.

Reid, T. B. W. 1956. "Linguistics, Structuralism and Philology." *Archivum Linguisticum* 8.

Reilly, Patricia Lynn. 1995. *A God Who Looks Like Me*. New York: Ballantine Books.

Re-Imagining Program Book: The Ecumenical Decade, Churches in Solidarity with Women. 1993. Minneapolis, Minn. 4-7 November.

Reynolds, William Jensen. 1963. *A Survey of Christian Hymnody*. New York: Holt, Rinehart and Winston, Inc.

Ricoeur, Paul. 1978. *The Philosophy of Paul Ricoeur: An Anthology of His Work*. Charles E. Reagan and David Stewart, eds. Boston: Beacon Press.

———. 1967. *The Symbolism of Evil*. Boston: Beacon Press.

Riekehof, Lottie L. 1993. *The Joy of Signing: The Illustrated Guide for Mastering Sign Language and the Manual Alphabet*. Second Edition. Springfield, Mo.: Gospel Publishing House. First edition, 1978.

Robinson, John A. T. *Honest to God*. Philadelphia: Westminster Press, 1963.

Romaine, Suzanne. 1994. *Language in Society: An Introduction to Sociolinguistics*. Oxford: Oxford University Press.

Routley, Erik. 1982. *Christian Hymns Observed*. Princeton, N. J.: Prestige Publications.

———. 1979. *An English-Speaking Hymnal Guide*. Collegeville, Minn.: The Liturgical Press.

———. 1978. *Church Music and the Christian Faith*. Carol Stream, Ill: Agape.

———. 1968. *The Musical Wesleys*. Oxford: Oxford University Press.

Rowthorn, Jeffrey, and Russell Schulz-Widmar, eds. 1992. *A New Hymnal for Colleges and Schools*. New Haven: Yale University Press in association with the Yale Institute of Sacred Music.

Ruether, Rosemary Radford. 1983. *Sexism and God-Talk: Toward a Feminist Theology*. Boston: Beacon Press.

———. 1985. *Womanguides: Readings Toward a Feminist Theology*. Boston: Beacon Press.

———. 1986. *Women-Church: Theology and Practice*. San Francisco: Harper and Row.

Saliers, Don E. 1993. "Our Hymnal Takes Hold: Initial Soundings." *Worship Arts* 39:2 (November-December 1993), 8-10.

———. 1994. *Worship as Theology: Foretaste of Glory Divine*. Nashville: Abingdon Press.

Samarin, William J., ed., 1976. *Language in Religious Practice*. Rowley, Mass: Newbury House Publishers, Inc.

Sanchez, Diana, ed. 1989. *The Hymns of The United Methodist Hymnal*. Nashville: Abingdon Press.

Schalk, Carl F. 1981. "German Hymnody: The Early Reformation Period (c. 1517-1577)." In *Hymnal Companion to the Lutheran Book of Worship*. Marilyn Kay Stulken, ed. Philadelphia: Fortress Press.

_____. 1990. "German Church Song: Pre-Reformation Models and The Lutheran Reformation." In *The Hymnal 1982 Companion*. Raymond F. Glover, gen. ed. New York: The Church Hymnal Corporation.

Schilling, S. Paul. 1983. *The Faith We Sing*. Philadelphia: The Westminster Press.

_____. 1991. "God and Nature." *The Hymn* 42:1 (January): 24-28.

Schmitt, Mary Kathleen Speegle. 1993. *Seasons of the Feminine Divine: Christian Feminist Prayers for the Liturgical Cycle*. New York: Crossroad.

Schüssler Fiorenza, Elisabeth. 1985. "The Will to Choose or Reject: Continuing Our Critical Work." In *Feminist Interpretation of the Bible*, Letty Russell, ed. Philadelphia: Westminster Press.

Singing Church, The. 1985. Carol Stream, Ill.: Hope Publishing Co.

Sizer, Sandra S. 1978. *Gospel Hymns and Social Religion: The Rhetoric of Nineteenth-Century Revivalism*. Philadelphia: Temple University Press.

Slough, Rebecca, ed. 1992. *Hymnal: A Worshipbook,* Prepared by Churches in the Believers Church Tradition [Mennonites and Brethren]. Elgin: Ill.: Brethren Press; Newton, Kan.: Faith and Life Press; Scottsdale, Pa.: Mennonite Publishing House.

Smith, Elizabeth J. 1993. "On Singing Hymns." *The Hymn* 44:2 (April): 12-16.

Song Goes On, The [Covenant Supplement]. 1990. Chicago: Covenant Publications.

Songs of Zion. 1982. J. Jefferson Cleveland and Verolga Nix, eds. Nashville: Abingdon Press. First edition, 1981.

Sosa, Pablo. 1983. "Himnodia Metodista—Los Wesley--EE.UU. y América Latina." In *La tradición protestante en la teología latinoamericana: Primer intento: lectura de la tradición metodista*. José Duque, ed. San José, Costa Rica: Departaménto Ecumenico de Investigaciones.

Spencer, Jon Michael. 1990. *Protest and Praise: Sacred Music of Black Religion*. Minneapolis: Fortress Press.

_____. 1995. *Sing a New Song: Liberating Black Hymnody*. Minneapolis: Fortress Press.

Struever, Nancy. 1970. *The Language of History in Renaissance: Rhetorical and Historical Consciousness in Florentine Humanism.* Princeton, N.J.: Princeton University Press.

Surin, Kenneth. 1993. "Process Theology." In Vol. 2 of *The Modern Theologians: An Introduction to Christian Theology in the Twentieth Century.* David F. Ford, ed. Cambridge, Mass.: Basil Blackwell Ltd. First edition, 1989.

Swimme, Brian, and Thomas Berry. 1992. *The Universe Story.* San Francisco: Harper and Row.

Sydnor, James Rawlings. 1990. "Why a New Hymnal?" *Reformed Liturgy and Music,* XXIV:2 (Spring 1990): 58-59.

Tamez, Elsa. 1993. *Amnesty of Grace: Justification by Faith from a Latin American Perspective.* Trans. Sharon H. Ringe. Nashville: Abingdon Press.

The Baptist Hymnal. 1991. Forbis, Wesley L., ed. Nashville: Convention Press.

"The Hymn Society Book Service." *The Hymn* 49.1 (January): 31-34.

The New Century Hymnal [United Church of Christ]. 1995. Arthur G. Clyde, ed. Cleveland, Ohio: The Pilgrim Press.

The Presbyterian Hymnal: Hymns, Psalms, and Spiritual Songs. 1990. Linda Jo McKim, ed. Louisville: Westminster/John Knox Press.

The Worshiping Church: A Hymnal. Worship Leaders' Edition. 1991. Donald P. Hustad, ed. Carol Stream, Ill.: Hope Publishing Co.

Thompson, Bard, comp. 1961. *Liturgies of the Western Church.* Philadelphia: Fortress Press.

Trible, Phyllis. 1978. *God and the Rhetoric of Sexuality.* Philadelphia: Fortress Press.

Troeger, Thomas H. 1982. *Creating Fresh Images for Preaching: New Rungs for Jacob's Ladder.* Valley Forge, Pa.: Judson Press.

_____. 1987. "Personal, Cultural and Theological Influences on the Language of Hymns and Worship." *The Hymn* 38:4 (October): 404-413.

_____. 1992. "The Hidden Stream That Feeds: Hymns as a Resource for the Preacher's Imagination." *The Hymn* 43:3 (July 1992): 5-13.

_____. 1994a. *Borrowed Light: Hymn Texts, Prayers, and Poems.* New York: Oxford University Press.

_____. 1994b. Telephone conversation with the writer, September.

_____. 1995. Letter to the writer, 3 July.

_____. 1996. Letter to the writer, 5 February.

Trooien, Roberta Peirce. 1990. "The Rhetoric of Hymn Texts: A Feminist Perspective." Ph.D. dissertation. University of Minnesota.

United Methodist Book of Worship, The. 1992. Nashville: The United Methodist Publishing House.

Vajda, Jaroslav J. 1984. "Notes on the composition of God of the Sparrow." *News of Hymnody* 9 (January 1984).

_____. 1987. *Now the Joyful Celebration: Hymns, Carols, and Songs.* St. Louis: Morning Star Music Publishers.

_____. 1988. "Interview." *The Hymn* 39:2 (April 1988), 7-9.

_____. 1994. "Jaroslav J. Vajda: Hymnwriter." Received from author.

_____. 1995. Letter to the writer, 18 July.

_____. 1996. Letter to the writer, 1 February.

Wahlberg, Rachel Conrad. 1975. *Jesus According to a Woman.* New York: Paulist Press.

_____. 1978. *Jesus and the Freed Woman.* New York: Paulist Press.

Walker, Alice. 1983. *The Color Purple.* New York: Washington Square Press.

Wallace, John. 1995. Conversation with the writer, 22 November.

Wallace, Robin Knowles. 1982. "The Language of Hymnody: The Hymn Texts of Fred Kaan." Master of Theological Studies thesis. Candler School of Theology at Emory University.

_____. 1993. "A Study of Names for God Using the Semantic Differential." Unpublished paper for course on "Linguistics and Gender" at Northwestern University, 7 December.

_____. 1994. "A Study of Three Verbs: *Free, Liberate* and *Emancipate.*" Unpublished paper for course on "Lexical Semantics" at Northwestern University, 20 March.

Warner, Marina. 1983. *Alone of All Her Sex: The Myth and the Cult of the Virgin Mary.* New York: Vintage Books.

Warner, Mary Alice, and Dayna Beilenson, eds. 1987. *Women of Faith and Spirit: Their Words and Thoughts.* White Plains, N.Y.: Peter Pauper Press, Inc.

Watkins, Keith. 1981. *Faithful and Free: Transforming Sexist Language in Worship.* Nashville: Abingdon Press.

Westermeyer, Paul. 1995. *With Tongues of Fire: Profiles in 20th-Century Hymn Writing.* St. Louis: Concordia Publishing House.

Wheelwright, Philip. 1954. *Metaphor and Reality.* Bloomington: Indiana University Press.

White, James F. 1978. "The Words of Worship: Beyond Liturgical Sexism." *The Christian Century,* Dec. 13, 1202, 1206.

_____. 1990. *Introduction to Christian Worship.* Revised Edition. Nashville: Abingdon Press. First edition, 1980.

Wichelns, Herbert. 1958. "The Literary Criticism of Oratory." In *The Rhetorical Idiom: Essays in Rhetoric, Oratory, Language and Drama*. Donald C. Bryant, ed. Ithaca, N.Y.: Cornell University Press. First written 1923.

Wilder, Amos. 1976. *Theopoetic: Theology and the Religious Imagination*. Philadelphia: Fortress Press.

Williams, Delores S. 1993. *Sisters in the Wilderness: The Challenge of Womanist God-Talk*. Maryknoll, N.Y.: Orbis Books.

Winter, Miriam Therese. 1991. *WomanWisdom: A Feminist Lectionary and Psalter, Women of the Hebrew Scriptures: Part One*. New York: Crossroad.

_____. 1992. *WomanWord: A Feminist Lectionary and Psalter, Women of the New Testament*. New York: Crossroad.

_____. 1993a. *The Gospel According to Mary: A New Testament for Women*. New York: Crossroad.

_____. 1993b. *WomanPrayer/WomanSong*. New York: Crossroad.

World Council of Churches. 1992. *I Will Pour Out My Spirit*. Geneva: WCC.

Wren, Brian. 1977. *Education for Justice*. London: SCM Press Ltd.

_____. 1989a. *What Language Shall I Borrow? God-Talk in Worship: A Male Response to Feminist Theology*. New York: Crossroad.

_____. 1989b. *Bring Many Names: 35 New Hymns by Brian Wren*. Carol Stream, Ill: Hope Publishing Company.

_____. 1989c. *How Shall I Sing to God? A Video Workshop with Brian Wren*. Carol Stream, Ill.: Hope Publishing Co. Videocassette.

_____. 1995a. Letter to the writer, 5 July.

_____. 1995b. "Wren Defends Updating Hymn Lyrics." *The Christian Century* (September 13-20): 842.

_____. 1996a. "Christ Is Alive: Hymn Interpretation." *The Hymn* 47:1 (January): 50.

_____. 1996b. Letter to the writer, 25 February.

Young, Carlton R. 1993. *Companion to The United Methodist Hymnal*. Nashville: Abingdon Press.

_____. 1995a. *Music of the Heart: John and Charles Wesley on Music and Musicians*. Carol Stream, IL: Hope Publishing Company.

_____. 1995b. *My Great Redeemer's Praise: An Introduction to Christian Hymns*. Akron, Ohio: OSL Publications

Young, Carlton R., ed. 1989. *The United Methodist Hymnal: Book of United Methodist Worship*. Nashville: The United Methodist Publishing House.

INDEX
General

Adey, Lionel, 31
Advent, 16, 196, 225, 227, 228, 229
Aldredge-Clanton, Jann, 81
Alleluia Aoetearoa, 177, 179n3
Ambrose, 6, 51, 193
"Amen", 30, 31-32, 36
American Sign Language, 83
anamnesis, 87-89, 171, 192-93, 199, 204, 230, 234-35, 239, 240, 243
androcentric liturgical language, 55-56
Anselm of Canterbury, 88
anthems, 107n3, 120n1, 127, 143
Aquinas, Thomas, 62
Aristotle, 176, 180
Arius, 6, 45
Assman, Hugo, 68
Augustine, 3, 101, 158

Baker, Frank, 23
Bakhtin, Mikhail, 21, 29-37
Baldwin, James, 238n2
baptism, 18, 67, 82, 85 86, 88, 136, 154, 157, 184, 197, 198, 216, 219, 221, 228, 244
Baron, Dennis, 71
Barth, Karl, 11
Batistini, Robert, 50-51
Beardsley, Monroe, 28
Beethoven, Ludwig, 45
Berger, Teresa, 1, 13, 14-15
Berry, Thomas, 110
Biber, Douglas, 38
Black, Edwin, 103, 152
Bower, Peter, 107n2, 111, 112
Brock, Rita Nakashima, 77, 84, 138
Brook, Stella, 37
Burke, Kenneth, 25, 100, 101, 103, 108

Bynum, Caroline, 45n4

Calvin, John, 7
Cameron, Deborah, 72, 76, 91
Campbell, Karlyn Kohrs, 41-42, 75-76, 91, 179
Cannon, Katie, 70
Cardenal, Ernesto, 68
carol, 6, 27
Caron, Charlotte, 77
Chalice Hymnal, 10, 16-17, 18, 49, 94-95 106, 120, 123, 127, 142, 162, 164, 176-77, 179, 189, 193-4, 202, 237
children, 19, 50-51, 55, 57, 68, 73, 79, 85, 91, 106, 108, 110, 114-15, 117, 130, 135, 148, 151, 157, 159, 169, 171, 173, 182, 192, 199, 211-214, 218, 224, 229, 235
Chopp, Rebecca, 61, 66, 67
Christ United Methodist Church, Bay City, Mich., 208, 212, 215, 218, 221, 224, 227
Christmas, 8, 73, 110, 173, 228
Cicero, 41, 42, 101
Civil Rights Movement, 6, 10, 45, 47
Clark, Linda, 17, 19, 51
close reading, 49, 94, 95, 96, 97, 99, 205, 211, 209n1
Coffin, Henry Sloan, 9
communion (Eucharist), 33, 67, 85, 87, 88, 134, 149, 171, 213
community, 12-19, 30, 32-33, 38, 42, 47, 61, 63, 68, 81-82, 84-85, 87, 88, 90, 94, 113, 168, 177, 178, 192, 205, 240
Cone, James, 9, 68
conversion (*metanoia*), 8, 62-63, 70, 91, 244
Copland, Aaron, 35

INDEX
Hymn Texts and Tunes

Hymn Tunes

INDEX
Biblical citations

About the Author

Robin Knowles Wallace is currently Assistant Professor of Worship and Music at Methodist Theological School in Ohio. Robin holds a bachelor's degree in music from the University of Cincinnati, a master of church music education from Scarritt College in Nashville, a master of theological studies from the Candler School of Theology at Emory University, and a doctorate in theology and worship from The Joint Program in Religious and Theological Studies at Northwestern University and Garrett-Evangelical Theological Seminary. She has served as a church musician for over thirty years and has written for various journals on worship, hymnody, and church music. In 1994, she published *Things They Never Tell You Before You Say "Yes": The Non-Musical Tasks of The Church Musician.* She has contributed to *Leading the Church's Song, Worship Leader's Companion to Chalice Hymnal, Hymns of The United Methodist Hymnal, 100 Meditations for Advent and Christmas,* and *Worship Music: A Concise Dictionary.* Robin has served as editor for a number of church music and worship journals. She lives in Columbus, Ohio, with her pastor husband and two teen-aged daughters.